SOCIAL MEDIA ANALYTICS STRATEGY

USING DATA TO OPTIMIZE BUSINESS PERFORMANCE

SECOND EDITION

April Ursula Fox

Apress®

Social Media Analytics Strategy: Using Data to Optimize Business Performance

April Ursula Fox
Las Vegas, NV, USA

ISBN-13 (pbk): 978-1-4842-8305-9   ISBN-13 (electronic): 978-1-4842-8306-6
https://doi.org/10.1007/978-1-4842-8306-6

Managing Director, Apress Media LLC: Welmoed Spahr
Acquisitions Editor: Susan McDermott
Development Editor: Laura Berendson
Coordinating Editor: Jessica Vakili

Distributed to the book trade worldwide by Springer Science+Business Media New York, 233 Spring Street, 6th Floor, New York, NY 10013. Phone 1-800-SPRINGER, fax (201) 348-4505, e-mail orders-ny@springer-sbm.com, or visit www.springeronline.com. Apress Media, LLC is a California LLC and the sole member (owner) is Springer Science + Business Media Finance Inc (SSBM Finance Inc). SSBM Finance Inc is a **Delaware** corporation.

For information on translations, please e-mail booktranslations@springernature.com; for reprint, paperback, or audio rights, please e-mail bookpermissions@springernature.com.

Apress titles may be purchased in bulk for academic, corporate, or promotional use. eBook versions and licenses are also available for most titles. For more information, reference our Print and eBook Bulk Sales web page at http://www.apress.com/bulk-sales.

Any source code or other supplementary material referenced by the author in this book is available to readers on the Github repository: https://github.com/Apress/Social-Media-Analytics-Strategy. For more detailed information, please visit http://www.apress.com/source-code.

Printed on acid-free paper

To my grandfather, Maximiano Gonçalves, who proved through his many books that writing and sharing knowledge is amazing and possible.

To my father, Maximiano Gonçalves Filho, who never gives up on me no matter what and taught me the discipline that shaped me into who I am.

To my mother, for giving me more than I ever asked for and supporting all of my huge dreams with infinite light, love, and strength.

Contents

About the Author   vii

About the Technical Reviewer   ix

Acknowledgments   xi

Introduction   xiii

Part I: **Data**   I
Chapter 1:   Social Media Data   3
Chapter 2:   From Data to Insights   23
Chapter 3:   Luis Madureira   49

Part II: **Defining Analytics in Social Media and
                 Types of Analytics Tools**   55
Chapter 4:   Analytics in Social Media   57
Chapter 5:   Dedicated vs. Hybrid Tools   71
Chapter 6:   Alexander and Frederik Peiniger   83

Part III: **Differences of Social Media Networks**   93
Chapter 7:   Social Network Landscape   95
Chapter 8:   Tam Su   113

Part IV: **The Analytics Process**   123
Chapter 9:   The Analytics Process   125
Chapter 10: Armando Terribili   147

Part V: **Metrics, Dashboards, and Reports**   153
Chapter 11: Metrics   155
Chapter 12: Dashboards   193
Chapter 13: Reports   219
Chapter 14: Milan Veverka   237

Part VI: Strategy and Tactics   247

Chapter 15: Strategy   249

Chapter 16: Tactics   269

Chapter 17: Michael Wu   281

Part VII: The Future   293

Chapter 18: Prescriptive Analytics   295

Chapter 19: The Future of Social Media Analytics   303

Index   309

About the Author

April Ursula Fox has over ten years of professional work experience in social media analytics and strategy. In this book, she maps the paths to success in implementing and running analytics without losing our human qualities along the way.

Her professional experience includes passages in Socialbakers and quintly, in client-facing roles, implementing and training organizations in the use and strategy of analytics. Working with clients of all sizes, including global companies such as Peugeot & Citroen, Danone, Autodesk, Bosch, Samsung, P&G, and Monster Energy, as well as global PR and marketing agencies such as Ogilvy, Leo Burnett, Publicis, Mediacom, Mindshare, Havas, and many others, her global and professional experience has given her a deep understanding of the different contexts of digital marketing around the world.

April has lived in the United States, England, Germany, Czech Republic, Portugal, and Brazil and highly values the cultural diversity of our world.

April was born into the technology industry. Her father created the world's largest technology convention of its time: Fenasoft (http://bit.ly/2uFoQgu). As a child, April clearly understood technology's immense power for positive change. When social media technology came along, she embarked on a journey to uncover more of its secrets, seeing it as a possible core system in all human-related technological operations.

By April's calculations, in more than ten years of working with analytics in social media, she has spoken to more than 9,760 people, for more than 24,400 total hours of conversation. She feels that this qualifies her as passionate for the subject, a trait that she will surely honor when contacted by anyone interested in talking about social media and social media analytics. So please be encouraged to get in touch!

You can contact April at www.linkedin.com/in/aprilursulafox/.

About the Technical Reviewer

Paulo Gomes graduated in IT with a degree in digital marketing and communication. He has a great experience creating communications projects for different companies from different countries, always using data as the base of his strategies. Besides his professional life, Paulo spends time with his family, most of the time traveling as it is one of his passions.

Acknowledgments

This book became possible thanks to the amazing professionals I had the chance to meet along my career, and the amazing clients I had the chance to work with, who pushed me with their eternal curiosity. It was in the trenches of social media that I understood how important it was to prepare this book as a compendium of the necessary knowledge to take every reader to the next level. I am absolutely sure that if we have worked together, either as a colleague or as a client, you will notice in this book some or a lot of what we spoke about.

An immense thank-you to the guests in this book who believed in me and through their interviews offered their insight and knowledge. In order of appearance in the chapters, I give a very special thank-you to Luis Madureira, Alexander and Frederik Peiniger, Tam Su, Armando Terribili, Milan Veverka, and Michael Wu. I am a great admirer and fan of your work, vision, and drive.

An extra-special thank-you to Alexander and Frederik Peiniger for giving access to use and for publishing of quintly's analytics metrics in the book, which are used to illustrate many concepts that we explore.

A huge thank-you to my dearest friend Paulo Henrique for bringing in his knowledge and insight as technical reviewer.

Eternal admiration and gratitude for the work and spirit of the entire team at Apress: Todd Green, Susan McDermott, Shivangi Ramachandran, Laura Berendson, and in special, for being my superhero along so many contacts in the everyday process of this book, Rita Fernando. A very special thank-you also to Jonathan Simpson, who introduced me to Todd Green and the Apress team. And for this second edition, also Jessica Vakili and Jim Markham, who offered me guidance and so much support.

Last, but most definitely not least, a hearty thank-you to all my friends and family who are present with me every step of the way, in my heart, giving me the drive to push forward and believe.

Introduction

Analytics is the pursuit of truth.

We want to find the truth because we want to make the best possible decision in the face of any given situation.

The concept of analytics is to understand all the different parts of a problem and then be able to find improvement points from facts in the past and to predict the future outcome of present decisions.

In social media, we are faced with many challenges when it comes to analytics. Many of us don't come from a technical background and become slightly confused by the details around data sources, integration, available data, and data processing systems. We might not have time to constantly use all of our mathematical knowledge either and may become slightly confused when creating and working with new metrics to accurately measure what we need. On top of that, social media is a field evolving very quickly, and analytics is evolving far beyond social media and into artificial intelligence (AI).

To get ahead in social media analytics, we essentially need to cover the following two points:

- **The foundation of social media analytics:** How to understand and deal with any social media network, strategy, or campaign
- **The broader picture:** How social media analytics integrates with and affects other areas of business

This book focuses precisely on these two points. It takes you on a journey of discovery, where, by the end of it, you are ready to tackle any project or process using social media analytics. Naturally, as in all interesting topics around technology and business strategy, you are able to continue your studies as you grow further into it. The journey of this book, in relation to that, drops you off at the point where you are ready to jump into advanced studies around analytics. You will be prepared to understand the current state of analytics in the world and to have a strategic view into what works and why.

To give real-world context and insight, the book brings exclusive interviews with six global experts in fields that cover social media analytics specifically, but also business intelligence, data integration, artificial intelligence, machine learning, project management, and even the "human side" of things. As you will see throughout the book, the "human side" of the analytics process is key to its ultimate success.

The ultimate objective of this book is to help you shape the best version of your "analyst self." We can truly become thinkers in the field and reach a point in which we can effortlessly approach any project with a sharp analytical mind.

On a last note, please don't be hasty as you progress through the book. Many concepts are built on top of the understanding of smaller parts, so even the "simple things" can matter along the way. It is important that you can make all the connections in the end and truly become fluent in analytics; so please enjoy each step of the way.

Data

Social Media Data

The Foundation for Analytics

Social media brings a very unique set of data to marketing and business intelligence. It also offers unique ways to access this data. Many of us who come from a creative background, or work with data that exclusively belongs to our company, find that social media analysis is an interesting new field to explore.

One interesting difference between social media analysis and traditional business intelligence is the competitive information highly available on social media. Historically, companies have mostly dealt with their own data and eventually added studies based on external data published by research organizations and so forth. Even in the digital age, website analysis and digital advertising still bind most of the useful data to its owners, and being competitive has never been an easy task.

Competitive intelligence and other aspects of social media data and analytics create a new context for social media and a data-driven strategy. It is in many aspects a new beginning, where we can revisit key concepts around the use of data, analytics, and strategy and make the most out of new technologies.

© April Ursula Fox 2022
A. U. Fox, *Social Media Analytics Strategy*,
https://doi.org/10.1007/978-1-4842-8306-6_1

The future success of marketing is highly based on the amount of data we have: data about our company, about our consumers, about our market, and about the world. The time is now to jump into a better understanding of data, and update continuously, becoming fluent in processes that run our data-based business.

Analytics is entirely based on the use of data, so the better we understand what data is and how it can be used, the easier it is to understand and make use of analytics to effectively add analytics into our business strategy.

Because we are facing new data sets on social media, a good first approach is to quickly revisit a few fundamental aspects of data in general—specifically, social media data, even if we are already familiar with working with data.

A Look into the Evolution of Data and the Digital Gap

Data is information. A simple concept, in essence, with a simple ultimate objective: *to enhance any given process, to change something for the better, and to improve upon a current condition.*

Keeping it simple, while going one step further, we can see data as a storage unit for a piece of information. So when someone hits the Like button on a social media network, for example, that action generates data, and the data stores this information. Technology makes use of this data—of these storage units—to access the information they carry and generate an output that fulfills an objective, such as delivering a graph showing how many "likes" a piece of content received over time.

The essence of the process around the use of data is very simple. Let's compare it to the construction of a building or to the baking of a cake. We are putting ingredients together to form a new product. What is complicated is the process itself. We all have different ways of reaching a given objective—some better than others, and we have only a limited set of data that we can access. Even with huge amounts of data being produced, we may not be able to access everything we need at one given time, so we face limitations in the real world of data-based business.

To better understand the use of data in a global civilization, we need to realize that there is a digital gap in our society, which can negatively affect our business. It is good to take a quick step back and look at the evolution of information generation, storage, and exchange. This gives context and helps us to decide on the best possible path to reach a data-driven level.

The evolution of the process of creating, storing, and exchanging information is very familiar. We began with grunts and strange noises, but then evolved to painting walls on caves, then reading books, and now to hiding information inside somewhat mysterious electronic equipment. We have always been on a journey of externalizing all the information from our minds into storage that can be accessed by other people. What is happening now is that the current digital format we use has made this process very fast; most of us cannot keep up with it all. This is where things become more complicated and where nontechnical humans begin to lose grasp of what data means, how it is stored, how to access it, and how to work with it and put it to good use.

On top of the technical challenge, today, data is not only created by humans and their activities in the world but also by machines—without human intervention. The amount of data created grows almost out of control. It sets constantly new challenges in terms of storage and accessibility. The need for the use of all of this data is pushing us into a higher level of technology advancement, whether we want it or not. There is no turning back now, so we might as well embrace it and grow with it.

To work with information today means to work with code. Code is instruction; it includes the different languages that command the data that instructs equipment on how to use the data. Today, we face a need to translate knowledge and information into many different languages so that information can perform better when applied to the equipment used to interact with it. This need is mainly related to the use of large amounts of information at very high speeds and to the interface between raw information and the specific equipment to interact with it, such as a computer or a mobile phone.

We do not have to become specialists in working with code to be good digital strategists and analysts. We do not have to be *coders*. The knowledge that different code runs processes, however, is important in understanding how far we can go with our strategies. It helps us understand our limitations and with knowing where to look for help when needed.

With this in mind, sometimes we notice that a social media analytics platform makes compromises to deliver data to users. One simple example is sacrificing a long-period analysis in the name of speed. Some data sets are too big to be delivered very quickly, so shorter periods are selected by default. Longer periods take more time to load and be presented.

Many compromises have to be made in data-based processes. A feature such as a look-alike audience, where a piece of content is sent to people with similar traits to an original sample or target, is a solution based on a compromise around not having enough data to send unique content to each individual. So the look-alike uses whatever data it can to match people to a target group. The logic is that if our message works with one group, sending it to a similar group can also work well. The ideal scenario would be an individualized approach; after all, we are all very different from each other in all sorts of ways—from our interests, to our culture, and our daily lives.

As a natural result of the evolution of the use of data, we create layers of distance between the people who have and the people who don't have the required skills to work directly with data. Hence, there is a divided landscape of people with different levels of knowledge who are trying to access available information; this ranges from the data-ignorant final users of devices and data-based technology, to developers and data architects, and everyone else in between.

This current gap in data knowledge is a known issue, and there are many initiatives working to close it. Some propose that children need to learn how to work with code. Others work on the development of simple and graphic interface layers for nondevelopers on which to build applications. And yet others are dedicated to the creation of intelligent machines and artificial intelligence, which shape the use of data in innovative ways.

It is well understood that we must have easy access to data and ways to work with it in order to break into our next evolutionary stages. This access is needed so that we can truly take advantage of all that we have created up to this point in time. There is really no point in creating a world where information management becomes increasingly overcomplicated, so we are sure to see this gap close as we go, even with more data being created in one day than it was in all of our existence before the year 2000.

It may happen that once we have artificial intelligence automating most of our decisions, covering much of our work, and by consequence helping us have higher personal growth and fulfillment because we have more time for ourselves, we will look back and see that this point in time was close to being a dark age of technology, where we were not yet able to easily make it all work. For now, however, we keep pushing hard to reach that stage in which technology works for us fully.

As we understand how fast and broad the world of data is, there is no shame in feeling that we have a hard time closing the gap sometimes, especially when dealing with technology related to creativity, content, ideas, and very subjective matters. It is perfectly understandable to reach out and create the necessary bridges for our own technical and strategic advancement. It is best when we are humble enough to admit that we have a gap to cross, instead of assuming that we know something that we truly don't. The idea that technology should be instinctive and easy to use must not keep us from learning what is out there in the present moment, and on the path of learning, there will always be new gaps to cross. It can be a very interesting process to research new technologies and new possibilities without creating pressure on ourselves, accepting that there is much we don't know but can enjoy discovering. As a wise voice once said, "The path is the destination."

Sometimes, we work on a team in which each team member has a different level of understanding about data. These situations can eventually lead to problems, especially when setting objectives for projects. Team members with less knowledge of social media data might create goals and expectations that are impossible to reach. Therefore, it is never a waste of time to quickly revisit the foundation and understand what is available at a certain point in time.

Moving forward, and stepping now into social media specifically, a few key elements come into play when dealing with social media data for analytics. One of them is the knowledge of data sources, or simply put, identifying where our data comes from.

Social Media Data Sources: Offline and Online

A good starting point for understanding data sources for social media and marketing is to separate the origin by offline and online sources. It seems simple enough, but many times we may expect that certain information is available to us when it is not. Therefore, this starting point helps us to later understand why we have easier access to some data sets than others.

- **Offline originated data**: Data that has been generated with no connection to the Internet, and then registered into a system, which may be accessed via the Internet later. Examples include physical retail, printed press, live events, telephone marketing and customer support, traditional television audience measurements, and so forth.

- **Online originated data**: Created from systems connected to the Internet. Examples include websites, ecommerce, media streaming, email, mobile applications, social media, online devices, and so forth.

Going further into online sources, we can also look at them by defining which systems are generating the information. Each social media network, for example, is a different source, even if the person, brand, or company behind each social media page or profile is the same. Then we have blogs, websites, apps, and more.

Within these systems, we might also have different points of data generation. The social media post itself is one source, for example, and the comments under that same social media post come from a different source, or a different point within the social network database. Now think of everything that happens on social media, with all the different types of interactions and quick sharing of content, there are many data sources within each social media network.

This simple and initial separation of offline and online data sources is interesting because it helps us understand the sources that are accessible for our projects' needs.

Sometimes people might ask us for specific information that is not available. So if we quickly identify the source, we won't waste our time looking for something that doesn't exist.

Also, later in the book, I talk about how to reach estimated results and integral results from a process of analysis. This means that in some cases, we have 100% of the data we need from clear and reliable sources; but in other cases, we have only a part of the information, and we have to estimate results for our analysis.

Having knowledge of the sources also helps us in cases when we know that we can reach that data, even if partially. In these cases, we won't waste time and can get straight to the point with our request to potential data providers.

As an example of how the knowledge of data sources can be helpful, consider the following request.

> *I wish to see all the mentions of my brand on the Internet, separated by geographical region, and including the demographics of the people making the mentions, plus an analysis of the relevance of the people mentioning, and if my competitors are also mentioned.*

To answer this request requires a very complicated process, which most likely will produce an estimated result; let's understand why. First, let's dissect the request and point out the different needs that it brings:

- All the mentions of the brand on the Internet
- Per region
- With demographics
- The relevance of the people mentioning
- If the mentions include competitors

Now let's see what we can do, what we cannot do, and how easy or difficult it is to access this data and answer to the request.

All mentions of the brand on the Internet. We will likely only have a sample here. The Internet is a vast space, and tools will likely miss a few mentions of the brand.

Region. We will reduce the sample of mentions we found into a smaller sample here. It is likely that many mentions will not provide a clear indication of the region, so we will lose a few more if we exclusively want to work with the regions.

Demographics. This will likely be an estimate, or it will be entirely unavailable in some cases. Mentions have to be connected to user profiles that include the age, gender, and other information about a person making a mention. This information is usually not directly available; most users don't need to fill out a form providing their age, gender, and so forth, before posting on the Internet. Some systems try to estimate this data based on people's connection location, their names, and even the kind of content they interact with. Other systems try to apply census data or match users to research information. And yet other systems try to cross-reference a user profile to their mobile phone to gather more information.

There are many attempts at estimating demographics. In essence, this is a very complicated task and quite impossible to reach a precise result. It can be a very good and useful estimate, but it will most likely always be an estimate when dealing with an open search, such as in this example. If we start our study with data that already comes from systems with precise demographics, then, of course, we have such details in hand. It is important to understand your sources so that you can decide on which type of study to perform. Depending on the strategy, a smaller sample with very precise demographic information can be the way to go.

The relevance of the people mentioning. Relevance is subjective. If we take the network size of the people who are mentioning the brand as a basis, we might be missing someone that would be a hardcore user of the brand's product if that person does not have a big network of friends/followers on the Web. So establishing what relevance means is a hard task on its own.

If the brand objective for this request is to optimize the awareness and to find *influential* people that have large networks of followers, then some systems give us that information directly.

That does not guarantee that people with large networks are the ones generating the most engagement for the brand. Perhaps someone with a smaller network has contacts that are much more related to the brand's niche, sector, or value proposition. There are ways to understand how interactions and conversions by potentially relevant people or partner channels are generated, so you can approach your research in that way.

Competitor mentions. This process would start by listing the competitors. Some platforms try to search the mentions and automatically find which brands are related to each other, but in this case, if the request is to look for specific competitors, a list is a good start.

Then, because we are not looking for random mentions of competitors but instead trying to understand if the same people who mention our brand are mentioning competitors, we will have an extra challenge to connect the mentions to their specific sources. Some platforms let us create a competitive group and have an idea of followers mentioning all of the brands in that group.

The issue here is usually the limitations of using only certain social platforms, such as Twitter.

Twitter is great for this kind of study because every user has a unique social handle that is easy to access. Mentions are easy to track on Twitter; the content is short, so it is easier to track more from the same sources. Everyone has a potential public-level profile, so anyone can see who they are, their network, and what they talk about. But if we only have proper access to Twitter, this makes our sample even smaller, now limited only to Twitter.

Competitive information on social media is highly available, but here we are touching some of the complicated spots, which are followers, individuals, and their private information. So while we can easily see the number of followers a brand has and how that evolves through time, it is harder to research further details of a follower base that does not belong to us. Even our own follower base can be hard to decipher sometimes, and a lot of that difficulty is related to the push for advertising on social media, in which networks limit much of this information to be used only by paying customers.

So as analysts (even if that is not our job title), we have to consider all of these variables when taking such a request into account. Our consideration of the variables, and how we choose to use them for analysis, can then be described in our reports, so that we deliver the most accurate insights that we can, and properly influence any decision-making process related to our study. In other words, we must disclose all the limitations of our studies so that the decisions are well informed.

There are ways of pointing out what is more important as an indicator for performance, so that a better decision can be made. This means that even for complicated requests, we always have a way to find actionable insights. You will see how to get to that as we go further into the book.

Also, it is important to mention that there are different types of social media tools on the market, such as analytics, listening, ads analytics, and CMS analytics; some are a better fit for certain requests. On top of that, companies are building their own analytics structures and integrating all of their data. We will look at these points in further detail later in the book.

In a brief look into the possible future of analytics, taking into consideration the technologies that are in the early stages today, it is likely that marketing data will be available via *intelligent* platforms. These platforms will gather and display data in an excellent manner, both graphically and in performance, and also perform much of the thinking for analysts. They will directly display the actionable insights that analysts today are spending a lot of time looking for. It is what we call prescriptive analytics, where the system prescribes the solution to the user. We will look more into this as we go.

Humoring a future beyond that, marketing optimization will very likely be entirely done by machines, and humans will gather around the strategy, the creative aspect, the brand values, product quality, and so forth. Humans will train and guide the intelligence of machines. But we are not quite there yet.

So as a next step, once we understand the importance of data sources for our studies going forward, it is important to define what social media data means, even if that definition may evolve as technology evolves around us.

Defining Social Media Data

Within online generated data, only a portion of it is considered truly social media data. There is always a gray area of debate on *what social media is and what it is not.* But to make it simple, we can define social media data as *data generated within a self-proclaimed social media platform.* So we rely on how the platforms present themselves and on their level of publicly available data.

If we are limiting our analysis to only social media data, we exclude from our list of data sources the websites, blogs, mobile apps that are not social platforms, streaming services not social by design, and so forth. They are sources that do not proclaim themselves as social media technologies. These sources are important for a digital marketing strategy, and we will look at integrated analytics as well, but focus mainly on social media data sources and metrics.

We include in our studies and examples concepts that directly relate to well-known platforms such as Facebook, Twitter, LinkedIn, Instagram, YouTube, Pinterest, Snapchat, and others.

The main focus is not to tackle every single specific point of every network, but instead to develop your knowledge to a level where you can tackle any of these networks as targets of your marketing strategies, and be ready for cross-network strategic planning and analysis.

Patterns of Data Sources in Social Media Platforms

An easy way to look at social media data sources is to think about how humans interact with social media platforms. Each platform has a set of possible actions that can be taken by a human interacting with it, and most of these actions are common across all social media platforms.

A few platforms may not offer certain features, but as we look at what is offered, we are most likely able to fit whatever feature we find into a common human action on social media.

The following are common human social media actions (in no particular order):

- Create a profile.
- Publish content.
- Praise or react to content (e.g., likes, favorites, etc.).
- Comment on content.
- Share content.
- Create groups and content only available to the group.
- Send direct messages and chat with other users.
- Connect to another profile (as a friend, follower, etc.).
- Purchase products and perform transactions.

There are different details in these common features from one social network to the next. The following are a few examples:

- Different available fields for creating the user profile (e.g., gender options, interests, etc.)
- Limitations and regulations over content interaction and visualization
- Content types that can or cannot be published
- Methods to send messages or to *tag* other users

The user features also have a different effect on other features of a platform—meaning, for example, that a "like" on Facebook generates a different exposure to the content than a "like" on Pinterest or Instagram. This is in line with the concept behind the algorithm of a certain network timeline, and the manner in which content is distributed, among other effects.

So even though many features are common to all social networks, when performing a study or analysis, there are specific challenges related to each social platform in terms of what data is actually available, how easy it is to have access to the data, and how to interpret the value of each piece of data related to performance and content distribution. The differences from one social network to another have an impact on how an analyst interprets the information qualitatively. One hundred "likes" on Facebook has a different impact than the same number of "likes" on Instagram.

These aspects also call for understanding the brand strategy and the network that resonates the most with the brand. The qualitative work of the analyst is as detailed as the analyst wishes it to be or has the time to spend on. It is always possible to go further into a certain study, but we have to make compromises based on our limited resources—time being one of them.

We will look more into these specific points of analysis. For now, my objective is only to point out the importance of understanding data sources, so that you have a clear basis for the upcoming concepts in the book.

Estimated vs. Factual Data Sources

It is important to understand when data sources represent a fact and when they represent a possible fact or an estimate. Especially when going into paid media and content promotion, we come across many estimated, or sometimes questionable, sources.

These estimated metrics include views, impressions, and reach, for example, which provide the number of times a user has potentially seen a certain piece of content or advertising.

We can consider these metrics questionable in some cases, from a performance standpoint, because we are never really sure if someone has actually seen our content unless we get a reaction from them. Who knows if anyone really saw the content? When we relate metrics to facts, we get a better value from them in terms of performance.

During an event I attended, a presenter defended his performance by showing a huge graph of his reach growing from one year to the next. He showed that his reach grew to double the size of what it was before he joined the company. Later, away from the spotlight, I asked him how the average interactions changed? How much did the top posts hit? How were the conversions? His answer was that it did not change as much as the reach, but on stage, he preferred to show only the big number. While this is somewhat understandable, and he was trying to impress his audience, it was also clear that he knew that reach alone was not telling the entire story, even if he didn't tell that to his audience during his talk. It is interesting, therefore, to know the true meaning of metrics when approaching an analysis of estimated metrics, despite the buzz.

These metrics have special value for understanding the distribution potential of a certain network, and sometimes reflect the value and quality of our copy, and how we compose our content specifically so that it navigates further within the network.

For example, when analyzing some content performance, we might see that we have higher reach if we have a certain amount of interactions early in the life cycle of a content piece. These estimated metrics can be great for such an analysis, because they reveal the behavior of the algorithm of the network, and we can then work further on the content if we are having a hard time getting actual interactions from the audience. We can also work hard on building a stronger group of core followers, who will interact positively with our content very quickly after it is published, boosting our reach.

As an analyst, it is good to question the nature of metrics, especially in digital marketing and social media marketing, so that you are on top of your game when it comes to understanding the meaning and effects of each performance metric.

Interactions (likes, comments, shares, clicks, etc.) represent facts; for example, a user clicked the Share button. Factual metrics are more reliable in most cases; they are easier to understand and relate to and can even be more valuable as a stand-alone metric if you are looking for a quick performance check.

Let's discuss paid social media and promotion, where the idea is to promote content to as many people as possible with the hope of having a high amount of conversions by these people. Metrics such as impressions provide a reference for the distribution side of the results.

As an example, let's take two days in content promotion (investing the same amount of money):

- **Day 1 results**: 500 impressions, 30 conversions
- **Day 2 results**: 500 impressions, 50 conversions

In this case, using the number of impressions as a reference, we can securely understand that day 2 had a higher performance. In this example, I used the same number, to make things easy to understand. From the same number of impressions, day 2 had more conversions. Neither impressions alone nor conversions alone would have given this view.

The final judgment of performance involves more variables than just a reference of interactions against distribution. We will look further into how to evaluate performance later in the book. At this point, you need to understand that usually the size of our audience, our impressions, reach, and views do not have much value unless there is a good amount of interaction included in the results.

If awareness is the goal, then these metrics will be a little more significant, assuming that people who *potentially* saw our brand content *potentially* remember us when it is time to purchase.

Promotion on social media is a game of its own, and it drives us into dealing with aspects of digital promotion that are common to digital marketing in general. When it comes to paid content, social media has a certain common ground with other digital advertising standards on the Internet. Soon, we will go down a path where we negotiate impressions, clicks, conversions, actions, and so forth.

If paid content success is our main objective in using social media, and it is our main interest when applying analytics, we can still cut through the clutter of information on paid strategies by mapping very clear, measurable, and relevant goals to our business, such as

- Registration for a newsletter or any content channel
- Purchases in a digital store
- Downloads of a new app

You can set the goal as something that brings you a clear business benefit. It helps measure the success of campaigns, independent of any other metrics and sources. Optimization of processes is always good; it will most likely always be needed. But best to place your feet on solid ground with clear goals first, and feel safe knowing that you are going in the right direction. Setting clear goals at the start also makes the work in strategic analytics much easier. When the goal is to only improve a specific metric, no matter what, things become more confusing. This is neither helpful nor reliable in the long term. Even if you need to focus on certain metrics as part of the journey toward a broader business goal, you can still have your higher goals very clearly guiding your work.

What this means is that if we focus, for example, on conversions without being true to our business goals, we might lose the identity of our brand and the perception of our brand in the market will be harmed. This includes how aggressive we are in our promotions, with our copy, the quality of our images, and so forth.

Paid social media strategies are affected by the organic effects of content and marketing in general. We will look more into this going further, but I want to point out that a conversion-based strategy that ignores organic effects is a compromise, because of the lack of time or other resources. Such a strategy can be the best way to go for some companies at certain times, but it is not the only way, and probably not the way that generates the highest possible long-term growth.

Many times, because of the focus on conversions, conversations around performance take only the estimated metrics as a reference. So we can hear or read about strategies that had a huge amount of impressions, and that's it. This can give some reference to some aspects of the strategy, but these numbers alone will not prove if a strategy is ultimately successful or not. They also rarely lead to an action point because they require more information and details to generate an actionable insight.

As a final note, the understanding and relationship between estimated metrics and factual metrics will be part of the core of current and future strategies in social media and social media analytics. It is likely that whoever owns the data (e.g., social networks) will not release too much of the factual data for free. The bottom line is that there is value in social media data, and that will translate to financial measurements at one point. Organic performance will never die, but if you wish to control your performance, then you will likely need to join the paid game.

With a large amount of high-quality data, we can reach very high-quality estimates, to the point where we get our estimates correct and statistically validated every single time. That is the point in which machines take over the decision-making process, and automation kicks in to take care of such tasks. When artificial intelligence comes in, we don't have to worry about data sources so much. Since we are still driving most of the decisions at this point in time, we should think more about this so that we can detect the nature of data sources and successfully apply this knowledge to our analyses.

Public and Private Data

Another element of data and its sources is whether the data is public or private. This causes confusion and can be a long ongoing debate. *What is public and private in the world of social media?*

Sticking to principles and regulations of data gathering and analysis, and not to the deep ideological privacy debate that will most likely push into eternity, we can think of public data and private data in a very simple way:

- **Public data** is what anyone can see when navigating a social platform.

- **Private data** is what only the owner of the social media profile can see.

We still face privacy limitations over certain profiles of certain individuals in certain networks, but this general rule of thumb can help us when we are looking for data sources. This helps us understand how third-party providers of social media analytics get so much information from certain sources. You will learn how (in some cases) information is shut behind locked doors or "walled gardens."

So if we are looking for competitive analytics and social media benchmarking, which is really a *must-do* for optimizing social strategy, we need public data for that. Public-level data allows us to see the performance of our competitors' social media channels or any of the available information that is not generated by us. Two points are important to remember:

- What is public can be easily compared.

- What is private, if it does not belong to us, can only be estimated.

Some services, for example, offer to detect paid posts on Facebook. Paid information is private, so it is not available if we don't own the data. Paid detection offers an estimate of it based on a machine learning process. Strategically, this can be extremely useful, but it is important to understand that it is an estimate based on indicators from the content. They show that a certain post has a high chance of being paid or not, but won't be exact. Even without exact information, sponsored post detection is a great insight into the competitive strategy of paid social media. We can use it, of course, but it is always good to keep in mind that we are dealing with an estimate, so we should consider that in our conclusions.

This is an example in which blocked access to a private data source became somewhat accessible through the intelligence of social media analytics platforms. Paid post detection is usually powered by machine learning, and this is the kind of insight that we will see more of in the future, following the advance of these technologies. Machine learning and artificial intelligence will play a big role in the future of social media, in many ways.

In conclusion, understand that paid detection does not come from the same data source as private data. It is not the private information being revealed. It is a new data source coming from the intelligence of the machine learning system—so that you can get your notion of the data sources involved well covered.

Keep in mind what is real data and what is a calculation made by a data provider. If you find yourself in a discussion in which one estimate is said to be better than another estimate, or *this sponsored detection is better than that one*, you really need information on how each program calculated everything to reach a conclusion or have enough tests made. So estimates can be great, as long as you know it is an estimate and how it works. When private data of others is unavailable, you will likely need to have processes for estimating these numbers.

Data Gathering in Social Media Analytics

Data can be gathered in two ways when it comes to pulling human action and interaction information from social media platforms:

- Via API (application programming interface)
- Web crawling or scraping

Social Media Network Support of Data Collection

How much does a social media network support the collection of data by third-party companies? An easy way to think of it is this: If a social media network offers an official API, it supports data collection.

Crawling a social media network for data can be a complicated task in most cases. Networks have all sorts of specific restrictions on data gathering for all sorts of different reasons. From privacy issues to very simple server performance issues, social network platforms control the way external parties plug into their data. They also control how much of the past data, or historical data, can be accessed. This means that it can be impossible to access past data in certain cases.

The idea around studying this topic is that we, as data-driven marketers or analysts, understand that data collection involves specific processes—and being supported, or not, by a platform is included in this. So it is good to know if a social media network supports data collection or not, because it helps us understand what kind of data we can collect, how easy it is to collect, and what challenges we might face.

It is also important to keep in mind that we don't need to go too far on this issue; we can keep it simple. Many people think that ultrapowerful access channels are needed for quality data to be collected, but that is just not true.

In some cases, social media networks offer different access channel options to connect to their data. Some access channels are more robust and dedicated to specific users, which pull a huge amount of data very quickly. That process is usually tied to the performance of the platform technology more than anything else. This means that there are no differences in the data itself, but rather in the speed in which it is collected, or the amount of data collected over time.

A copy of a piece of data is exactly the same as the original data. If I get the information from one access channel, and someone else gets the same information using a different channel, it is still the same information. Corrupted data is an entirely different problem. It is not related specifically to the channel from which data is gathered; it can be related to several other aspects. Missing data is not related only to the channel used to collect the data. Having tested many analytics tools, I have noticed that problems with data can happen, but are usually related to different issues every time.

So we should be extra careful when defending data consistency and quality based on an overview of so-called special access channels. We must do a lot of homework before we start a debate about data consistency and quality. This topic becomes very technical and requires updated knowledge of the tiny details of technology on the social network side. So we don't need to go that far to become good analytics strategists. We can always rely on the very technical people around us, and the software providers themselves, if we need to deal with a specific situation regarding data consistency.

When in doubt, the best way to go is to perform a few tests. We can compare the same data request across different providers and look for the differences. Then, we can ask the providers to help us understand the details, and go from there.

Once, I had a conversation with a client who wished to view Twitter data. This client would only work with me if I confirmed that the data that I was gathering came from a channel called the Twitter Firehose.

He wished to see very simple data, such as the evolution of followers through time and the evolution of interactions through time. I told him that he did not need Twitter Firehose for that. Twitter Firehose would be needed for different objectives.

But he had a misunderstanding that this specific channel was the only one able to give him quality data. He was wrong, and it took him a very long time to realize it. He lost a lot of time on his project. If he had just looked at the Twitter Firehose web page and read the following, he would have found out that he didn't need special access.

> *This endpoint requires special permission to access. Returns all public statuses. Few applications require this level of access. Creative use of a combination of other resources and various access levels can satisfy nearly every application use case.*

If we are going to dive deep into the technical details of data-gathering mechanisms, we must be sure to research the official sources of information.

API: Application Programming Interface

An API is a structured channel of access into an application. It allows a programmer to see a clear structure of the information that is stored in the application. This structure points the programmer straight to the data that is being sought.

Facebook offers API access to its data. A programmer can look into Facebook and request any specific information, for example, "total likes for a certain page post" (I'm not using any specific programming terms here). Facebook then shows the programmer exactly where the number of the "total likes for the post" is located inside their database, and the programmer can then easily get that information by adding that access point to their data request.

The programmer can then safely add to a data accessing program the places in which the data is stored inside any application that the program is trying to access, because the data will always be at the same spot. With this safe and reliable access, the programmer can then work on the access program, so that it can always find the data from the other application it is connecting with.

So it is very easy to use API access to create a repetitive action. If one program always needs the same data from another program, an API helps programs connect and the data is always perfectly exchanged.

Web Crawling or Scraping

Everything we see on the Internet has a source code driving it—a set of instructions for all the systems connecting and interacting with the data. A good-looking website full of images has a set of hidden instructions telling the browser how to display all that information.

A programmer can tap into the source code and then *crawl* for any specific information needed. Other terms are also used to describe this process, such as *scraping*.

Web crawling/scraping is a very fragile and unstable way of gathering data, because when anything changes on the website, the source code is changed, and the programmer has to reprogram a new way to *crawl* for the information.

It is also likely that *crawling* can bump into privacy regulations from websites; the owners of these websites will not like that very much. So whenever possible, API access is the way to go. APIs are what most analytics platforms rely upon.

Key Takeaways

- Data is information, simple in essence, but becomes complicated as you need to store, access, transfer, and manipulate.

- Separating marketing data in offline and online sources can be a good first step to find what you need.

- Analytics requests can be approached by first separating them in parts and then identifying the availability of the data you need.

- Social media analytics platforms will likely become *intelligent* in the future, and take you directly to insights, but for now, that is still your job.

- Social media data can be defined as data generated within a self-proclaimed social media platform—let's stick to that in this book.

- Data sources on social media are conceptually based in human actions and activity on social media platforms.

- Human actions across social media platforms always fall into one of a few common categories, for example, create a profile; publish content; praise or react to content; comment on content; share content; create groups and content only available to the group; send direct messages and chat with other users; connect to another profile; purchase a product.

- Similar human actions can have very different meanings across platforms. You cannot assume that a Facebook like has the same value or impact as an Instagram like.

- Some data sources deliver estimates; others deliver factual data. It is important to know when you are dealing with one or the other.

- Promotion on social media is a game of its own. As a general rule, you should focus on what can be measured and what has true meaning to your business. If you wish to control your performance, it is likely that you will need to join the paid game.

- Public-level data is comparable and is the basis for competitive analytics and benchmarking.

- Understanding processes around data gathering helps you understand how easy or difficult it is to retrieve what you are looking for.

From Data to Insights

Shaping Data to Work for Us

Insight is the holy grail of analytics. The faster we reach an insight, and the more relevant insights we have from a process of analysis, the more successful we can consider that process. To reach the insights we need, we first shape the data into metrics and then work with the metrics to find what we can from the data. Metrics can be seen as an interface between us, and our human way of understanding, and the raw data we are using.

Analytics are driven by metrics. Metrics are the building blocks for our analyses. A metric is a collection of data that is put together for a specific objective, such as understanding the interactions on a piece of content over time. Therefore, as a natural next step in our studies in this book, we start to see how data is shaped into metrics and a few basic elements that drive us to use our data in a certain way.

Later in the book, there are chapters dedicated to more specific studies of metrics. At this point, what matters is that we can finish our overview of the use of data in analytics, and have an initial big picture, which will better prepare us to move forward into analytics strategy.

© April Ursula Fox 2022
A. U. Fox, *Social Media Analytics Strategy*,
https://doi.org/10.1007/978-1-4842-8306-6_2

The Key Is to Be Actionable

Actionable is the word of choice when dealing with analytics. At some point, hopefully soon into the analysis process, we must reach insights that push us to clear action paths. Being actionable is a major objective when shaping data into metrics and when using metrics to perform our analyses and build reports, dashboards, and any output.

When it comes to being actionable at the metric level, you can notice that some metrics immediately give actionable insights, while others create the need for further analysis.

An Example of a Single Metric Giving Actionable Insight

The *posts/interactions comparison* metric in Figure 2-1 shows the time of the day and day of the week when the content is driving more interactions. Being specific, it counts the posts, checks for the time they are created, and counts the interactions they generate. It is a simple example of a metric that gives an actionable insight straight away, even before it is correlated with other metrics. I used quintly analytics for this book, but you can approach all of the metrics and studies here proposed using any social analytics tool with similar capabilities.

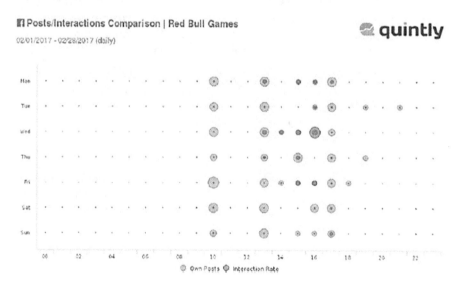

Figure 2-1. Posts/interactions comparison

From a simple graph, we can then adjust our posting times to fit what the data is telling us. In Figure 2-1, the dark circles represent interactions, while the light circles are posts with not as many interactions. So the more we have big dark circles in this case, the better. This is a very simple example, and more complex studies can be made about best times to post, but even being simple, this is already an easy-to-understand example of what it is to be actionable.

In other cases, a metric may lead to a new question, and the process may extend itself toward a final actionable insight. This does not mean that the metric was badly shaped or is irrelevant in any way. It will not always be possible to jump into actionable insights from one metric alone. The process of one metric leading to another, and one question leading to another, is very common in analytics, and we will understand how to better deal with this when we look at metric correlation, reports, and dashboards.

An Example of a Metric Leading to New Questions

The *interactions distribution* metric in Figure 2-2 shows what type of interactions the content is driving. We see how many people are reacting, commenting, or sharing the content.

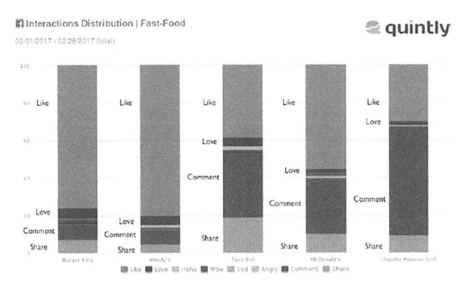

Figure 2-2. Interactions distribution

Figure 2-2 shows the different types of interactions distributed from top to bottom in the order they are presented, where the first area shows the percentage of likes and the last area shows the percentage of shares.

If we look at the metric and see that we are driving a huge amount of likes, some comments, but much fewer shares, we then will have a second question to deal with: *Why?*

The answer will then call for a few other metrics that can help to understand the reason or give us a pattern behind the behavior of the community over the content.

One possible next step is to look at a table with all the posts from the page in the period, then rank the content by top posts for each interaction type, and ultimately go through a few of these posts to detect a pattern behind the numbers. Figure 2-3 is an example of an Own Posts Table metric that will help us investigate patterns of interactions related to the content.

⨍ Own Posts Table |

02/01/2017 - 02/28/2017 (total)

≈ quintly

Post	Total ...	React...	Com...	Shares
Nordstrom - 02/18/2017 06:08:02 View Post Fall in love with flats. Shop the shoes of the season: http://bit.ly/2kSsN96	100,535	97,528	1,884	1,123
Nordstrom - 02/01/2017 09:13:25 View Post Say hello to the new Ivy Park Spring 17 collection. http://bit.ly/2jDllq4	95,412	90,444	2,515	2,453
Amazon.com - 02/18/2017 13:01:03 View Post Naps in space 🚀💤http://amzn.to/2lYljkL	73,637	59,447	4,044	10,146

Figure 2-3. Own posts table

A pattern can be anything that the content pieces have in common. Maybe a certain product of the brand always drives shares, and another product doesn't, or the style of the text in our content promotes different patterns. It could be anything, and we will see more ways to quickly look for patterns as we go further in the book.

Another way to explore the reasons behind certain interaction patterns is to perform a hashtag detection or keyword search over the content and look at the kind of interactions connected to each topic, subject, or theme published on a channel. Figure 2-4 is an example of a hashtag detection filter. It searches the content of the selected channels for the presence of any hashtag and shows the interactions related to the posts in which such hashtags are used.

Hashtag Detection | Fast-Food

02/01/2017 - 02/28/2017 (total)

Hashtag	Posts	Reactions per Post	Comments per P...
#1	1	4,407	1,440
#Monday	1	4,830	385
#AmazonPrime	1	4,830	385
#PrimePet	2	3,970	357
#Caturday	1	3,110	329
#AmazonSweepstakes	6	938	2,113

Figure 2-4. Hashtag detection

These filtering mechanisms are great to save time when we need to go through a lot of content at once. We are basically grouping the entire content of a channel very quickly and easily, to then analyze the performance per group—a group in this case being a theme, subject, product, or any relation of a specific hashtag to the content it is present within.

A third way is to look at interactions distribution by content type and start by seeing, for example, if photos drive more reactions and videos drive more shares. Figure 2-5 is an example of the interactions distribution by post type metric.

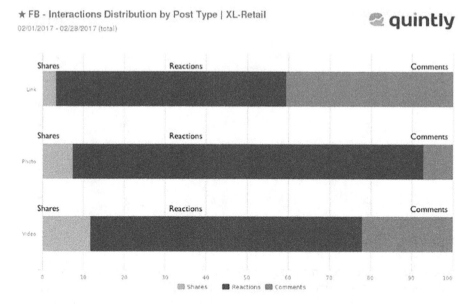

Figure 2-5. Interactions distribution by post type

Ultimately, we want to clearly understand what is driving our engagement with the community. Having an idea of what is driving each type of interaction leads us closer to that objective. It comes down to some experience as an analyst, combined with a well-built dashboard of relevant metrics, to reach these conclusions very quickly. We will look at this later in the book.

Once we get there, and we have all the information we need, then we are facing the actionable stage again, in which we go back to our content creation and planning stages, and adjust the details based on what the data has told us.

In this example, if we found that a certain type of content drives more shares, and we want to have even more shares, we can then take action and post more of that type of content. We can also explore that content type and enhance it even further.

So being actionable does not necessarily mean that we need to have only a single metric or very few metrics to work with. In many cases, we need a broad amount of metrics to get to that point in which we can propose the next action or the next step in our analysis or our social media strategy.

Later in the book, we look at specific metrics, the kind of information they bring us and when we should use one metric or another for better results. For now, it is important to understand that even before we start our analysis, we can think about what we want to see from all the numbers available. We can have an objective and test a hypothesis. This makes it much easier to select what we need out of the huge number of metrics that we have available to us.

Also, we will see that we can create custom metrics from the data we have, and these primary points help us shape the data into a metric that is very relevant to our specific project. We will explore custom metrics later in the book as well.

Focus on Being Objective Even When Everyone Else Is Not

When walking the analytics path in search of the best data, it is a good idea to be very careful with subjective goals. Trying to find "which brand is performing better" might not lead us to a clear idea of what to look for in terms of data and metrics to then answer that question.

Instead, these subjective goals such as better, creative, innovative, successful, and disruptive will require an initial step of definition to describe what they actually mean or what we want them to mean specifically for our project.

Subjective goals with clear meanings allow you to define which data and metrics are needed to reach insights. If this stage of transforming subjective goals into objective steps is neglected, we might end up with a very confusing process, not only for us, but for anyone reading our reports if we ever manage to get a good output from such an unstructured approach. If in our reports we feel the need to bring up subjective goals, then we can link the meaning directly to the metrics we are using to reach our conclusions. We must explain to the audience what we are doing.

For example, if our goal is to point out which brand is doing better in a competitive analysis, and we reach that conclusion after an analysis of several metrics, we can display a checklist on our report, showing in which metrics a certain brand is doing better, to then make it clear why it is doing better overall. When looking at each of those metrics, we set parameters for what is a good result or a bad result; positioning brands against such parameters provides an analysis of the level of their performance.

The tricky part is that there is no exact formula to this. It varies by the value that we give to the metrics and the strategy that we believe is the best.

For example, some people may decide that a higher number of average interactions per post is better than higher overall interactions (independent of number of posts), so it is up to the analyst and the team to decide what they will judge as being best during the analysis.

We will look further at this later in the book, when I discuss metrics, reports, and dashboards.

When setting up our goals, some goals can be set very objectively from the start and still be clear to the audience. When deciding on the set of goals that we judge important to our brand and our analysis, we can pick as many of these objective goals as we need, to quickly generate insights into the best performance, and easily communicate this to our audience.

Goals may include the following:

- The fastest growing audience
- The highest average number of interactions per post
- The most shareable content
- The most interactions with video
- The highest number of mentions
- The highest number of total interactions

These are very objective goals—and some even match the name of the metric. These goals lead us directly to equivalent metrics, and we will have the answer to our study ready very quickly.

If we have such studies happening on a constant basis, we can even prepare a few dashboard templates with the common goals that we usually deal with in every project; it speeds up our work even more. The more familiar we are with our goals, metrics, the data that we need, and our tools, the faster we can deliver reports and insights. Once the principles of analysis are clear, becoming familiar with social analytics tools, or building relevant metrics and dashboards for any project, becomes very easy.

It is our responsibility as an analyst (independent of job title) to translate subjective terms to objective ones, and from there drive the metrics to deliver the analysis. If we are working in a team and we are the one responsible for the analytics part of the process, we must not be afraid to ask as many questions as we need until our team establishes what is required for the project. Simple questions, such as *What do you mean by better?*, drive the conversation to an objective point.

If we are not the person primarily responsible for the project, we can still question the responsible person about the reason why they chose certain metrics and parameters to answer the project objectives.

As a quick reminder on this topic, there is no obvious meaning to any of these subjective terms, so we just ask, and ask again, until we have something objective to work with.

- Better? Worse?
- Good? Bad?

- Right? Wrong?
- Success? Failure?

These words are subjective until placed into context.

- Better than…?
- Success compared to…?
- Right for…?
- Good based on…?

When going into analytics, the key is to correctly determine the specific context behind objectives and then relate to this context in our results.

Creating a Plan to Shape Data into Insights

On the road to insights, it is useful for an analyst to scout ahead. We will eventually look at strategic planning for analytics, but note that a good skill is the ability to project the available quantitative and qualitative data into potential insights, even before the actual analysis takes place. This is not as hard as it seems.

After working with analytics for a short time, you are able to create a plan to make the best possible use of analytics—even before jumping to an analytics tool or using any technology. Think of it as a director creating a storyboard for a movie; he sees the movie in his mind even before he starts to figure out all the technical details and have a final judgment of capabilities. This is very useful because it saves a lot of time on our project, and if we are paying for technology (which is very likely), we cut costs by saving time.

Much of the knowledge for projecting our needs is shared throughout this book, and much of it comes with experience. Once we are more familiar with specific metrics, and we have gone through entire processes of analysis and reached insights and conclusions a few times, we are naturally able to scout ahead and project or estimate our needs.

Once the process starts, however, we must be open to what the data shows and to be surprised by what is revealed. So whatever we project or plan only serves as a very important, useful, and time-saving guideline.

The Planning Stage: Projecting Possible Insights

The ability to project insights is a skill that greatly improves over time. As you work with more and more data, and go back and forth in search of what matters, the ability to project which insights can come from each data set becomes a natural, or effortless, skill.

In essence, the principle is simple: understand the data that is available, and realize how it can be converted into an insight.

A Very Simple Example: The Analysis of a Social Media Post

What can we get from a post?

We know—even just by being social media users ourselves—that a post includes certain data, such as

- The time of publication

- The content (text, image, link, audio, video, etc.)

- Interactions by people who have access to the content, such as likes, comments, shares, retweets, replies, and so forth

Additionally, there is less obvious data related to a post, usually hidden from the eyes of a common user, such as the paid vs. organic nature of that post (if it had investment behind it to promote exposure or not).

Leaving the complicated data aside for now, we can then think of what insights can we find with what we have?

The following are a few examples:

- **Time of publication**: Determine if it is a good or bad time to connect with the audience, based on the comparison of the interactions made by the community on different posts and different times.

- **Content**: Determine if the type of content is enjoyed by the audience, again based on interaction comparison to other posts.

- **Interactions**: Determine what impact the content had on the audience. Was it worth being shared? Did it provoke comments? Good comments?

There are more interesting correlations that we can make around the data from social media content. The example here is just to illustrate our line of thought on projecting what we can get from what we have.

The point of this stage is to think about the process of transforming data into insights and how this process happens before the analysis. It begins inside the mind of the analyst. Throughout the book, we dive deeper into the analysis process, so consider this example as simply getting your feet wet.

Sticking to the human aspects of what is behind the data is very helpful in determining what the possible insights are and how to reach them.

If we are investigating possibilities involving human interactions, we can always start by asking ourselves, *What data can humans generate by interacting with that post or participating in that conversation?*

A Glimpse into the Analysis: The Process of Comparison

During the analysis is when an analyst attempts to measure enough comparisons or correlations to reach enough conclusions and answer enough of the questions that were brought up in the first place. It is also a process of discovery, in which the data can also be surprising and reveal more than we asked for.

The best analysts and the best analysis processes inevitably create new questions as they go along. They pursue a very specific story that a certain data set is trying to tell. By *best* I mean they generate more of the useful insights or more of the strategic material that can be applied to decision-making in less time.

This curiosity in asking *Why?* every time something peculiar is spotted is an inevitable impulse of an analyst. It is a natural part of the analysis process. It is with this instinct that the connection of the subjective human side to the objective data side of the analysis is made.

This is why we are approaching the use of analytics from its foundation: so that we can train ourselves to naturally think of relevant questions that may lead us to new discoveries. The questions themselves are very simple at their core:

- Why?
- When?
- Who?

- What?
- Where?
- How?

Why did I have a spike in interactions? When did it happen? Who generated it? What is it related to? Where does it come from? How relevant is it to my past performance? To my objectives? To my competitors?

The trick is to answer such questions quickly, to know how to ask the right question at the right time, and just like a chess player, to think ahead about the possibilities of the game.

We will dive deeper into the mindset of an analyst in this book and work on ideas to enhance our way of thinking throughout the process of analysis. For now, remember that a principle of analysis is comparison, and curiosity is the fuel for a good analysis process.

Going beyond the human analyst, we can see that machines are now taking over and running processes that uncover unexpected results and even predictions based on factors that are either overseen by the human eye or part of a data set too complex or too large to be used by a human-driven process.

These machines are being built to be as intelligent as technically possible and inevitably start thinking for themselves (and for us) sooner or later.

When we hear of machine learning or artificial intelligence, we can be sure that from these processes a new era of analyses will come to be. All of us will eventually become familiar with these processes when dealing with analytics.

The subjective world of humans, therefore, will need to become even more objective under the eye of machines. It is intriguing to think about how machines will make such connections and process human subtle behavior to reach actionable insights. It is very likely that we are much more predictable than we imagine. We create machines and give definitions to their parts, and in turn machines will analyze us and give their definitions to our parts.

Without extending too much into machine-based analysis processes, a common issue today is that machines are reaching mind-blowing results from the analysis of large data sets but are not quite able to clearly explain how they reach such results. So part of the challenge that technologists have is to generate a more clear explanation of how a result is reached. This is a very interesting area of study and one recommended to all who are interested in strategic analysis and the use of analytics.

Remaining within the human-driven approach to analysis, we can then highlight a few crucial elements that help us along the way, such as the way we choose our objectives, our analytics tool setup, and the tools themselves.

Objectives: Keep Them Simple

To quickly relate a human world to the world of data under a process that we are capable of working with: keep it simple.

Ask yourself: What do people do? What do they do when they wake up? How do people relate to content? How did people relate to content throughout history?

Some aspects of people are simple in essence, so we can make that connection when preparing our objectives and preparing to analyze people. People's motives can be complex, but we can leave the area of motives as a second stage in the analysis. In content marketing and social media marketing, where we are looking at the interaction of people to technology through physical devices, many times the answers to our questions are simple ones related to timing, format of the content, and capabilities of devices and of the software. From there, we can get into more complex questions.

When dealing with objectives, always have quick and easy wins along the way. Even when dealing with a complex issue, if we create a series of simple-to-answer objectives along the way, we give ourselves an advantage against a big and complex task. We feel motivated to keep pushing as we get our positive stimulus from answering the simple objectives, and we build up a set of basic insights that serve as material to answer the complex question in the end.

The examples that we have seen so far, in which different metrics answer simple questions toward a conclusion of a more complex research, can well illustrate this process of creating simple milestones during analysis.

Preparing for Anything with a Template Setup

When working with analytics in social media, we inevitably reach a point when we feel prepared for almost any challenge coming our way. Such challenges usually come with a short deadline and people not experienced in analytics involved. Independent of the challenge, we feel empowered to face it not only because of our experience but also because of the setup of the technology we use.

With experience, we build a clear understanding of the most useful KPIs (key performance indicators) for each situation, and we are able to have our analytics tool setup in a way that helps us to be ready for almost anything. Naturally, we face situations that are unexpected, but even then, preparation based on previous experience is helpful.

Some analytics tools, for example, let us create custom dashboards and templates that we can fit into many different projects. We can then use these dashboards and quickly adapt our templates with only the metrics that are truly meaningful for a specific given project. Facing many similar KPIs throughout different situations, we can build a set of template metrics and dashboards where each dashboard can focus on one specific area of investigation or analysis.

One dashboard can be focused on quantitative KPIs, another can dive deep into content analysis, a third one can perform keyword and hashtag filtering, a fourth can work on detecting paid content and delivering paid content analysis, and so forth.

If we are using an array of different tools at the same time, we are able to bring them together onto the same dashboard by using a few tools that integrate other tools.

Dashboards are covered in more depth later in the book, but for now, remember that we are most likely able to prepare our analytics process for any given case. Prepare your formulas to reach as many actionable insights as you can very quickly. The analytics technology that we use, being it one tool or a collection of many, is a lot like a Swiss Army knife—ready to handle almost any situation.

Notes on Choosing a Good Analytics Tool

When choosing an analytics tool, it is important to dedicate a bit of time to explore a few different tools along the way. We can take some trials, get in touch with the technology providers to answer our questions, and dive into the features and limitations of what each solution can offer.

There is no easy way out of this. Some of us learn about the capabilities of different tools faster than others, but all of us will grasp details of each tool sooner or later.

In this book, we prepare for use of any given tool. The idea is to think beyond specific tools, and be in a position where you first know what you want, and only then seek the right tool for the job, not the other way around.

As much as I admire many of the companies offering fascinating tools, I would rather not hear about how useful a tool is before I know what I need for my project. Once my goal is set, I am happy to increase my knowledge about a product. But the process has to start on my side, within my project, so that I have a strong basis to judge what I need.

One useful process for making choices and learning about tools is listing the needs for your project. This sounds very simple, I know, but believe me when I say that most of us don't do this when we look for technology. We want to be surprised and to discover what is new, so we feel that an initial list of needs is irrelevant. But on the contrary, the more diversified the market, the more valuable such a list will be.

From our initial list, we can break down our needs into important subsets, identify what is most valuable to us, and use it as a good checklist to evaluate and choose the ideal tool. In some cases, we find tools that take one or more of our needs up to the next level. Usually, these are the tools we select.

As an example, let's say that we are looking for customized reports and we find more than one tool offering this. We then notice that one tool also offers customization of reports to different audiences and a live link to your dashboard as a report format. That is a motivating value. Another tool has an amazing graphic display of reports and decent customization capabilities. So then, we have to ask ourselves if we need the more attractive visuals or the more flexible set of features.

One good and simple question to keep in mind when going through tools and demonstrations is, *Why is that important?* We can ask that as many times as we need. We don't need to pretend that we already know everything when we approach a new tool; the only ones missing out with such an approach will be ourselves. So really, we can just ask, and ask, until we have a clear understanding of what that technology does.

A big quality of most early adopters of certain technology is that they grasp the capabilities of such technology very quickly. You notice this a lot in the gaming industry, where gamers are beating games only days after the release. These early adopters reach this level of interaction with the technology because of the huge amount of curiosity they have and the drive to answer to that curiosity. We are safe in making good choices if we approach our process in such a way. We naturally have expectations from previous technology we have used, but that will not keep us from learning what is new and from enjoying the learning process and the process of mastering a new technology afterward.

I discuss more tools in this book, but when talking about shaping data into insights, being actionable, and having the right metrics for the job, I need to mention that the process is eventually driven by a tool. So having a good tool is an important part of shaping data into insights.

Data Aggregation, Calculations, and Display

In many analysis cases, we benefit from bringing different data sources together in one metric. We also benefit from creating indexes and use formulas to reach a certain insight faster. Then we choose the best way to display this data so that we can quickly read what it is trying to tell us. Data aggregation and calculations are important elements for shaping data into insights. Although this process is reviewed in the metrics and dashboards sections of this book, now is a good time to cover a few of the basic concepts and ideas.

Aggregating Data: Avoiding Common Mistakes

At any given point during an analysis, we may find ourselves building metrics with a sum of different sources, or an average, or an index calculation. This is a normal part of the analytics process, a natural step in finding the insights and answers to our questions.

However, by doing this, it is quite easy to lose track of how relevant a certain calculation can truly be in the end. A good first step in this process is to understand the data sources that you are working with in each case. Then you can relate that to your final objective to make sure that what you are doing makes sense.

A Sample Case

An analyst is looking for the total reach of a social media page over the period of one month. He comes across a data source with the total daily reach for that page. He then sums the values and takes the sum of the days in that month as the total reach for the month.

Does this make sense?

It would seem like it does, but the analysis will actually not work well. The problem lies in the nature of reach as a data source.

Reach, by definition, shows the unique people who saw the content. When creating a total sum from one day to the next, it is likely that the same people are going to be counted. Maybe they were unique on one day and unique on the next, but the sum is not showing the number of unique people. So the analyst would need to find a source for the monthly reach, which is not a sum of the daily reach.

Cases such as this happen all the time. What matters is that we check our sources as we start working with certain metrics.

Indexes: There Is Usually a Bigger Story

We see indexes used in many cases of analysis. The idea behind an index is that it can *tell the entire story* in one number. It brings many metrics together and saves the time of having to go through each metric individually.

In other words, it brings data sources together in calculations and creates insights with multiple sources in one formula. Again, the key here is to check our sources and understand what exactly the index is telling us. One social media index that suffers from great debate is the engagement rate.

The following are the usual original variations of the formula:

- Interactions divided by fans
- Average interactions per post divided by fans
- The reach variation: with unique or nonunique interactions divided by reach

Eventually, there will be even more variations. Each of these variations will have a different purpose and will tell a different *story*.

In the first two variations, the immediate questions that come to mind are sources of debate among social media analysts:

- Why divide by fans?
- Why use the average per post?

Division by fan base compares social media pages of different sizes to create a relation between each page's content and its fan base, taking into account the possibility that a larger page that has more fans will generate more interactions.

The problem here is that the size of the fan base does not have as much significance to the interactions as it once had. Pages with fewer fans can generate more interactions than the bigger ones. Pages are now publishing to nonfans as well and paying for that.

But when the analyst is trying to compare a small page with a big one, what should be done?

For the lack of a better metric, this engagement rate formula will end up being used competitively, since it uses public-level data. Another option is not to use engagement rate and take a completely different approach.

For a page in which the analyst is the administrator or owner, and assuming it is a noncompetitive analysis, the reach engagement rate is a better option, since the view is counting only the people that have potentially been exposed to the content. Reach is a private metric, which is why only the owner of a page can see it.

For competitive analysis in this case, the analyst has the option either to use the engagement rate with fans (for the lack of a better metric) or to ignore it entirely and find metrics that translate more precisely into what is truly being searched. The objective set by the analyst and the team plays an important role in the choice of the metric.

With engagement rate, you may ask:

- *Does the relation between interactions and the fan base matter?*
- *Why do I want to have this relation set inside one formula?*
- *Is this unique number (the result of the formula) helping me more than having the metrics separate?*

Keeping interaction growth separate from audience growth can be a good option in a competitive analysis. We can better understand the evolution of each metric over time. We can also take a snapshot of total interactions and audience for a certain period and quickly visualize the relationship between brand interactions and the size of the audience.

Figure 2-6 displays interactions and audience at the same time.

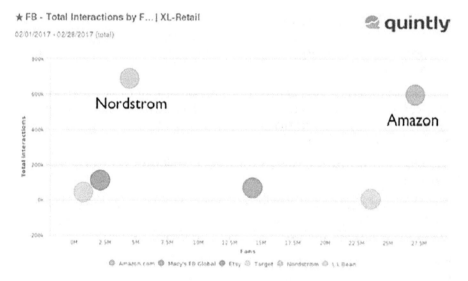

Figure 2-6. Total interactions by fans

Figure 2-6 shows that Nordstrom has fewer fans than most competitors, but more interactions. Besides Amazon, the other brands on the chart do not match the assumption that more fans lead to more interactions. Looking at this chart by engagement rate, with one number to represent the performance of each of the brands, it would be very confusing to understand what is actually happening to them. This separate view of audience and interactions is, therefore, a better metric to report.

With the engagement rate, if the audience grows and the interactions grow, the number displayed might even stay the same. So what is it telling me about the page? Engagement rate, therefore, does not tell the entire story. It needs the help of other metrics.

We will further discuss engagement rate when we look at metrics and dashboards. For now, keep in mind that some formulas are not as magical as they seem. An analyst should always question the sources and understand the formula when choosing to work with it.

Data Display: Keep It Simple and Easy to Understand

An important part of shaping data into insights is the visual side of the analysis. Many times, the way that we display data improves our process for reaching insights.

Keep data display simple. The more time needed to understand a graph, the less time you sustain working with an analytics process. We become tired of looking at graphs at a certain point. The purpose of graphs is to avoid fatigue, to get to the insights as quickly as possible, and to pinpoint relevant aspects of the metrics at a glance.

When you look at any metric that is not immediately comfortable, you can consider how it could be better displayed. Sometimes changing the way a graph looks helps more than you'd imagine. Good examples are metrics that display an entire period of time (as opposed to a snapshot). These metrics come as line charts, in which you can spot the spikes in the general trends of the line, making it easy to grasp performance. However, depending on the context of the analysis and metric, you might want to see it differently.

A Simple Example: Changing from Line to Column

If we wanted a visual of the monthly average interactions per post for a group of competitive pages over one year, a line chart, such as Figure 2-7, could be a little confusing.

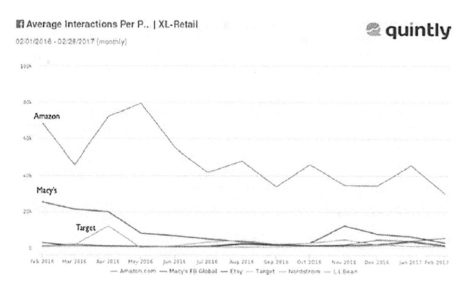

Figure 2-7. Average interactions per post

If we change the display to columns, it is likely that the comparison of one competitive page to the other will be easier to understand, and the comparison from one month to the next would be easier to make. Figure 2-8 is a variation of Figure 2-7, where the line chart is replaced by a bar chart.

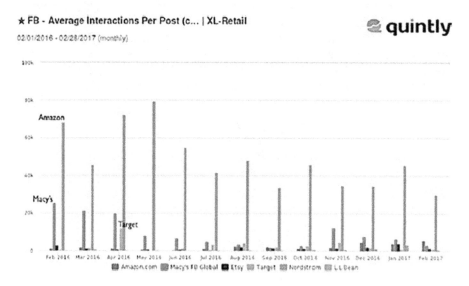

Figure 2-8. Average interactions per post (column view)

So we can always keep an open mind about the display and never assume that the graphs cannot be changed. In analytics, we can most of the times have such elements set precisely the way we want.

We will explore graphs when we look at metrics and dashboards, but it is important to consider this in our current studies.

Social Media and Big Data

As a final thought about our data overview, it is good to grasp the very big picture of what social media data represents. This helps us understand the challenges of the technologies involved with social media and social media analytics. It helps us when building our strategy and choosing technologies to work with.

Social media data definitely belongs in the big data category. Sometimes we might relate big data to an amount of data that cannot be handled by common types of technologies, so there is confusion about social media from our user perspective, since we are interacting with it all the time from devices that are very common to us. Social media data is huge. It is also part of a very fragmented landscape, and this makes it very confusing to work with from the data perspective. Therefore, all the challenges under the definition of big data are applied to social media data as well.

For marketers, it is good to start looking at social media from such a perspective, so that we can all work in making the most out of what is there today and in the future.

It is remarkable to think about the amount of data social media generates and also quite easy to grasp the idea of social big data once we think about the fact that social media data is generated by billions of people using these channels every day.

Possibly the most intriguing aspect of social media as big data, however, is not the amount of storage and infrastructure needed to work with it, but the incredible results that can be pulled from working with all of this data—the incredible potential.

Many of our projects call for insights into a broader view of the audience, the behaviors, and the use of social media. Sometimes, I receive requests for metrics about an entire industry, an entire country, or an entire social network. We certainly love to make use of huge potential, but practically, we are not quite there yet.

To kick-start a few thoughts about this, let's separate things into potential challenges and potential gains when thinking about social media and its value.

Potential Challenges

While challenges and the future of analytics are explored later in the book, this is a good point to start evaluating strategies and technologies with certain challenges in mind.

The Fragmented Landscape: How to Unify Social Data?

This challenge is huge. The scenario is such that we have many users on different social media networks generating data that is being stored separately. The same people and the same brands have their data spread out through many different databases of different companies. As users, we think this is normal, we are used to using different applications, but as data analysts, and in the position of anyone who wants to make sense of all this data, this is a terrible landscape to deal with.

It is complicated enough to simply access all of the data from each of the different social media networks. On top of that, it is also complicated to correlate users across these social networks and understand which data was created by the same person or the same brand.

The data collection challenge also bumps into privacy issues when trying to unify everything. It is likely that some kind of opt-in mechanism is needed for that privacy to be unlocked. Not everyone wants the world to know who they are; much less relate them to all their social media profiles on other networks. Most people that I have spoken with about this say that they prefer having their profiles separate.

Many services are offering people the chance to connect more of their social media profiles to the service. From dating apps to music streaming services, we are connecting our social media assets within certain environments sometimes without even thinking about it or noticing.

To do that on a larger scale is a very different game, but one worth playing. We can be sure that every social media data company out there is playing this game, and eventually, this collective effort from technology developers will come together in one big effort that benefits everyone involved. This is nothing but a hope I have as an analyst, and maybe a fool's hope.

The most likely outcome to this challenge in our competitive world is that one social media network manages to connect more data to its user profiles than others, such as data from smartphones connected to Facebook and WhatsApp, for example. It is unlikely that we will see social media networks sharing data among themselves, even for legal reasons.

Therefore, the fragmented landscape continues to be a huge challenge for the strategic use of social media data.

Who Can Pursue a Big Data Unification Approach?

One possibility is for a third-party company (not any of the social networks) to pursue the goal of unifying social data and deal with the bigger picture. This third party will likely have a very interesting product as an outcome, with insights that go beyond marketing. They will likely make use of machine learning and maybe even AI during their process. They will be part of a future when data manipulation will be easier to perform, and network APIs (connection points) will also be easier to work with and offer more data sources than today.

The need for AI and machine learning within this process is related to the speed in which we need to access and work with the data. These intelligent machines will be able to understand the needs of the application they are working on and deliver results that are likely to be unexpected by humans. It is hard for us to think the way that machines do, so these processes, in which a machine is learning how to be the best at what it does, are essential to our evolution.

Another possibility is the growth of data integration companies. These companies do not store data, but seamlessly integrate the data sources into any applications necessary. This seems to be the future of the technology world. It preserves the rights of the companies doing the hard work of data gathering, or data generation, so it fits well in the business models we currently work with.

Data aggregation companies are also great partners for innovation. Even if we are only trying to validate a certain idea we have for a new technology, we can use the power of such companies to test the application we are building before we start gathering the data ourselves.

When it comes to analytics, these companies can bring all the important data sources that we need to the same place and even into the same metric. So with the use of such an approach, we can put social media analytics together with all of our digital marketing efforts and our internal business data. So we move closer to finding the return on investment of all our digital marketing strategies, for example, among so many other use cases.

Thinking on the positive side, if we overcome all of our challenges, what is the best that can be done with social data? Marketing comes to mind immediately, of course, but what else?

To find the *jewels* within the data is also an interesting challenge for marketers and technologists.

Potential Gains

The thought of potential gains helps us find innovative uses for social media data. When we ask ourselves about what else can be done with social data, we may stumble upon ideas that generate exciting applications, like finding the best gifts for friends, choosing the best route to avoid traffic, picking up the takeaways from a new book in 5 minutes, understanding details of the emotions behind people's favorite music, and so forth.

Marketing and Targeting: The Eternal Goal of Sending Only Truly Relevant Content to the Right People

Once more information about people is known, they can be served only what they need and want. The dream of marketers always hitting their target audience might actually come true in the future. It could be even good for the audience, because suddenly, for once, something actually relevant and interesting would show up on our screens without us asking for it or looking for it.

Reference: What Do People Think About ... Everything?

Imagine a new way of learning about people's opinions about everything. This would help the world shape itself into a better place. On the commercial side, companies would be able to make better products, leading people to better lives. It can be a cycle of upgrading everything we use in a truly beneficial way. Maybe it is a utopian thought, but the effective analysis of social media big data can add to outcomes in this direction. Some technologies already do a lot of this, but under very limited conditions.

Community Growth: "Power to the People"

With easier access to social data, communities can grow stronger independently. The dependence on big budgets will likely be less relevant, and easier connections between people with common interests can be made. Communities are already formed under social channels today, but also under certain limitations.

Our Personal AI

With a lot of our conversations, interests, and purchases passing through social media, it is likely that social media data can educate artificial intelligence to learn about us. This "personal AI" of ours can then help us with a lot in our lives, just as a superpowered personal assistance. It would remind us of any and all important events. It would help us monitor our health and even help us with ideas about our next topics for study and intellectual growth.

The applications for the "personal AI" are huge, many companies have this in mind already, and parts of it are already built. We will see how far it goes.

Let's Think Big, But Not Too Big—Not Yet

Currently, we still need to hold our horses when planning for a very big project on social media and the use of social media data. In many cases, we know what we want, but the means to get there are not available and may or may never be. If we are on the development side of the coin, then maybe we can be the ones to push forward and take the benefits from so much available social media data.

There are challenges: data integration within and between social networks; privacy and permissions; data management systems and storage; final application design and programming.

In conclusion, it is important that we have a clear view of how data flows within social media networks and in social media analytics tools and in our studies. The idea here was to explore an overview of the many aspects related to the processing of data, to the work of shaping data into insights.

Technology today often seems like it should provide a plug-and-play solution, where we don't have to give much thought about the benefits it provides. While that can be a remarkable goal for many technology companies, we are not quite there yet when it comes to the strategic use of technology and analytics.

Strategy involves the understanding of all the moving parts related to our object of study, of everything we have access to that can help us in reaching our objectives more effectively and with greater success.

Your success is my ultimate objective with this book; therefore, we will together explore as much extra information as we can so that we have the necessary foundations for your strategic work.

Key Takeaways

- Being actionable does not mean using few metrics; you can use as many as you need. Some metrics are immediately actionable, while others generate further questions and call for more metrics.

- You must convert subjective goals into objective ones to find the metrics you need to apply to your projects.

- It helps to know what you want before searching for the right tool. It is a better starting point, even if you discover features unheard of along the way.

- When dealing constantly with different projects, you can set up templates to anticipate any analysis request.

- Check the nature of data sources when aggregating data.

- Understand the formula behind an index to find out if the index is telling you what you need to know.

- You can separate metrics from the formula of an index to have a clear view into what you are dealing with.

- The display of a metric (the graph or table) can usually be changed to fit better into your interpretation. You can explore this as much as you like.

- Place subjective words into context to make them objective and useful to plan your analysis.

- Look ahead to the potential insights that the data can deliver in project results; this is a skill that will greatly improve over time.

- Analysis is based on comparison. What are you comparing to reach your conclusions?

- Machines will take over a larger part of the analysis process in the future. They already deliver interesting insights today.

- Some aspects of people are simple in essence. You can take that into consideration when planning your analysis, and only as a second step deal with more complex human aspects.

- Social media data is big data.

- Huge potential exists for the full use of social data and integration of social data with other business and marketing data.

- Challenges to fully use social media data are currently immense. They include integration of different social media networks and dealing with privacy of users.

- Ambitious projects on social media data currently face challenges that are likely too big to overcome. Analysts and marketers must approach such projects with caution and a critical view.

Luis Madureira

SMINT Author and Design Thinker on Competitive Intelligence, Strategy, Innovation, and Growth

Luis Madureira has a brilliant career in competitive intelligence and strategy. He is a thinker, a visionary, and an executive who takes theory into practice and not only validates his innovative methods and his science but also generates immense success for his clients and partners.

I met Luis when he was heading global competitive intelligence as a partner of OgilvyRED, based in Lisbon, Portugal. I was working with Ogilvy on social analytics at the time, from the platform vendor side, and had the chance to experience a walk-through of a very robust platform and method he created to gather and correlate competitive information. I was impressed with his vision, his methods, his technology, and with his character. His excitement about competitive intelligence is motivating, and he is a great person, bearer of the famous friendly spirit which people from Portugal are well known for. From that point on, I continued to follow his work and learn from his insights.

When the time came to invite guests to this book, I immediately thought of bringing on Luis to share his vision with us. The reason for that, and the connection to the content we will see in the book, lies in the fact that Luis

© April Ursula Fox 2022
A. U. Fox, *Social Media Analytics Strategy*,
https://doi.org/10.1007/978-1-4842-8306-6_3

has a vision that values and understands social media, but that will also go beyond social media and into any area of an organization that will benefit from innovation. He is a true analyst and strategist, one that understands all the different factors that can affect business processes and their outcome.

You will see in the book that, as analysts, we benefit from having a broader vision on our object of analysis. The impact of social media analytics to a business will be much more significant when that process is truly integrated with the business in all relevant ways.

My questions during this interview with Luis Madureira range from details about his methods to his vision of social media. As with all the interviews in this book, this is a chance to read a real-world approach to strategy and analytics.

You can find Luis Madureira through his LinkedIn profile at www.linkedin. com/in/luismadureira/.

Question 1

Luis, you are author of SMINT, which stands for "social market intelligence." Could you share with us more details about SMINT, and the importance of certain aspects of the approach, such as agility and brands' attention to what is happening in the market?

SMINT is competitive intelligence in real time. The aim is to support decision-making or build a strategic flux that allows organizations to succeed in real time.

This is particularly relevant in a VUCA world—volatile, uncertain, complex, and ambiguous. As such, SMINT can be used to navigate the competitive environment by supporting organizations at all levels, from corporate level, passing by marketing, innovation, digital, and even content or messaging.

Only by focusing on the five strategic vectors—external and internal environments industry, customer and consumer, and players within any given geography—the organization can understand the opportunities and threats, as well as the strategies of its competitors, to position itself strategically and address change in the utmost agile way.

One of the greatest contributions of SMINT (the approach) in the development of social market intelligence (the outcome) is the usage of social web listening to integrate consumer and customer feedback.

According to J-P De Clerck, social business is the understanding of how your business can evolve by effectively embracing the fundamental principles of a business era in which social technologies and sociological changes affect the ways in which organizational and customer success is achieved.

SMINT therefore, by addressing the social consumer, and inherently the social business paradigm, develops the actionable insights that enable the development of a social business strategy. Based on a design-thinking mindset, it is human centered, and as such, it promotes customer centricity. On top, since it does so in real time, it also potentiates agility.

A real-life example comes from a competitive analysis performed for a global customer of ours. After identifying the competitor's route-to-market strategy, focused on six verticals, we investigated whether their marketing communications would follow a pattern. We discovered a pattern in their marketing communications across several levels, all the way up to the social networks. What we found was a *hockey stick* approach with posts that started by identifying the potential problems that customers face and ended with a call to action to buy the service. This had been going on for around ten months. This pattern, similar across all six verticals, allowed our customer to foresee exactly what this competitor's marketing communications would be. Most importantly, it allowed our customer to concentrate its efforts in the six middle months, in between the competitor's ten-month campaign, to close the deals for itself, thus potentially gaining market share at the competitor's expense.

Companies that overlook the competitive environment, or that do take notice of what is happening but in a reactive way, are taking a big risk. This risk can take several forms. They go from overlooking emerging competitors, namely, disruptive innovators that enter via the low end of the market, to game changers who can turn your industry upside down.

Another obvious risk is losing the first-mover advantage. Most times, being first is half the way to success, especially if economies of scale are critical. Obtaining a critical mass from early adopters, for example, can also be critical to a certain business. In this last case, getting there first is essential. The only way that I know to get there first is to identify and exploit opportunities before competitors, or be prepared to mitigate threats in case there is no possibility to be the first to market.

A quick note to highlight is that, as most companies do not develop competitive intelligence in real time, they also overlook the protection of critical information. This augments the opportunity to understand the competitive environment but also increases the threat in case your competitor has a competitive intelligence capability. In any case, you need SMINT.

Question 2

Going further into applications and implementation of SMINT, what are the challenges that will be faced in the practical aspect?

The challenge to implement a SMINT function in our organization is twofold. On one side, we need skilled analysts who not only dominate the frameworks and methodologies but also the industry and the different functions within a company. Examples range from marketing, digital, social media, sales, operations, finance, commercial finance, research and development, innovation, HR, and so on. On the other side, these analysts need to dominate technology and can creatively put that technology to use, to distill even better intelligence. This is the main reason why I set up my company, Uberbrands, to perform social market intelligence for global customers.

This leads us to a well-known Pirelli campaign: "Power is nothing without control." This is precisely the case we are facing. A capable analyst will be outpaced by a junior one using technology to his advantage, and a tech-savvy analyst will be outpaced by a senior analyst who knows his industry and is able to "read between the tea leaves" by using the frameworks and methodologies to his advantage.

Another example would be a data scientist who uses the latest technology to find relationships between the variables, but without understanding the full picture, it will be extremely difficult to find the most value-added relationships between the data points.

Question 3

What advice would you give to teams or any stakeholder looking into building a more agile and competitive company?

The best advice I can give to someone looking to build the agile company would, again, be twofold. First, always start with the consumer perspective at the heart of whatever issue you are considering. Second, build up the capabilities both from the intelligence side, as well as from the technological side. Third, perform SMINT on your competitive intelligence capabilities to always be at the forefront of your game.

Question 4

An interesting point I have read in many of your articles is related to the challenges with connecting causes and effects in the current digital era of the world. With analysis processes in mind, what can be interesting for analysts to consider when dealing with such issues?

The inability to connect causes and effects increases the complexity and ambiguity of the competitive environment, the C and A of VUCA. Digital has potentiated these factors because we become more connected and interwoven in our relationships, both personal and professionally. This created a big network where sometimes finding the cause and consequence is almost impossible, especially if you are considering the problem for the first time.

Complexity is characterized by the situation having many interconnected parts and variables. Some information is available or can be predicted, but the volume or nature of it can be overwhelming to process. This happens, for example, when an organization is doing business in many countries, all with unique regulatory environments, tariffs, and cultural values. To address this, organizations must restructure, bring on, or develop specialists, and build up resources adequate to address this complexity.

An ongoing approach is needed so that the analyst can develop a greater understanding over time, and when a problem occurs, he may process the incremental data points instead of becoming overwhelmed with the situation he is trying to shed light onto.

Ambiguity happens when causal relationships are completely unclear. No precedents exist, and the organization is facing a state of "unknown unknowns," meaning it was not aware that those data points, problems, and so forth were even possible of existing.

This happens, for example, when an organization decides to move into immature or emerging markets or to launch a venture into products outside its core competencies. In these situations, organizations face a myriad of potential blind spots that is only brought to their attention when the product is in the market, or a competency is needed that the organization did not know was needed. This problem requires a different approach. Organizations need to experiment. Understanding cause and effect requires generating hypotheses and testing them in the market. Designing experiments and lessons learned can then be more broadly applied. Once again, if an ongoing competitive intelligence capability is active, the number of unknown unknowns decreases dramatically. A good methodology for this is war gaming, a simulated strategic exercise that forces the organization to deal with current or future scenarios of the competitive environment.

Question 5

With the processes of gathering and use of data in mind, knowing that many times we will be dealing with estimates when it comes to data analysis, can you share some thoughts on how an analyst can approach competitive intelligence, and the worth of working with estimates in certain cases?

Competitive intelligence is the development of actionable insights on the competitive environment. An insight is an understanding of the information in the form of a hypothesis. To deal with the hypothesis, an analyst must consider the supporting data, observations, and even his strategic intuition. On top of that, the analyst must use the analysis of competing hypothesis (ACH) to gauge the level of trueness in the insight he developed. In a VUCA world, there is increasingly lesser time to respond to events, so an iterative approach to insights is critical to deliver the right intelligence (actionable insights), to the right person, at the right time, or at least in time to add value to certain decisions. Without sacrificing accuracy, an analyst must balance the trade-off between such accuracy and timeliness. As a summary, I would prefer to be 80% right than totally wrong, or maybe even worse, outdated.

Question 6

Another key topic in many of your articles is big data—how it grows even faster with the Internet of Things, and the challenges that it creates for analysts and processes of analysis. What should an analyst keep in mind when dealing with big data?

Big data is just that, a considerable amount of data, which increasingly grows at a faster pace, includes different formats, and includes data points that are untrue. The Internet of Things brings an exponential quantity of data to the table. This leads to the necessity for the analyst to focus on the most relevant data points, thus orienting the big data processing. In my opinion, one of the most critical capabilities of the analyst of the future will be to focus his work on the right data pool, as well as orient big data crunching with highly relevant insights from small data. In other words, big data is used to complete the picture that small data hypothesized.

Question 7

When it comes to decision-making, what can you share with us regarding the use of competitive intelligence and technology in the process?

Using intelligence in the decision-making process is quite challenging when the current *zeitgeist* is that a goldfish has a longer attention span than a human. Considering a case where an analyst can overcome all the challenges linked to "connecting the dots," he then still needs to "implant" the critical insights into the minds of decision-makers so that they can take the best decision. This leads us to the ultimate challenge, which is presenting a considerable amount of insights in both a quick and clear way, ready to support the decision or the strategy development.

Technology can help a great deal in this realm. Communication, I believe, will be the ultimate frontier for the competitive intelligence professional. As such, the only way to keep pace after reaching the insight is using the technology at his fingertips to guarantee that it is understood clearly, with no room for being actionable in the wrong way, or left with no action at all.

Defining Analytics in Social Media and Types of Analytics Tools

Analytics in Social Media

Defining a Very Broad Term

Analytics is indeed a very broad term. In the digital marketing world, it is as broad of a term as it gets. It becomes even more confusing when we go beyond marketing and start noticing that there are analytics available for any business process. So how can we differentiate analytics when working with social media?

The word *analytics* simply indicates the following.

Noun

1. (Used with a singular verb) Logic. The science of logical analysis.

2. (Used with a singular verb) the analysis of data, typically large sets of business data, by the use of mathematics, statistics, and computer software: digital marketers with a strong knowledge of Web analytics; selecting the best analytics tools.

© April Ursula Fox 2022
A. U. Fox, *Social Media Analytics Strategy*,
https://doi.org/10.1007/978-1-4842-8306-6_4

3. (Used with a plural verb) the patterns and other meaningful information gathered from the analysis of data: an abundance of actionable analytics to help you deliver a better customer experience.

—Dictionary.com

Confusion about the word *analytics* happens as we try to understand which type of data we are dealing with and how such data is collected. Different types of social media analytics tools gather different types of data from different sources.

The objective of this section is therefore to clarify what analytics means in social media, related to all possible aspects of the analysis of social channels, campaigns, influencers, and buzz.

What does each type of social analytics tool deliver to us?

Types of Analytics in Social Media: Analytics, Listening, Advertising Analytics, Analytics from CMS and CRM

The type of analytics in social media varies by data sources and search patterns that feed each process. In essence, all of it is "analytic," but if we go out into the market searching simply for "analytics" in social media, we will see that the offerings are quite different from one another.

To make it simple, let's divide the analytics types into the following categories:

- Analytics
- Listening
- Advertising analytics
- CMS analytics
- CRM analytics

On top of premade analytics tools, many companies are building their own structure for analytics and including social media into the mix. These processes involve integration of data from different areas of a business and from specific data points within digital assets created for specific purposes. An app that supports the launch of a product is one example of this. The paywall created by publishers such as *The New York Times* and others is another example. Any digital touchpoint of the company can be optimized to deliver insights through analytics and even become part of an automated feedback loop that optimizes processes and offers based on the data collected. This means that some analytics are integrated into software in a way that the program learns what is best and starts applying that learning into what it is doing. In other words, the software can optimize itself without human interference.

Although I touch on such cases throughout the book, the focus is on ready-made technologies currently available on the market and easily integrated into a social media analytics strategy. From this foundation, it is possible to jump into a broader analytics process knowing how to fit social media data into the mix.

Analytics or Channel Analytics

When the source of the data is exclusively the social channels that we add into an analytics tool, we can stick to the term "analytics." Data sources that are included under "analytics" are the content that the channel publishes, interactions related to the content published, number of followers, and some information on these followers.

It is important to make it clear that the term "analytics" alone is often used as a name to this category or data set, for the lack of a better term. It is also the term used in the market by the tools that offer this specific data set. All the types of analytics we are looking at refer to the official terms used by the market to describe or define them.

The reason behind the different analytics types on the market is mainly related to the way that social media networks are structured. There are different data points on social networks feeding different tools and platforms on the market, or even different features of a same tool, as we see happening with hybrid tools.

The social media networks offer many different connection points for their data. Some tools only connect to one or a few of these connection points. So by watching the labels that the market gives to these tools, we are also filtering the tools by the kind of data we need so that we can quickly find the best tool for the job.

Inside this analytics category, we also find data from the "native analytics" tools. These are the tools offered directly by the social media networks. Most social media networks offer some kind of analytics directly to their users. Usually, they are not complete or are not easy to work with on a professional level, hence, the growth of the third-party tools.

This does not mean, however, that you will find all of the data offered from native tools present inside third-party tools. Many times, the networks offer a set of data that is exclusive to users that connect to them directly. This usually happens while a social media network is still structuring its technology to then enable third parties to connect to it and pull data. It is demanding for one system to be open to external programs to pull data from it. As a social network matures (i.e., builds up its technology, hires more engineers, enhances its software, etc.), it is likely that it will offer direct analytics connections to third parties and be ready to handle the demand of external programs pulling its data.

So a third-party tool that may be missing a certain data set does not necessarily need to be considered a bad tool; it is important to investigate further information before making such a judgment. It is never a bad thing to ask the makers of a social analytics tool why they don't include certain data. We usually learn a lot by asking such questions, especially about the technical aspects of social media data.

Data that we can expect to find in an "analytics" labeled tool:

- Audience size and growth of a channel
- All the content published by a channel
- All interactions to published content
- Top interacting followers from that channel's audience
- Timed view of metrics: hourly, daily, weekly, monthly
- Benchmarking the data against competitor channels

The goal with the analytics tool, therefore, is to have a strategic approach for the performance of the channel and the growth of the community around official channels. The concept of community is explored further in the book, and in this case, it refers to the fans or followers of a brand, people that have the brand or a channel as a common interest point.

With an analytics tool, an analyst can easily understand important points, such as what the community is interested in and the best way to deliver that content to them.

Professional analytics tools allow you to perform competitive benchmarking, features that let us compare our analytics to other pages and channels. These can be our competitors, or partners, or any page that we are curious about and wish to learn more about what they do. This feature is very powerful, and within an analytics tool, it can be an integral part of the strategy, perhaps even the main reason to use analytics.

With such tools, we are usually dealing with 100% of the data from a channel. So when we reach any insights, we know that we have evaluated 100% of what happened within our channel or any external channel we are looking into. This is important, because we can approach the analysis from any angle we like. We can see what is working best and also what is the worst. This can truly help us shift our strategy into a better performance and make the correct references to the overall business strategy.

Social Media Listening: Keyword- and Mention-Based Analysis

Social media "listening" received this name because it relates to the analyst being able to "hear" what the market is saying about the brand via social media channels. Many marketers also refer to it as *social media monitoring*.

The process starts with a keyword-based search, and the data source in this case is any possible source where a mention of the brand (or any keyword searched) is found. It does not need to be a channel that belongs to the brand; usually it is not. It is most of the time content generated by profiles and sources external to the brand.

Please note that I make reference to brands, but listening and analytics in general can be used for broader market research as well, and different approaches that are not related to marketing, such as academic research. There are remarkable studies on happiness and other more philosophical or sociological themes that use social media analytics and listening to find results. This book does not address the depth of academic research, but if you are an academic, please be encouraged to get in touch, and we can explore those topics together and exchange resources on that.

Listening is a process that can be easily related to what a search in Google can do. It is similar to Google in the way that it is performing a search all over the Internet, but it is focused instead on finding information from social media channels. Some listening tools go beyond social media and gather information from news channels and from nonsocial channels such as websites. The objective of such additional sources is to enhance the context of the analysis, which can be fascinating.

The process in listening is based on using keywords or expressions for our search. The listening tool then crawls the Internet for the best results it can find. This means that the results in listening are often a sample of what is out there. They are not 100% of the mentions of a brand on social media or on the Internet. This is because the Internet is too broad of a space and not a problem caused by the type of study or by the listening tools. For most studies, a sample is good enough to indicate actionable points and insights.

Within official brand channels, it is likely that brands can retrieve all the comments and content from their audience or community. Therefore, when the objective is to be more precise on the analysis, an organization can create incentives for the audience to come into the official channels to express their thoughts. Listening is initially aimed at covering cases in which the official channels are not the channels that people are using to talk about the brand— cases that will likely happen a lot, despite activity within official channels. Some organizations like the beauty retailer/brand Sephora have very strong incentives for clients to be part of their internal social networks and forums, giving them unprecedented insight to their audience.

Listening tools face challenges to gather the data they need. Many social media networks are not open for listening-type searches, and the Internet is a big space to begin with. So a good listening tool is often judged by how far its search can reach and how many extra insights it can offer on top of the search.

After the trigger from keywords (the search results), most listening tools then add a few processes to enrich the data with more details.

Some of the features of these processes are related to

- Demographics: gender, age, location
- Interests of people mentioning
- Sentiment of mentions: positive, neutral, or negative
- Influencer factors, such as the number of followers of the people making mentions, or how relevant they are to the brand based on what they talk about or the number of people interacting with their content

It's important to note that these processes that go beyond the keyword search results are usually run by calculations and the technology of the social media listening tool, not by gathering the extra information directly from the social networks, or even directly from the description that people insert into their profiles.

What does this mean?

Let's look at an example.

The user performs a simple search for the keyword "Toyota."

The tool then finds the following results (different tools offer different features):

- 100,000 mentions (count)
- Mention sources: social media profiles, blogs, maybe more
- The mentions themselves (the content)
- Share of voice: mentions separated by brands if people are also mentioning competitors
- Demographics: age, gender, location
- Interests of the community making mentions
- Sentiment: positive, negative, and neutral mentions

Some of these results are pulled directly from the social media network themselves, and others are generated by the social listening technology.

The results generated by listening tools are a mix of data from social media networks and calculations or processes that run on the listening platform. Social media mentions and sources, in this example, come directly from social networks. The remaining points are processed by a tool.

Let's take a deeper look.

Demographics

Demographics depend on the network that you are searching. When available, it is often not fully accurate. If a social network gives direct demographic information from user profiles, it is likely incomplete, mostly for privacy reasons, or for the simple reason that people do not include their demographic information in their profiles. Think about it: Do you include your age, gender, and other demographic information in all the social media networks that you use?

Tools sometimes use unreliable demographic elements, such as the name of the person to determine gender.

Interests and Sentiment

Interests and sentiment are usually not provided by the networks directly. Tools use several methods to deliver this kind of information—methods that go from simple data correlation to more advanced machine learning processes.

Some tools filter the content posted by the people mentioning to determine their interests, what they talk about, and who they mention. Other tools gather general studies: offline research not specific to the search, which may only have a minor connection point to the search, such as the region or industry segment of the brand. The tool then applies these studies to the results with the intention of positioning them within a certain demographic.

An example of this is to search for "Toyota" and get information from offline studies about automobile brands. Perhaps offline research discovers that most people in the region searched who buy a Toyota are from a certain demographic, and that information is included in the results of the search.

Sentiment is also a process run by the listening tool. Listening technologies go through content to find out if what people are saying about the brand is positive, negative, or neutral.

It is very easy to understand how challenging this can be. Humans are subjective in nature, and language is not always logical and easy to update into a digital system. Sometimes, there are expressions that use negative words, but are actually expressing positive interest. Slang words such as "bad ass," "insane," and "killer" are examples; so are mixed expressions such as "hate the red hat, love the blue one."

Listening technologies are pushing the line on advanced analysis in many fields. It is very interesting to follow what these tools are doing and how they are innovating in many ways. Some listening tools are designed for image recognition to generate insights from content that has no text. It is very likely that this will be at the core of future social media analytics.

Many times, a tool does not openly tell that it is running processes on its side or pulling results directly from social networks, so we must be careful about their processes when we see a listening or analytics tool offering audience interests, very detailed demographics, sentiments, and so forth.

Keep in mind that when it comes to processes run by tools, we should check the sources very carefully. It is great to make use of advanced technology, but also very important to understand what is behind the technology, so that we can understand which companies are generating the best value in the output we get from them.

Another important point about listening is that it does not cover all of the channel details, so the use of listening and analytics together is very common and even recommended. In fact, if we go into dedicated tools, having one tool of each type running together is ideal, as each tool offers different features and answers different questions we have. I will further discuss dedicated vs. hybrid tools later in the book.

Advertising Analytics: Focus on Conversions and ROI of Paid Social Media Campaigns

Social media is strictly an advertising channel for many brands. Many marketers treat it as simply that and are very oriented to conversions and the return on investment (ROI) of their campaigns. This is not right or wrong, it is a valid strategy, like any other. If a brand is seeing results from such an approach, great. Other strategies can offer great results as well, so the everlasting debate on paid vs. organic social media will never cease to exist.

I am personally inclined toward the creation of true communities, so I also value the organic performance very much. I also understand that when a company reaches a certain huge scale, it becomes increasingly difficult to manage "true" communities, and easier to just treat social media as an advertising channel with "true-like" content posted to it, or in other words, pretending that it is building a true community when it's really not. This book will not dive too deep into the content strategy itself, but I would advise you to take that critical look at the nature of the content posted and the effect on the audience. Does the audience think it is a "true community?"

Paid promotion on social media is useful for everyone trying to get more exposure than the channel offers organically. Paid promotion can be a good addition to an organic strategy. It can be used in crucial moments to help drive the awareness of the channel. Social networks have an array of options for marketers to invest in, and some of these options work better than others for each specific case or campaign.

This is where advertising analytics come in, the information that it delivers is focused on showing to the marketer what is working best and why, based on results from the direct investment on specific content.

Conversions: The Key to Digital and Social Advertising

The performance of digital and social media ads has one central point: conversions.

The term "convert" comes from the idea of a "transformation" where a potential client becomes an effective client. Since its creation, the term has become broader, and now it doesn't mean only that a new client has come in, but rather that anything which the marketer is trying to make happen toward that end has happened. It follows the concept of "call to action"—whatever action is taken from the "call" within the content is a conversion. Conversions, therefore, can be many things. It depends on the objective of an ad or paid content.

Social media networks offer different kinds of conversions for any paid content. With new formats for ads and promoted content, we see new types of conversions available as well.

The following are examples of conversions in social media:

- Following a profile or liking a business page
- Clicking a link in a post
- Signing up or downloading an app

Other metrics are also part of the strategy, such as views, impressions, and reach. These metrics also have a cost, which is very low when compared to conversions, because they mainly work as a driver to potential conversions.

Advertising analytics focus on providing an overview of all the dynamics of promotion. Since promotion in digital marketing is usually a numbers game, where the more we produce and invest, the more we get from it, typical metrics for ads display the performance based on a large quantity of ads. As an example, we could be managing the performance of 50, 100, or even 500 different variations of a piece of content distributed at different times across different regions to different audiences. This would be impossible to manage without a good advertising analytics tool.

These tools provide metrics such as the CPM, which means *cost per thousand.* There is also CPI, which is *cost per impression,* and other metrics that facilitate the understanding of performance when dealing with distribution of promoted content on a larger scale.

Impressions and reach have significant value when running such campaigns. They reflect the power of projection and distribution of the social network we are using, and of our strategy as well, of the quality of our content. They are the initial point of measurement, and from them we add factual numbers to the mix to find the ultimate value of the strategy. If we get good impressions and very low interactions and conversions, it is time to act and make some changes to our content. Included here are not only ads specifically but any form of paid or promoted content.

Some problems with impressions and reach can be related to the amount of investment in advertising as well, so there is also the monetary factor to consider when dealing with paid content. Perhaps our content is not performing because we do not have enough investment in it. Some advertising analytics tools help address such issues.

CMS Analytics: Measuring the Performance of the Content Management Team

Another big aspect of social media is the management of content on a professional level. When we have a brand identity to maintain, many different social media channels to publish into, and an ongoing significant amount of very specific content that we wish to publish, we need tools to help us get it done.

These content management systems (CMS) also come with metrics of their own. These metrics typically display the performance of each team member and allow you to mark content to better analyze the progress of each campaign. Here, we sometimes have a mix of traditional channel analytics and analytics on the individual team members or content campaigns. So we can eventually find a metric such as "engagement per team member" to see who in our team is creating the most engaging content.

CMS tools, being such a core element for a professional social media content team, usually include features from different types of social media analytics tools. They are usually what we call a "hybrid" tool, as opposed to a "dedicated" tool that has one unique focus when it comes to analytics. There are advantages and disadvantages related to hybrid and dedicated tools; we will look at that throughout the book.

CRM Analytics: Customer Support and Sales via Social Media

Usually, when we think of CRM, or *customer relationship management*, we don't immediately think of social media. This may happen because of how hard it is to maintain a long conversation through a social media channel and how easy it is to lose track of the conversations we had. Usually, conversations related to customer support and sales that start on social media quickly move to other channels in order to be continued.

The truth is that many brands are already using social media for longer conversations and are taking the conversation all the way to a successful conversion or resolution of a problem before inviting the client to use a different support channel.

Beyond common CRM, companies are creating bots to interact with people through social media channels. These bots can do many things, from selling products to directing customer support requests and even entertain people with games. Also known as *chat bots*, these virtual entities rely on different kinds of technologies to interact. They range from simple and basic sets of possibilities to systems that learn from the interactions and evolve into delivering more.

A very common social media channel for customer support workflow is Twitter. Many brands have special teams dedicated to speaking with clients via Twitter. Facebook is also a network where many brands try to dedicate a team to engage with people within the comments section of their content or to answer questions posted to the brand's timeline or via chat. The challenge on Facebook is that the content can be longer, not as limited as on Twitter, and the volume of comments within Facebook content is usually too much to handle. In general, the volume of community interaction is what primarily limits CRM on social media.

Facebook is trying to help on this aspect of engagement by creating messaging tabs for conversations within comments sections of posts, so that people can continue the conversation without leaving the comments section of a post. This feature was available before only when using direct messages; it was a chat feature. So there is an awareness about this issue, and there are many different initiatives to help brands relate to their communities on social media and to push social channels to become truly engaged communities. Facebook is also working on giving users the ability to praise comments of others, so a comment can receive a like or any other reaction that the platform offers. This type of initiative from the social networks will help social managers understand the sentiment in audience-generated content and community behavior by monitoring reactions within the comments section, since they cannot track what happens within direct messages between users.

Some CRM tools try to integrate social media in different ways. They use it to enhance the information that a brand has about its clients, to open a new lead to the sales team, to keep the conversation going directly from within the CRM, and to keep the historical information of the relationship registered.

The metrics here vary by task, ranging from the number of questions answered by customer support and how fast the team can answer them, to the lead score in sales, where a mix of metrics are used to determine if one person is a potential client or not.

It is likely that CRM technologies will add more from social media as they evolve. One of the main challenges they face is the collection of data. Because personal profiles are usually under privacy regulations, only a few social networks, such as Twitter, offer personal data at a public level; but not everyone uses Twitter. Independent of challenges, the idea of influence and influencers is one that is likely to merge into CRM tools; companies can then better understand how influential their clients are, correlate that to their purchases and interactions history, and engage people in more meaningful ways.

A Final Note

It will all come together eventually, but looking at each part separately makes it easier to understand the whole.

All the different initiatives and tools we are seeing here will eventually be part of the same social media strategy. What happens is that the technologies offered in the market today are all fragmented in terms of features and also data sources, so it is important that we can understand each *fragment* to then understand the *whole* and reach the objectives that we have or that are given to us by internal or external clients.

We can think of this in many different ways, but going by the analogy of a cook in a supermarket, we have a recipe and all the different sections to pick our ingredients from. So we can keep an integrated view of the data and metrics (our final cooked meal), but never forget that they may come from different sources (sections in the market).

Key Takeaways

- Different types of social media analytics tools draw data from different sources, are based on different search patterns, and also deliver different results.

- Analytics covers data from the channels themselves, based on searching into previously selected channels.

- Listening covers mostly community-generated data, based on an open search by keyword.

- Advertising analytics cover paid performance and conversions.

- CMS analytics integrates channel and content team performance.

- CRM analytics connect customer relations to social media contacts.

- The ideal strategy will likely include more than one type of social media analytics, since they are complementary technologies, and add value to each other.

- It is good to understand the different types of tools and data sources available so that we can understand what exactly we need for each project we are running.

Dedicated vs. Hybrid Tools

What Are They? Which Are Best?

After looking at different types of analytics tools, we can move forward to the differences between dedicated and hybrid tools:

- **Dedicated tools** offer one type of service, such as analytics, listening, publishing, or ads.

- **Hybrid tools** offer a mix of features from different types of services (e.g., publishing and analytics).

On top of this initial division, we can also make use of *data integration tools*, which can be a very powerful and in some cases inexpensive way to get all the different data we need in one place. As technology evolves and many different tools are offered, such data integration tools give us the freedom to use any technology.

The rule of thumb when comparing dedicated to hybrid tools is that a dedicated tool delivers much more from specific sources; hence, it will likely offer more options in its field and give the user the power to do more in that specific field. A hybrid tool brings the most useful features from different fields, but does not go too far into each field.

© April Ursula Fox 2022
A. U. Fox, *Social Media Analytics Strategy*,
https://doi.org/10.1007/978-1-4842-8306-6_5

As simple as it may seem, we must still approach this rule of thumb with caution. It does not mean that because a dedicated tool is focused on one field, it is good at it, or that every hybrid tool has its features fully integrated and picks the most useful features from different fields. We will find good and bad tools despite them being dedicated or hybrid.

Breaking the rule of thumb, very few hybrid tools are as powerful as dedicated tools. They might lack in advertising capabilities, but have great publishing, listening, and analytics. These powerful hybrids are usually very expensive as well. A single hybrid tool may be even more expensive than several dedicated tools that cover the same processes.

From the user's point of view, it makes perfect sense to integrate all the features needed for a social media marketing strategy into one tool. The technical complications behind this, however, are huge; hence, the costs of these top integrated tools become very high. As an alternative, it is possible for a marketer to go fully into dedicated tools and still have a very powerful setup for a good price. So the choice of which tool is best for our project is not as simple as it seems at first.

Let's point out the specific advantages of

- Dedicated tools
- Hybrid tools
- Integration tools

Common to All Tools

Before going into specifics, keep in mind that the best tools in any field always offer the following features:

- All possible reporting and exporting formats related to images, spreadsheets, and editable slides
- Customization of reports
- Automated reporting
- Detailed selection of the period of analysis
- Advanced user permissions management
- API access to the tool

It is important to note that processes such as machine learning and artificial intelligence run on top of any type of tool and will not affect our research at this point. While there is great value in such processes, we can safely approach this study as the basis for our knowledge going forward and dive into more advanced machine intelligence once we are comfortable with the descriptive side of analytics.

Dedicated Tools

A good dedicated tool is one that offers all possible features related to its field. The best dedicated tools in each field go further and innovate, pushing the entire field.

When scouting the market for dedicated tools, start with a clear checklist of features, and then round up the finalists for a check into unique features, user experience, quality of graphics in reports, support and training, and any elements that can influence your final call.

To make it simple, approach this topic with a quick look at the fundamental elements of dedicated tools—elements that influence the quality of such tools despite the evolution in technology. Take into account the objectives of these tools, which will likely not change anytime soon.

The following lists what the best tools in each field deliver.

Analytics tools offer the following:

- **More metrics and channel-based data sources**: Better tools offer access to more data in their field.

- **Competitive benchmarking**: Detailed channel-based data from pages that do not belong to us, with features to help us compare this data to our own in many ways. The very best tools do not have limitations in the number of channels you can look at once, and offer detailed analysis.

- **Include all possible information from native analytics tools**: For example, Facebook insights and Twitter analytics integrated into the tool, so that we don't need to access the native tools at all during our workflow. We stay within the environment of the dedicated tool.

- **Customization and creation of new metrics and dashboards**: Better tools offer advanced customization, which unlocks the power of having access to the data sources. This is very important, since there is no point in having so many data sources available, and be limited on the use of them.

Listening tools offer the following:

- **More social networks and data sources**: Some listening tools go beyond social media and into news channels to relate mentions and brand presence to important online and offline events related to the brand (or search term); this can be huge.

- **Relevance of mentions and of people or channels mentioning**: Measures relevance based on the size of the audience's audience, a view of reach and interactions on mentions by audience, and other elements.

- **Influencer analysis**: An extension of the relevance analysis. It detects channels or profiles that are already promoters of our brand or have the potential to do so.

- **Competitive benchmarking, measuring quantitative and qualitative aspects of competitor mentions**: Some tools detect and indicate potential competitors.

- **Audience demographics and interests**: This aspect greatly varies from one tool to another. We look for the most we can get from a tool, but need to always check how it gathers information.

- **Sentiment analysis**: This point also greatly varies from one tool to another. Some tools go as far as image recognition applied to sentiment.

Advertising analytics tools offer the following:

- All advertising-related metrics (CPC, CPM, CTR, CPI, etc.).

- Creation of social media ads within the tool. Some tools make A/B testing and the creation of variations of ads very easy.

- Suggestions on how to optimize your ad investments, including predictions of performance based on factors such as the amount spent.

- Access to more social networks to promote within and integrated management of the campaign.

CMS and social CRM tools offer the following:

- Full publishing features and management of content assets, such as pictures, videos, and links, and including marking content for campaign analysis

- Team member performance analysis

- Information on customer relations, with specific analysis on the number of questions, response time, activity and relevance of customers, and other elements

The Advantages of Dedicated Tools

The following are some advantages of using dedicated tools:

- More for our investment within a field

- Cover the full spectrum of features within a field

- Freedom to change tools independently by type, without having to change our entire setup at once in case we need a new tool

Think of a dedicated tool setup as a series of independent modules that you can swap if one of them is not working, but don't have to touch those that are working well. So we could change our analytics tool without changing our listening tool, and so forth.

Another advantage is that we usually have a tool that continuously improves in its field. So we do not have to worry about changing tools too often, since the best dedicated tools continue to be developed to be the best at what they do. A hybrid may improve a certain aspect of its technology, but that new feature may be something not relevant to you. The best dedicated tool improves all aspects so that it can stay ahead of the game in its segment.

The Disadvantages of Dedicated Tools

The following are some disadvantages of using dedicated tools:

- Lack of out-of-the-box integration between tools

- More providers to deal with

- More tools to onboard and learn how to use

Dedicated tools offer indirect disadvantages. Because they aim to be the best in their field, it is likely that the disadvantages are related to aspects external to the features and capabilities of the tool. Some disadvantages, such as the lack of integration between tools when choosing a dedicated tool setup, can be dealt with by choosing another solution that handles the integration. Solutions such as open dashboards and companies that build any integration for their users are great possibilities to work with in such cases.

Hybrid Tools

The concept behind a hybrid tool is that it can take good care of an entire process. When we look at hybrid tools, we see that the creators behind these tools are trying to understand what marketers need to do to succeed at certain objectives, and are delivering all the features needed to do so.

For example, we may find a hybrid tool that handles publishing, ads, analytics, and listening. The idea behind such a tool makes perfect sense. If we follow the reasoning behind each part of our process as social media marketers, we see that there is a clear logic behind each one.

- **Publishing**: Content is the trigger, or the first step of the applied strategy. Therefore, creating and publishing content is important.

- **Ads**: Then we may need to promote content to reach interested and interesting people.

- **Analytics**: We will then need to understand the effects of content within channels and optimize our strategy.

- **Listening**: Finally, we will also need to go beyond channel-based data and understand the buzz around content and further information about the audience.

So the hybrid tool is proposing to take care of the full process and offers enough features for the user to go through all necessary steps without having to change tools. This is a great concept for a social media tool, and the tools that can do all of it very well can truly put users ahead of the game.

As you can imagine, it is not an easy task for a company to offer such a broad array of features within one tool. The differences and variations among hybrid tools are huge. Some are more advanced than others in certain aspects, leading to evaluation and reviews about hybrid tools that mention points such as better at publishing, or better with ads, or better at listening, and so forth.

This means that things can get very confusing with hybrid tools, because we have to understand everything about the process that we want to run before we can judge if a specific hybrid tool is good enough. A checklist of what we need is always a good start in these cases.

Dedicated Tools with Hybrid Features

Some dedicated tools offer hybrid features. They are great at what they are intended to do, but they offer limited features in areas that are not in their main field of work.

It is not easy to find such tools, and it is hard to be certain that it is a dedicated tool with hybrid features and not just another hybrid tool.

Investigating the history of the tool can help here, but follow the developments after the new hybrid features were integrated. If the tool stopped focusing on its primary purpose, then it is likely now a hybrid tool.

You want to understand the focus of the team behind the tool. What will that tool become in the future? Where is it heading? We are investing our time to become experts in a tool in the long term, so it is good to be sure that our objectives and the developments of the tool are going in the same direction.

The Advantages of Hybrid Tools

The following are some advantages of using hybrid tools:

- All processes in one place
- Integration between processes
- One provider to deal with and one tool to onboard and learn how to use

The hybrid aims to be the one-stop shop for our needs. Its advantages, therefore, are extremely helpful when our needs match the features. If you are not looking for the best possible performance in every single field, you can find many interesting hybrid tools to cover your needs.

The Disadvantages of Hybrid Tools

The following are some disadvantages of using hybrid tools:

- Usually offers fewer features per field of work.
- Changing tools becomes a bigger effort because we have to change our entire process.

- Chances are that in the long term that tool will develop into something we don't longer need, or we evolve our business into something the tool cannot attend to.

- If there is an area we don't need, we usually cannot remove it from the package to save on our budget.

The disadvantages of hybrid tools are more or less relevant depending on the level of your current needs or in the planning and future objectives of your strategy. If your main focus is to create and publish content, and you have a limited budget, a hybrid tool with a very good content management system and good enough analytics support can be a great option. So the final judgment inevitably comes down to your professional goals.

Data Integration Tools

Data integration tools are a very good option to bring different data sources together.

These tools let us choose information from entirely different other tools and see it all in one place, with visual displays, dashboards, and reports to go along with it. This includes data not related to social media, so we can even look at integrating very different data sets here. We can think of this as a second layer of data gathering. The first layer is the dedicated and hybrid tools pulling data from social networks. Then the second layer is the integration tools pulling data from these specialized tools. Some integration tools also pull directly from social networks, but as a rule of thumb, the specialized tools (dedicated and hybrid) do a better job, so we would expect integration tools to perform better when pulling data from them instead of trying to tap directly into social networks.

Some data integration tools are essentially a dashboard to connect different data sources and have a visual display of it all in one place. Other data integration companies offer added services and the possibilities to have more complex processes using the data from different sources. These companies can integrate the data into our systems and even build applications with the integrated data.

Many marketers are not familiar with such tools or immediately discard the use of these tools because they seem too complicated or too expensive. Yes, there can be challenges in integrating data, but in most cases, the challenges will not be as big as expected, and results are worth it.

The Advantages of Data Integration Tools

The following are some advantages of using data integration tools:

- Integrates any available data source, even if they come from different tools or networks and beyond social media.

- Gives us the freedom to choose a modular or dedicated tool approach, and have the advantages of such an approach with integration between tools.

- Opens a universe of integration possibilities for a business. As you learn more about data integration tools, you may find that tools outside of social media marketing and analytics can also add to an integrated business analytics setup.

The Disadvantages of Data Integration Tools

The following are some disadvantages of data integration tools:

- Require a setup process that calls for technical help to conclude.

- Each new data source and integration likely requires some level of technical work.

Discussions on the disadvantages of using such tools can also touch on costs. It is ultimately a case-by-case analysis if such a setup is worth it at any given time.

Some open dashboard tools have a very low cost, for example. So if your need is to have a report with data from different tools in one place, this option is more than worthwhile.

If our needs include an integration that requires development or data processing from different tools to deliver the output we need, costs will be higher.

However, in the second case, where we are using data from different sources to build something that is more significant to us and has a greater strategic value to our business, it is likely that the investment will be worth it. The reasoning on this assumption is based again on our needs. If we are attending to our business needs in the best possible way, and that will generate a competitive advantage, we will likely see greater results from it, and investment can pay off.

The Best Setup: Focus on Our Objective

What matters most when choosing our setup of tools is that we can succeed with our objectives. To succeed, we need tools that offer the features we need, but also tools that make us happy about our workflow. The user experience within our tool of choice will then also be an influence, whether we understand that rationally or not (i.e., "I like the feel of this tool"), and especially when we find equivalent offers in the market.

Some people are more technical than others, and that aspect influences their judgment. If we consider ourselves less technical, however, we should still not be afraid of the technical aspects of tools. It is likely that such aspects will not be as hard to learn as we imagine, and even if the learning process takes a bit of time, once we have the tool working perfectly toward our needs, we will feel it was worth it.

If we focus on our objectives, everything else falls into place. So even when learning about tools, we can always relate what we learn to our business objectives and to our personal professional objectives as well.

Trials of Different Tools Before Choosing the Best: Heaven or Hell?

Trying new tools can be time-consuming and brain-consuming.

If you can avoid wasting your time on tools that are not going to cover what you need, that is definitely the way to go.

It is a good idea to start by having a clear list of features based on objectives. First, make sure that the items on your list are covered by that tool. If items are not covered, determine if it is a technical limitation external to the tool (e.g., a lack of data sources), or if it is just something the tool does not offer, but another tool does.

If the tool has more to offer, great! But we don't need to go into trial if our list is not fully covered or checked, and we have no time to invest in learning a new tool that we will likely not use. If we are out in the market for an overall knowledge of all the tools out there, then naturally we can trial everything.

Our checklist is based on what we need for our process, so the creation of a checklist is usually one of our initial challenges. We have to understand our strategic goals and have at least an initial view of how to reach them so that we can create a list of our needs.

As simple as this may seem, the majority of people I have met who go into the market looking for tools have not done any kind of formal checklist based on their needs. This checklist is also a huge time-saver, so the time we invest in creating such a list will likely be saved many times over later while going through all of the tools we find.

We can use the material that we have been studying so far in this book to help build a list.

Services: When Processes Are Done on Our Behalf

Some social media tool companies also offer services. If your business is not an agency, you might hire an agency to perform services.

The hiring of services becomes an interesting option when there is a specific need, such as lack of time, lack of manpower, or maybe lack of expertise. Many companies can deliver great results by using outside services. This option can take your business to the next level instantly.

When choosing a service provider, you need to know what this vendor can do on your behalf. Knowing the details is helpful if you ever decide to change service providers. It also prepares your internal team to take over at some point.

Before a service delivers analytics reports, for example, you should know what you want out of the reports before you get them. Once you receive the output from the service team, you should know how they reached the results, which tools they used, and the processes they ran, so that you can better judge the quality, and suggest improvements or changes that will better resonate with your objectives.

Key Takeaways

- Rule of thumb: dedicated tools are usually better on whatever they are dedicated to do.

- Powerful hybrid tools exist, they can be even more expensive than several dedicated tools put together, but it can be worth having it all in one place.

- When planning a tool setup, consider the effort of onboarding and the challenge of eventually having to change tools in the future.

- Data integration tools are very powerful and can be the key to a perfect setup of dedicated tools.

- Our specific goals lead us to a checklist of needed features, which makes it easier to choose the best tool setup. As simple as this seems, most of us don't create a checklist of needs before looking for new tools.

- If we are hiring third-party services, we should still understand what they are doing and which tools they use. This helps us choose, participate, and evaluate the service.

Alexander and Frederik Peiniger

Founders of quintly Inc.

In 2010, Alexander and Frederik Peiniger created the first version of what would later become quintly Inc. Working in digital marketing and facing the hard work of tracking social media analytics manually for clients, they built a technology that would automate that process.

Their journey from there, with the growth of quintly as a company and as a technology, was filled with challenges on the technical and business aspects of developing and running a social analytics platform. The experience they acquired and their vision of the social analytics landscape will be valuable to us. As with all of the interviews in this book, we are adding real-world context to our studies.

© April Ursula Fox 2022
A. U. Fox, *Social Media Analytics Strategy*,
https://doi.org/10.1007/978-1-4842-8306-6_6

I first met Alexander and Frederik in person in Köln, Germany, two days before Christmas 2014. Arriving in town by train, I was immediately impressed with the massive Dom Cathedral and the beauty and livelihood of its Christmas market. Little did I know that later that day I would be even more impressed by the quintly technology and vision as an analytics provider.

I had already been working professionally in social analytics for a few years at that point. I had also been integrating, from the developer side, custom dashboards, publishing, listening, and social ads technologies into companies of every size. I had extensive practical experience relating to problems on the client and technology side of the business. One such problem, that couldn't be solved in a simple way despite the resources of global brands, was the flexible access to data sources and the customization of metrics. Most analytics providers would offer only a fixed set of metrics, and any kind of customization would need to be newly developed, managed by a professional services team, and would cost a lot more than expected. The platform quintly developed came into the market to change that.

As you can imagine, the needs involving analytics can be as diverse as all the different aspects that make each company unique. Internally and externally, companies have different workflows, cultures, branding, and market strategy. Alexander and Frederik's vision for quintly is to be able to attend to that, to create a platform that will be as dynamic and flexible as needed, and still remain within the price range of an accessible analytics solution.

With such a vision in mind, we can then better picture the potential challenges they faced along the way. I am addressing many of these challenges in my questions for them, to help us understand how much falls on the technology side and how much of it relates to education and knowledge on the client side.

You can find Alexander and Frederik on their LinkedIn profiles at www.linkedin.com/in/alexanderpeiniger/ and www.linkedin.com/in/frederikpeiniger/, respectively.

Question 1

In the context of all the different aspects related to gathering data, data sources, eventual limited data availability from social networks, and delivering the data to end users, what challenges can you highlight from your experience? And how do you see things going forward?

Alexander: When I look at the analytics platform, I see three different parts. One is the data availability, which includes data quality. That is the part where no interfaces are involved. It's only about getting the data from the networks that are available, and getting it with high quality, resolving any issues and bugs from the networks. But then, from this process, you only have the data in the raw database.

What makes the analytics tool complete is then the ability to set up what you can do with the data, and this will also relate to the data source part of the question. A process that shapes the data into a form that is usable from the outside. Maybe adding some additional information, maybe getting something pushed away, maybe combining some raw data into data calculations, and so forth.

Then you have the entire visualization side, where it's a lot about *How can we make the data actionable? How can we show it in the right way? What can we do with it?* This last piece, the visualization part, will naturally include reporting. We will ask ourselves, *I have these visualization possibilities, but what is most important in order to really serve the processes of the client?* These are three main challenges.

When I think about what I expect to happen in the future, I see that many parts of the visualization aspect will probably be solved globally, for a company as a whole, where social media is only one part of the equation. This will touch a little bit into the discussion on BI (business intelligence). There will probably be a lot more intelligence on visualization also on the client side.

I believe the data source level is somewhat hidden from many clients at the moment because they have no clue what it is and what it does. It will likely be revealed further in the future when companies start their process by asking more about *What are my goals?* to then understand more on the data source level related to that, rather than approaching analytics only from the visualization level that they see at the moment from the outside. The analytics field in companies will likely move one step deeper into the process of analysis, or at least there is a need for them to go there to create more value.

Frederik: Going further into that, we can add a little more on what I would call the data challenge. It is also about making sense of the data and thinking about *What data am I looking for and what is helpful to optimize my strategy?* Besides that, of course, we also have the technical challenges.

As a true analytics provider, we definitely have the challenge to maintain all the APIs that we're getting the data from, ensuring that we get the right data points, keeping up to date with all the changes they bring and keep working around all the bugs that the networks also have in their APIs. It is always good to keep in mind that their products, the social networks themselves, are usually not bug-free.

There is also a technical challenge to maintain a huge data set, so we are talking about a large database, and also about scalability and how to import, for example, 100,000 profiles with a few thousand comments on average. How do I manage the sheer amount of data? How do I make it available in real time in a tool? In that sense, it's definitely a big data challenge as well because you have to handle all that data and then work with data mining on top to then find ways to visualize it.

Of course, that's the critical challenge for the business, to try to make sense of the data and to identify what data sets are most interesting or most useful for the problems of our clients. I also agree that there is a view of three parts: technical, data interpretation, and then visualization, which can be looked at quite separately.

Alexander: I think especially when you look at the data part, on how to take meaning from it, it's not a challenge exclusive to social media. You have it everywhere in the company, right? You have it with customer support data, with sales data, with any ROI data. It's probably a challenge everyone needs to solve somehow, again and again, and at the moment, it's done with a lot of different tools. I would say that a lot of the thinking is currently into the visualization part, but I think more and more companies are realizing that there's a lot of value on going deeper, more closely to the data sources in order to make more correlations, and so on.

What it will mean for the tool market in our space is that we need to be really good at integrating with all these processes so that we are flexible to cater to any client—from the ones who only want to get the raw data sources and do whatever they want to the ones that need a bit more hand-holding. I think this will be one of the challenges for the entire social media tools market.

Frederik: Part of the data challenge, besides the interpretation, will then also be the data availability. We rely on the platforms, such as Facebook, Twitter, Instagram, Pinterest, and others, to provide the necessary data set.

For them, the benefit of offering data is that they help the market to professionalize. As a tool, we participate in that environment. Companies become more professional in using social networks, and hopefully, for the networks, they start spending more dollars on their platforms.

If the data set isn't available, we can't use it for any kind of analysis, correlation with other data set, and so forth, so we're relying a lot on the availability, and that the networks themselves make it a priority to make the data available. That is always a challenge because some networks don't do it.

With Twitter, for example, we've seen a new challenge. With their private statistics, they decided to make it a paid access to their APIs. This then also brings some kind of challenge to us because we have to think about *How do we make that work with our pricing?* and our clients asking *Why we have different pricing for other data sets?*

We definitely rely on a lot of points from the outside, which are the networks in this case, but a good thing is that most of the networks will share a lot of the data. It is naturally in their interest because the data is from companies that are also part of their networks and their clients, and it will help them grow. This environment is the base for our business.

Question 2

One area that you focus on is competitive benchmarking. While I know many of us are familiar with and adopt benchmarking in our strategies, some of us are not yet quite sure why we should use competitive benchmarking in social media. Could you share your view on the advantages of competitive benchmarking for a social media strategy?

Alexander: I think no strategy makes a lot of sense without the benchmarking piece. Maybe what is still holding back a lot of companies from doing it is that they don't know that it's possible, because social media is one of the few markets, actually, where it's possible to be done as it is. In the "real world," it can be hard for a restaurant to benchmark what other restaurants are selling, but on social media, it's very easy because you can get access to all the data. Also, when you come from the technical web tracking context, you know that you can only track your own numbers.

You can always take a generic approach, but when you need to compare apples to apples, you will need specific benchmarking. The question of *Am I doing a good job or a bad job?* is basically not possible to answer if you don't benchmark your industry, because the interaction rate or growth rate or any metric could be really good in one sector, and the same metric in another sector could be pretty bad.

Frederik: I agree with Alex. Why wouldn't you want to use data that's available out there for your optimization, right?

You could also look into competitor Facebook pages without a tool and do it manually, but companies using a tool will simply think much faster. They can learn from their own mistakes but also from the mistakes of others.

Only learning from your own mistakes means you have to do all the mistakes yourself.

On social media, where everything is public related to company publications, the data is there, so not using it simply makes no sense to me.

Question 3

When it comes to investments, people think, "Should I invest? Should I not invest? How much should I invest? How early? How do I justify the investment? What's my ROI on that?" What are your thoughts for someone thinking about investing in analytics?

Alexander: I think it really depends. It will be directly related to the value you get from the data. One first approach can be to compare it to the manual process.

Even with a tool like quintly and others offering so much more around the process, such as a nice bit of visualization, giving you flexibility, giving you the chance to automate the reporting, and so on, you can still look initially into how much time it can save.

If you imagine you do it manually because you believe in the value but then it takes you ten hours a week, you can calculate your costs. Let's say that operationally you have a total hourly rate of $50 to $100 dollars. You would be spending $500 to $1000 a week, which is $4000 a month. If you can buy the same output or better for $200 to $300 a month with a tool, it's basically a no-brainer to do it. If the tool is too expensive and you can do it cheaper manually, then yes, sure, you would probably do it manually, or you would get less data and accept that you maybe have only 80% of the quality that you need.

I think the first question that needs to be answered is, *What is the value I'm getting from the data?*, and then the second step is, *Let's look at tool options out there that help us precisely with this process.*

What is also an interesting aspect of tool providers like quintly is that we see a lot of cases from a lot of different clients, so we may be able to help with finding value, finding what is good and what is bad, because we get all the feedback from all the different clients. We may even, on top of the pure process of automation, give more insights, more features that we have learned from all the other cases, so that's probably a second piece that can amplify the value you will get from a tool.

Frederik: Where most of the companies are struggling—and as a provider, we also want to help—is in education at the beginning. They don't know what data is valuable for their processes and what data will help them to optimize their initiative. So a big part of the process is identifying *What metrics, what data is valuable for me?*

This is where I sometimes see that the approach is a little bit on the wrong way around at this point. Companies are coming to us as an analytics provider asking, *What data is valuable to them?* While we are specialized in bringing the data in a fully optimized way, and we can help, much of that question must be answered by them first. Sometimes companies have not given any serious thoughts about their social media strategy yet. The strategy and goals will help with identifying what data you are looking into.

Naturally, if even without a proper strategy they decide to get inspired by data and by seeing what can be optimized, analytics will be interesting for pure KPI tracking. The approach can be to then first understand how good or bad you are doing on certain KPIs, even without a strategy on how to do better.

So there are different approaches that can bring value. As a reference, we see much stronger results from companies that come into analytics with a solid strategy in place. Without a strategy, obviously, the answer is mostly *No, I can't find value*, because they are not clear about what their goals are in the first place.

It is interesting to think about this contrast, and how sometimes someone will be looking for a tool, willing to get the numbers, while not knowing what numbers to look at. Being dedicated analytics providers, we can help with that on a more generic level, but we won't be the ones that tell you, *This is the best social media strategy for you specifically*. There are marketing agencies out there that can work with you on building a specific social media strategy.

Alexander: There's also one trend that I'm seeing, which is that all the marketers need to get more analytical in a way. We are all coming from times when we put billions of dollars into traditional television, where we basically knew we could not measure a lot besides some survey numbers at the end of the month. It was basically money thrown out and then hopes that it would pay off.

Now it's completely changing. There's so much data available, that if you use a tool like us or any other tool, even when you only get a 1% improvement on the budget that the company has involved, you will know all the details about it. It just takes a bit of time to develop the analytical skills, taking small steps on small improvements that you can measure, which can have a big effect when later you look at the results and the budget.

Question 4

Thinking about these changes, in terms of becoming a data-driven market overall, what are your thoughts about the future? Also, from the social network side, how do you see them supporting analytics in the future?

Alexander: If you look to the client side, things are moving. Every big company now has a centralized data strategy or is getting into it. Probably the smaller companies will follow a little bit later once they have the capabilities.

Many companies have a setup where the entire data strategy goes to the management board to try to push it through the whole organization. So that's one big change I'm seeing. At least from the client side, I'm expecting a lot more centralization of data—a lot more real strategy behind it, especially for the bigger companies.

On the network side, I think they also started to see more and more value in this over time. Facebook extended their analytics availability, bringing more and more depth into the data. I think all of them have understood somehow that the data is important. Of course, the networks have different things going on in the background and need to optimize their ads revenues, which can define which numbers they show in which cases.

In general, however, I think it's all going in the right direction where the networks basically open up because they know it works. If you look at the history of Facebook, for example, the open data strategy they have, not charging for it, basically giving it to anyone, was a big part of their success. It somehow belongs to their DNA, and I think also probably a lot of the other networks will see it as a key advantage.

Frederik: I agree, it's always a promotional advantage for their platform. Facebook has understood this better than anyone else, I think. We've seen, for example, LinkedIn turning off certain parts of their API and then re-enabling it. So for some networks, it's still not mature.

Probably what we will see is that they open in a more controlled manner, where you cannot just create an application with these networks and simply grab all the data, but they will want to know who you are, what are you using that data for, and how does that fit with their goals. You see that happening with LinkedIn, for example, also Facebook has a lot more checks nowadays. This trend is also visible when it comes to permissions on what kind of data you are able to ask about the companies you're monitoring. They want to better understand who you are and what you are using their data for.

This is a great extension of the entire ecosystem around their platforms, including the app platforms. The fact that they check who is using the APIs is a good trend, because that ensures high-quality integrations, and we are happy to have these integrations, and let them know what we do with the data. This will let them know how we can help their clients, who will, later on, also hopefully invest more in their platforms.

Alexander: Especially the clients we talked about before, the ones that need more guidance and don't have a strategy yet, these would probably be overwhelmed with the networks alone. So in the case, let's say, of the small company that cannot justify investment, maybe if they learn more about social strategy via analytics, and such details we educate on, they can end up spending on Facebook advertising or other app sponsoring, so it's a lot about professionalizing the market together.

Frederik: Again, it's about optimization, right? So another point is that all the networks have understood that companies are not just on Facebook or just on Twitter, and so forth. They will be reporting across various different networks. If Facebook or others would lock down, it would keep their client from cross-network reporting in an optimized way. That would harm their clients, and if their clients get angry, they can probably not spend more on their platforms.

From the platform's view, it then doesn't make sense to do something against the interest of their clients who spend lots of ads dollars on their platform. In that direction, I see many different reasons why they keep up these APIs and make them available to third parties while ensuring they know who these third parties are and what they want to do with the data, which is totally fine.

Question 5

The very last question is on machine learning and artificial intelligence. What are your thoughts on the impact of these technologies in social media and social analytics?

Alexander: I think we are starting to see all these terms, like machine learning and AI, move from buzzword status to actual implementations. A lot has been tested before, but now is the time that the applications start happening for few different reasons.

Solutions are coming out that make it easier for developers to work with it, to deal with data sets that are getting much bigger. With very big data sets, it basically makes sense to look at these solutions because machines can probably find patterns in the data that we can't spot as a human. Let's say you look at a billion different Facebook posts, it's basically impossible to make all possible correlations, I mean, you could probably do some filtering and certain calculations, but you will probably never find the correlations that the machine can find with the mass of the data.

In the upcoming years, it will probably be one major trend for companies to bring more intelligence to the data. This goes in line with finding elements in the data that are special, that you would otherwise need to look manually for hours or weeks. It could also be the case that the machine learns how to use different interfaces, the machine would understand what the intentions are behind the requests. So it can also be a lot about usage analysis and trying to make it easier for the clients to get to the results they actually are looking for or that they need.

In a sense, it can be about the software becoming some kind of concierge— guiding the user and helping him find the right things, rather than what we have nowadays, where we need to say exactly what we want to be able to get it.

Frederik: From a completely different angle, which is also very exciting, because we had a recent discussion about this, is how the communications, especially on social media, can evolve. If you look at what's happening currently, it's mainly companies broadcasting to users. You know they are using targeting and tailored content, and now they use more of that even into the broadcasting context, more specifically. If you drive that thinking further, it would be a logical step that, at some point, you will reach a mass-scale tailored one-to-one communication process, meaning that I tailor my content so far that it's really tailored toward the interest of a single person.

You see this trend, by the way, on websites or digital marketing and website optimization tools. They're also trying to reach the point where the website can be optimized for that one specific person and it would be strange if the same doesn't happen in communications overall. We see the trends already, for example, with the social bots.

The case for AI is mainly in the volume. Let's say that I want to tailor my communications one-to-one instead of broadcasting one post to 100,000 people. I then can't easily tailor to each person because of them being very different to each other. How do I then try to tailor to every single person? What most likely won't happen, which is happening today with some initiatives, is to have many people creating all those posts. The answer to such case is another example of where AI will come in.

Without AI, it will not be possible to deliver that experience of being truly customized to one single person. At the early stages of this trend, we see certain solutions in place that are still kind of "dumb," but it already shows how marketing and all communications will eventually change.

For analytics providers like us, that means it will be likely that targeting will be used more and more intensively until a point where it targets to a single person. That's a challenge for analytics providers, but foremost that's a challenge for communication itself, where if you want to do that, you have to use a lot of AI to make that happen.

This is where I see communications in ten or fifteen years from now. This will have a lot of impact on various different parts of organizations and also how things are managed, how the content producing happens. There's a lot to change.

Differences of Social Media Networks

Social Network Landscape

A Brand Strategy Approach

Each social media network differs from the others in many aspects. As much as we feel that we know it well, it is still very common to think of social media as if it were one big channel. We usually hear people talking about it in this way, even in the news, in professional research papers, studies, data-based reports of different kinds, and we do it ourselves many times.

This can happen, naturally, because the concept behind all social networks is similar. The intention of social media to offer users a voice is similar across different social networks. Technically, social media networks do, in fact, have many similar features; however, when we are working on seriously improving our performance and being more strategic about our activity on social media, we need to be more specific. In essence, each social media network is a different channel, with crucial differences that impact our strategy in unique ways.

As we investigate the landscape, we may find out, for example, that our brand better fits in only one or two social media networks. While we may have a presence in other networks, we can then save resources and focus only on

© April Ursula Fox 2022
A. U. Fox, *Social Media Analytics Strategy*,
https://doi.org/10.1007/978-1-4842-8306-6_7

what works best for us. Strategy is a lot about investing resources wisely into projects and activities that bring the very best results.

Despite differences in social networks, we know that branding on social media is naturally very much integrated and in synchronicity to all the activity of our overall business strategy. But to integrate elements into the same strategy, it is important to understand each element individually first, so that we can then understand how they relate to one another and how the entire strategy will play out.

Differences between networks vary from the overall user experience that each network provides, to their specific features, and to the social factor, or the interactivity within each network. These three elements are very interconnected, but we can still think about each of them separately, even if there is overlap.

To better understand how to detect the fundamental differences that impact our analyses, we can separate our study into these three areas:

- Concept and user experience (UX)

- Features

- Interactivity (How social are the social networks?)

Concept and UX on Social Networks

The understanding of the concept behind a social media network and its overall user experience, or UX, helps us give value to the information we get from each of them during analysis.

Social media networks have a certain concept behind them; a certain objective that they are aiming to reach; or a problem, if you will, that they are trying to solve.

Twitter is the fast-paced, short message platform. Pinterest is about pinning our interests onto boards and collecting the world. Instagram is about great images and videos and how we can easily be great photographers ourselves. Snapchat is about the thrill around ephemeral content.

The concept around each social network is so strong that when they try to add different features and leave behind their original concept for commercial or other reasons, most users still have the old concept in mind and don't adopt changes very fast.

A network such as Facebook, however, is conceptually bound to grow and be part of every aspect of people's lives. Many changes that we see on Facebook are still an integral part of its concept, so the users adapt to these changes very easily. The concept behind Facebook is connected to the identity of users, to becoming a space where users can express who they are to the world, and add all the many different aspects of their lives into what they share. It is natural that Facebook offers so many different features, including login capabilities to other services, instant messaging, and other broad sets of options for our profiles.

The connection of the user experience to the concept of networks will always be very strong. The success rate in which a social media network can deliver on its proposition is directly related to the connection between UX and concept. The better the UX, the easier it is for users to spend time and interact with the network. When users go through the entire proposed journey and reach the point where they are using the network for its purpose and following its concept, it is likely that such a network has become an integral part of their lives. As a brand, if we want to become part of the lives of people and create a community around our brand, following the concept of each network can then be an interesting strategy.

For analytics, understanding concept helps us interpret and give value to each event within each different network. We can think of events as any action that a user or brand may take.

Under the study of concept, for example, we can also look at users as content creators themselves and as part of an audience to other users (not brands). Some networks promote that aspect more than others do, and it can be another interesting element to consider during analysis. The different approaches of detecting influencers on social analytics will come into play here, and a careful analysis of certain events, such as comments, can add to it.

Going further into the UX as a basic element for valuation of events, we can take a simple example of likes on Instagram.

Instagram makes it very easy for users to double-tap and like a photo. Users see a huge image in their timelines and very easily "tap-tap" and the heart icon becomes red. Users don't have to think if they want to share the content, because there is no real sharing option, and comments are almost a heroic act of social interaction there, since we rarely end up engaging in conversations on Instagram and are not motivated to comment from the social point of view. So basically, the UX setup is pushing us into just liking everything and not thinking too much about it. It is also a "thing" on Instagram to "tap-tap." It is fun and it is what everyone does so we do too. It is a behavioral trend.

While this "tap-tap" mechanism is great for the user experience, a marketer can see that the value of a like on Instagram is lowered by the ease of interaction and because the effect of a like on Instagram does not affect the distribution of the content within the network. We do not see in our Instagram feed the content that our friends liked. The timelines are separate in this sense, so a like is mostly just a signal to the content creator that someone enjoyed the content for some reason. On the UX side, there is really nothing keeping users from liking a huge amount of photos. In a network such as LinkedIn, where our professional persona is on the line with every action we take, and everything is registered in our activity chart, we may think twice about liking a piece of content.

One approach to analyzing Instagram likes, therefore, is to have an overview based on overall volume, and go for metrics such as average likes per post, and eventually a long-term view to understand if we are keeping our audience interested in general. This kind of approach can be useful for all such types of interactions, where they are not a big deal for users, but can still give us understanding of basic audience interest in the content. The new experiments that social networks are making on "smart" algorithms allow people that like, or have basic interactions to our content, to see our brand at the top of their timelines (and other such content filtering); so for that purpose, it is good to keep the volume of such interactions strong.

The analysis of UX also offers ideas for experimentation with content topics and formats across different networks.

Interesting examples of this kind of thinking by marketers are happening in the social media advertising space. Because people consume content on the go, the time for the content to get the message across is extremely short, even down to three seconds or less in some cases. This brings a new challenge for creatives that have to think about a broader context for their message, from the storytelling tactics in a very short timeframe to the user experience with mobile on the go. If we are looking at being ahead of the curve with our brand, we can scout for such innovative formats and experiments, analyze their results, and apply the best ones into our content strategy.

Features and Their Strategic Value

Social media networks have similar features; but although very similar to each other in concept or in name, they have different capabilities or effects.

A like on Facebook is different from a like on Instagram or on Twitter. All of these actions are called a Like, but the result of a user liking a piece of content in one network or another may be different.

On Facebook, for example, a like may trigger the content to be shown to the user's friends. On Twitter and on Instagram, however, a like just sends a notification of praise to the owner of the content.

The likes also affect the hidden algorithm of the timelines and tend to show more content from a source that is linked to the people who liked it. By growing the amount of likes, a page is also amplifying its future exposure. This tends to happen because the algorithm is trying to serve content to people who are very likely to enjoy it. Each social network has a different algorithm.

Sharing on Facebook is different from retweeting on Twitter. Facebook gives the user more options on how to share the content within the network, with different effects on each option.

It is very easy to confuse the capabilities of features in different social media networks. The important point is that there are differences even in very similar features. The knowledge of features and capabilities then add to the understanding of the value of each event that we see displayed in our analytics report. When we are given the task of translating numbers into insights, the more we know about each network features and their effects, the better. Gathering such knowledge is an ongoing task, so we can have a planned effort to update ourselves on such details from time to time.

If we are working with social media analytics tools, we can ask the team inside the tool for information in this sense. We can ask them about the effects of different features in different social networks and update our knowledge with them from time to time. I would recommend this, because usually such people have direct access to the technical teams within the social media networks themselves, and they are happy to help us if we are their clients. So the relationship with a professional analytics service can go beyond our interface with the technology and become a relationship with the very smart people in their teams.

Because of the shifting nature of features and algorithms, the value of a list of their specific effects in each network is not very long term. For that reason, some elements of this book, such as this one, are present only to open our eyes to them, so that we have the necessary critical thinking when performing our analyses. Independent of being specific or not, we still consider the impact of such aspects as we explore metrics, dashboards, and reports in this book.

Interactivity: How Social Is the Network?

Some social networks are more "social" than others are. This is important to keep in mind so that you can better judge the value of the interactions and events seen in an analytics report.

But what exactly can we understand by being more or less "social"? The key here is to be able to think about two main points:

- The flow of content
- Interaction between users

This is not only a technical view of being "social"—it is also a behavioral view.

Technical aspects and features are likely the greatest influence on the shaping of behavior within social media networks, but there are also trends that are created by people despite the connection to technical features.

The Content Flow on Social Networks

How far can a piece of content go? How easy is it for a piece of content to reach every corner of the Internet?

Content experts will say that "good content will have a good performance." While that makes sense, it is not entirely correct when we think about the structure of networks.

There are a series of "hurdles" for a piece of content to cross and then become "viral" (for the lack of a better word).

Depending on how the source of the content is positioned within the network, its content will have higher or lower chances of being seen, and then shared and spread all over. The power of a good piece of content alone will not do the trick, so what else is there to help spread it around?

The short answer is money. Sure, the more we pay, the more visibility we get, but even then, we want our content to be spread organically. We always love that people can find it, share it, and help us project it into the world. This is where the flow of content within networks comes into play.

Many brands do very well with organic content. The main reason usually involves high interest of their community in the brand and its content. Studying the concept of community can be helpful here, so that we can give people enough space and motivation to join and build a lively group. As analysts, understanding these aspects plays a role in our interpretation of data and suggestions toward improvement.

Despite the tactics we use to spread our content, social networks offer different structures of content flow, which may help when going viral.

Snapchat positioned itself as the ephemeral content network. They created, with this, a sense of urgency in people, so that the content must be seen before it is lost forever. Beyond that, it also creates that craving for another piece of content, since we can't go back and have again that cool experience that we just had. So while this can create high initial interest in content, the chances that a piece of content in such context will not break through from the first circles of connections to its source are very high.

Pinterest, on the other hand, goes in an opposite direction. When a person creates a pin, it becomes part of the Pinterest universe forever. It may be found by other people a long time after it was created. So the longevity of content on Pinterest tends to be much longer than in any other social network.

In general, excluding Pinterest, social media networks offer a very short life cycle for content. It is all about "the next best thing." This is another reason to think carefully about how content flows within each network when working on our strategy.

Instagram, for example, does not allow people to share content on their timeline. It can be copied and embedded somewhere else, but how many people will go through that when they like a certain piece of content? Not many. Instagram tries to compensate for that with the use of hashtags and a few areas of the network dedicated to the discovery of content. This is still limited compared to a network with direct sharing capabilities for user profiles. So for one piece of content to be "spread all over" Instagram, it would need either "all of Instagram" to be connected to the profile which created the content or that all of the people would use an external app to share the content within their own profiles. Either way, it is not easy for a certain piece of content to "go viral" on Instagram. So on Instagram, in this case, the audience size will matter a lot.

Facebook, on the other hand, does not only have many sharing capabilities but has mechanisms for content to show up on the timeline of the friends of people who only liked it, for example, increasing exposure very easily.

On Twitter, people love to retweet everything. Maybe because it is a network of short snippets of content, so we need to be very busy to be actually showing up on someone's timeline. Maybe it can be also because it is just something that people do instead of creating all of the content themselves; maybe it's just "a thing" to retweet a lot. The conclusion is that for whatever reason, this behavior helps content "go viral" on Twitter.

On top of this, we have now the smart algorithms trying to learn what we are most interested in and give us more of that. So some content will never be shown to an audience if the profile publishing it is not popular with the audience or isn't paying to suddenly show up in their timeline.

This book does not dive into all the tiny details in content flow on every social network, but I do mention more of this as we dive into metrics. It is interesting to go through this line of thought when giving value to engagement on social networks and suggestions on tactics.

The Power of Copy

Within the concept of content flow inside and from social networks to external sites and searches, it is also vital to point out the importance of the copy we create.

The term "copy" in digital marketing refers to the text of our content, including headlines and any formatting we use. In some cases, the names of the files we use for images and videos also count in copy.

When we take the role of the analyst (independent of our job title) and start looking for reasons why certain content performed better or worse than expectations or than average, the copy comes into play.

It is not easy and not always very straightforward to perform an analysis of copy. This effort, therefore, is highly dependent on the amount of time we have to invest in this specific analysis after the content is published and the amount of preparation and research before the next piece of content is created.

Copy quality affects the searches people make. It also drives people in the call-to-action part of the content. It can also affect further reactions, such as shares and comments, which promote an even higher awareness of that piece of content on the Internet. It can then affect the impressions and reach of that content as well.

Prior to the analysis, content creators follow a series of preparation steps before creating copy, such as searching for top-ranking words in search engines. There are many tactics for creating good copy. If we wish to perform a good analysis, we can hunt for such tactics on the Internet ourselves and then experiment with metrics to measure them. If you only wear an analyst hat, it is a good idea to synchronize your work with the content team to work together to effectively measure the performance of copy.

Metrics that can relate to copy will always have a trigger that is related to text. When we filter hashtags or keywords, pull word cloud graphs, and relate text to specific interactions, we can start building potential patterns around certain elements in the text.

A simple example is to use very clear words as a call to action in our content. We can even use the interactions themselves, such as the words "share, comment, retweet," and so forth. We can test if when we ask people to share, we then get more shares, and if when we ask people to comment, we then get more comments. We can also test for elements such as question marks and check if we get more comments when we ask questions.

More complex tests can be made, and those usually work best when aligned with the content team. So the content team can prepare a few unique conditions that can then be added to the analytics tool for a quick evaluation later. This can involve the use of certain words or expressions, content length, punctuation, or even the specific order of words in a sentence.

Processes such as machine learning can be applied to the analysis of content, so we can look for experts in this area to help us run such analyses. Sentiment analysis is one example of this, but more specific analyses can be made, such as understanding the influence of specific words on the quantitative aspect of performance, and also on the qualitative, on what people are saying in the comments as a reaction to those words, for example. This goes into the predictive side of analytics, since we are using these insights as a basis for our future content. We will look at predictive and prescriptive analytics later in the book.

Interaction Patterns Between Users: Can Networks Put Us in a Sharing Mood?

The interactivity between people within social media networks ultimately results in a higher amount of content sharing.

A natural part of any real-life conversation we have is to ask the person if he or she has already seen a trailer to a movie, or tasted a certain brand of ice cream, or seen that there is a crazy sale going on in a shop somewhere. On social media, these conversations likely involve digital links, where people share content related to what they are talking about. Some features of a social network, such as groups, promote sharing content, which happens even if we cannot detect or track the specific source in analytics. What this means for analysts is that it is great to look at behavior and behavioral trends on social media as well, despite our technical knowledge.

The easier it is for users to interact, the better it is for the content. The more active these users are, the better it is for the network. Many measurements of network success are related to active users. We hear about this on the news and on evaluations by industry analysts and investors. Daily active users, monthly active users, and the time they spend on average on the network are more than buzzwords on social media. These measurements are directly related to potential content exposure and performance. So in theory, the higher these numbers are, the more business a social network can generate, hence a higher market value. What these studies tend to forget is to include the interactivity between users as a factor. Such interactivity translates into an even higher value to the network.

Networks offer different features to promote user interaction. Tagging is a feature in almost every network. Using hashtags to search and tag the content is also there and can promote connections among strangers. Groups, direct messages, endorsements, recommendations, the list goes on.

On top of the features, we can then look at patterns of behavior.

On Twitter, for example, people usually do not engage in long conversations via direct messages, so a tweet may have a couple of replies where a very short conversation happens in an open environment, and it ends there.

On Facebook, with its messenger app, a conversation that starts in the comments section of a post can be easily moved to a direct one-on-one chat. To keep the conversation within the comments section, Facebook (and other networks) lets us reply to a comment and create parallel conversations within comments, for example.

On Instagram, a comment is a very rare type of engagement, a reply to a comment is even rarer, and a third response is even more than that.

On Pinterest, comments happen under certain communities more than others. I have seen a large amount of comments under cosmetics and beauty-related pins, for example.

Behavior is highly influenced by the UX of a social network, which can be our connection point to understanding them as data analysts.

A behavior spontaneously becomes a trend for the simple reason that human nature creates and increases trends on everything. The "selfie" is one example, and the "boomerang" is another. Our curiosity as humans always leads us to experience something that we see someone else doing and that we imagine we would like to do ourselves as well. This subjective aspect of behavior is harder to detect in the numbers, and it comes down to the awareness and vision of the analyst going beyond the numbers to reach actionable insights. In our example, if we detect that a content piece with high interactions is a "selfie," we can add a note about that trend in our reports.

So again, while our objective in this book is not to go too far into the specific behavior trends on social media, as these also change constantly through time, it is very useful for an analyst to understand that this exists when translating numbers into insights. It is also a fun and interesting field to research, and we will discover much about ourselves while at it.

How Friendly Is a Network to Brands?

Brands are attempting to create communities since the early days of social media networks, but how friendly are social networks to brands? Are they giving brands an easy time and letting them get all the organic interactions? Or are they making things harder and harder and forcing brands to play a tough game of paid promotion?

Truth is, it depends on each network, on each brand, and on each community, as most aspects relating to our analyses will.

"Pay to play" continues to happen until a better business model is found. But again, at the end of the day, everyone wants to get some of that organic performance on top of what was paid or simply better understand the value behind the performance of the content.

Although the balance between paid and organic changes from time to time (networks usually experiment with that), some networks are naturally better shaped for a brand to promote itself in a certain way.

This is where things get a little tricky.

Depending on the objective of a certain piece of content, one social network is better than the other. Also, depending on the concept of the brand and what are its products, one network will perform better than the other.

For us, as analysts, this is important to understand when we reach insights via analytics. A good analyst is able to grasp the objective of the brand and give a high-quality reading of the performance of campaigns based on a contextualized view.

When the time comes to judge if a brand is doing better or worse than in the last period of analysis, this type of understanding can play a big role. The view of the brand positioning, the culture, and the adaptation of the brand universe into the concept of a certain social media network gives it meaning and suggests certain interpretations for what the data shows.

Take Instagram as an example: It is easy to see how very visual brands perform very well in this network. A brand that has stunning images to share in a network where it is very easy for a follower of the brand to like that image is a recipe for success. A brand offering business consultancy services can probably find its audience friendlier on LinkedIn, unless it understands the language and behavior of a different network, and is prepared and creative enough to explore aspects that are initially and instinctively averse to their branding. So the business consultancy on Instagram could explore the visual side of brands they work with, or the profiles of the people running the businesses they work with, taken with extremely high photographic and artistic quality. This would likely even open a new market for them, for example. This kind of strategic thinking comes from an analysis of the difference in power between each social network related to content and brand context.

The best analysts offer a well-rounded analysis, considering elements that are beyond the numbers. This is what we are doing in these initial chapters of this book, preparing ourselves to think beyond the numbers and become masters in translating these numbers into actionable insights. A well-done analysis touches the core of business growth. It is more than a nice-to-have process, becoming a key element in decision-making.

Looking further at the "friendliness" aspect of social media networks toward brands, we also understand that it comes with a behavioral factor, a trend in user behavior within each social network.

LinkedIn is an interesting example to look at in this regard. While working with a global organization, it was noticed that the content shared by the institutional page did not have any performance, whereas the same content shared by its executives had a very good performance. This pattern was then observed on the analysis of competitor brands and brands unrelated to that industry segment.

The reason for the low performance of the brand page could be related to the lack of deliverability on LinkedIn. Even users following a brand are rarely exposed to its content; it could eventually show up in their timelines, but it will likely not be seen as more content from other sources push it away.

On top of the lack of deliverability from the network side, we can speculate about the interests of the community on LinkedIn being higher on the personal networking side. This could mean that people prefer to participate with other people's content, so that they can develop their personal relationship and enhance the professional networking effect of LinkedIn. With this in mind, I went out to ask everyone I could about it, which added up to more than 500 people, and everyone agreed they were more likely to interact and especially comment on content from other users than from content posted by a brand page. One of my contacts even asked me an interesting question: "Why would I expect IBM and Google to ever respond to my comment?" It is indeed food for thought.

For analytics and analysts, this is bad news because up until now, LinkedIn does not yet provide data on individual profile performance from within their API. It is private data, and I haven't come across yet to an analytics tool that would give insights into individuals. Analysts, therefore, can't work on dynamic studies about the performance of executives against the brand. It will take manual work to get that done. It will take a lot of time.

So this case pushes LinkedIn to the "unfriendly" side of brands, despite the professional networking concept that the network is all about. This does not mean that if our audience is on LinkedIn, we should look elsewhere only because of a certain factor, not at all. Knowing that the network performs a certain way gives us enough material to create a successful strategy around it. Knowing about a weakness only helps us overcome it.

On top of the conceptual match between brand and social network, there are features that point the direction for a certain specific strategy to be used, making a certain network very good for a certain task.

Some brands choose to make Twitter an extension of their customer support channel, for example, and that usually works well because of the short length of content and ease of using the reply back and forth. There is focus on the actual problem (and not on the emotional effects of such problem), which in return helps brands to be faster about fixing the problem.

Facebook offers brands an array of features, including direct shopping, making it very friendly.

Instagram makes it hard to even post links into content, so it becomes unfriendly in that sense.

Although I do not get into each individual feature of each social network in this book, the conceptual element of each network, and its "friendliness" to brands, is important for us to keep in mind during strategic analysis.

Social Media As a Two-Way Channel

One element that brands often "forget" to explore is the direct connection between social media and their other digital assets, such as institutional websites, ecommerce, and support channels. There is often a lack of continuation in conversations started on social media.

When there is a connection, the trigger is usually the use of links, but sometimes even that is "forgotten" by content creators, and a piece of content generating a lot of buzz around a product does not even have a link to the product within the brand's website or other sales channels.

On top of the lack of links and information within content pieces, brands very rarely participate in the comments, which is where the potential buyers are expressing their thoughts.

Maybe brands don't have the manpower to do so. It takes qualified people to do this job and sometimes a big team. Or maybe brands really don't care about the comments. Or do they?

A major part of the analysis is judging and measuring the performance. Defining what is good or bad, though, can be a challenge, as you will see in the chapters on metrics. A high number of comments under a post risks being judged as better than one with a low number of comments. But aren't the comments qualitative information that need interpretation to give insight to any conclusion?

Yes, of course they are.

A quantitative opinion that more comments are better than few comments shouldn't happen unless we think that *good or bad, what matters is that they talk about my brand*. A high number of comments could mean that people are unhappy about what they see. There could be very important feedback about the brand from users. And on the best side, there could even be some direct purchase intentions.

Whatever is in the comments under a post, it is very likely that a brand is not seeing it all or not seeing it in the right way.

Some analytics tools offer an automatic sentiment of mentions about the brand. Although this can be very interesting, it is not specific to each content piece. It doesn't do the job of looking at every comment under every post and delivering a visual of what is going on there.

This flow of qualitative information, whether we like it or not, is what social media is all about. Marketers that focus on social media as just another advertising channel are in fact assuming that they cannot win on the interaction with qualitative information. It is not smart to discard all the qualitative aspects of social media in the name of traditional advertising and simple pay vs. conversions metrics. It is simply a way out, an escape from the responsibility and opportunity to engage with the community.

It is not an easy task for brands to "be social" on social media. The amount of time for a manual approach to that is huge, and at the end of the day, the final judgment of many brand marketing teams is that "it is not worth it." The simple "use it as an advertising channel" approach is enough for many brands. If a strategy works and delivers results toward the business goals of a brand, that is great. It does not mean, however, that because one strategy works, another strategy could not work just as well, or even better.

As analysts, we have a responsibility to point out the truth when we find it and to point out possible truths when we have evidence to support it. Despite what a brand can or cannot do on social media because of the lack of resources, an analyst can at least point out what the brand is not doing and what is being left untouched by the analysis.

A big technical issue here is that even for analytics tools, the amount of data in comments is quite big. This not only increases the cost for tools to store every single comment in every single post for every single brand channel included in the system, but it also brings the challenge of the user experience. How to display this data? How to help an analyst reach insights?

Some tools offer metrics such as word clouds, giving an overall view of what was said in comments. This is interesting, but it will not lead a brand to continue the conversation with the individuals. Even if an analytics tool can detect and point out the most relevant comments, a manual approach is still necessary to keep the conversation going. So when we are delivering an analysis report, we can be very careful in judging the value of qualitative information such as comments.

Today, brands generally do not have the resources to fully make use of social media as a two-way channel. Maybe at early stages of their strategy, they can handle every single comment, but it is likely that as they grow their audience, it will become impossible. Some brands still respond to direct messages and to people publishing questions to their walls, and many brands keep doing as much as they can within the comments section. These brands often see great results from such efforts, even when unable to engage in 100% of the conversations. The understanding of the value of two-way social activity is very clear to many brands.

New technologies offer new resources for brands to deal with large amounts of people wishing to speak to them. Chat bots have that task as part of their playbook for the future. It is likely, however, that a lot needs to happen for brands to be able to handle the qualitative information and engage in one-on-one conversations with everyone on social media. Brands may have to change their core structure to be able to do so. Historically, brands have never done that, they never needed to speak with people watching their TV commercials, so there is also a general mindset still lingering with some marketers that this kind of interaction is not needed at all. Social media was born to change this, and as social media analysts, we can be true to that, even if the decision of not engaging directly is the one that prevails in the end.

Goals or Trends? What Is the Best for Brands?

A big part of any analysis is relating the information to goals and higher objectives of brands. Among the first questions that an analyst can make before starting an analysis are

- Are there any specific goals or objectives?
- If yes, what are they?

The real question is if brands ask themselves that question even before they join social media networks. It has been said that "brands should be on social media because if they are not, people are talking about them without their presence, and it is best to be part of the conversation." While this is true, and it is always better to be part of the conversation, should brands really be present in every social media network? Should they be following the trends without specific goals?

Part of the insights of an analysis can eventually show that a brand is not gaining from the investment in a certain social media network and that the resources invested in it can be used elsewhere for a better outcome of the overall marketing strategy. It is the job of the analyst to point that out and to be able to suggest what to do with resources instead. Having brand goals as a reference greatly helps that judgment.

We can naturally also perform analyses without direct contact with a brand and without a context of specific brand goals. We can take our own experience, added to as much knowledge about the brand and the market we can get, and reach very interesting results based on generic goals of audience growth and content interactions. Competitive benchmarking is a lot like this. When working directly within a brand, however, goals are extremely helpful.

When brands join social media without thinking too much about strategy, it is very likely that they will have an inconsistent performance, and the numbers will reflect that. It is also harder to relate the numbers to an evaluation of what is good, what is bad, and how things can be improved. It is easy to say that "this brand has fewer interactions from this network, so it needs to improve interactions there." The hard part—and what makes a good analysis stand out—is identifying the reason behind fewer interactions and suggesting how to improve it. The less strategy a brand applies during the planning stage, before joining certain social media networks or before launching campaigns on those channels, the more an analyst has to figure out the reasons behind the performance and then suggest improvements.

As analysts, we should be ready to engage with brands and help them set their goals. We can bring into projects our experience of what we see working elsewhere, or even in certain specific aspects of that brand, and share that with the creative and planning teams of the brand we are working with (assuming that we are not part of the brand ourselves). An analyst should not be only an extension of a technical service, simply helping to display numbers. The analyst should be a thinker.

While trends are important, and a brand does not want to be left behind under the eyes of the market, the process of following such trends can be done together with goals.

The following are some examples of common goals on social media:

- Increase brand awareness

- Promote sales

- Get feedback on products

- Offer customer support

- Enhance customer satisfaction

- Find brand advocates and evangelists

- Promote flux to other digital assets

As you can see, none of these goals translates directly to exact metrics from analytics. Objectives are usually not specific, such as "increase in followers" or "more shares," or "more likes," or "more link clicks."

Metrics and numbers in analytics are part of the process of reaching such objectives; they are not typically the objectives themselves. This means that metrics and numbers need to be related to each other and to external events to be able to generate insights. This is why our studies include a view of the social media landscape, so that we can think strategically about investing our resources and measuring our results.

Key Takeaways

- Similar features in different social media networks still have a different effect on the network and hence generate a different value and meaning upon analysis.

- The user experience generates a different value for features on social media networks and influences the marketing strategy in each network.

- To understand how socially active a network can be, we can look at the flow of content within the network and the interaction possibilities between its users.

- The assumption that good content will go "viral" because it's good is not true, and does not help us to work toward making such content viral. The structure of networks facilitates or complicates the virality of content.

- The factor of how social a certain social media network can be influences the analysis of performance within that network or in a cross-network environment.

- A brand can look for the social media network that is most friendly to its concept, positioning, content, and community for a safer bet on high performance.

- An analyst can take into consideration how friendly a social network is to a brand and its performance when making an analysis. This aspect enriches the analysis and generates important insights to be applied strategically by the brand.

- Social media networks constantly change their algorithms and the balance between organic and paid performance; keep an eye out for that.

- Brands are missing many opportunities because of the lack of attention to the feedback from their community on social media and the lack of connection from social to their other digital assets.

- The challenge for brands to effectively be social on social media is huge, but as analysts, it is part of our task to point out what is missed when a brand decides to not invest in using social media as a two-way channel.

- A higher number of comments does not necessarily indicate that the content has had a good performance. Comments are qualitative information, and a qualitative analysis is necessary to reach a conclusion on performance.

- New technologies such as chat bots are coming to help brands establish a better conversation with a huge audience or community.

- Social media was born to change the traditional noninteractive broadcast/advertising mechanism; let's stay true to that.

- Goals and objectives help brands optimize resources into what really works for them. Not every social media network is good for every brand, and investing in all of them at once is not the best strategy in most cases.

- The analyst can relate the numbers from analytics to the goals, objectives, and historical positioning of brands to deliver an analysis much richer in insights.

Tam Su

Founder of Studio TSU

Tam Su is a product innovator with a unique vision. His pursuit of all the different areas of knowledge on shaping product innovation toward real-world success led him to perform in key roles in companies that have excelled in their fields.

One such company, which is part of the reason why it is great to have Tam as a guest in this book, is Crimson Hexagon, a social listening and analytics provider. Crimson is an innovative company, pushing the boundaries of technology to deliver insights to its clients. A lot of that innovation culture is influenced by Tam.

Tam's work goes far beyond Crimson and social media specifically, diving into aspects that involve the manipulation of data, user experience with products, human behavior, and best practices of project management and processes that deal with a broad range of elements.

My contact with Tam was made through a common friend, Christine Berry, who worked for Crimson Hexagon. She told me about a brilliant colleague of hers and how she was inspired by his work, his knowledge, and his vision. I kindly insisted, as friends do, that she ask him to be interviewed for this book.

Times were somewhat turbulent then; Tam was moving across the country and had just opened Studio TSU, his product innovation company. Lucky for us, once settled, he was happy to join the book as a guest and share some of his knowledge.

© April Ursula Fox 2022
A. U. Fox, *Social Media Analytics Strategy*,
https://doi.org/10.1007/978-1-4842-8306-6_8

During the interview, I tried my best to keep an open conversational tone, so that Tam would feel comfortable in sharing any points he thought would be interesting to us. My questions went beyond social media for a broader understanding of the key aspects concerning data, the user experience, product, behavior, and so forth, which influence social media and social analytics, our sense of strategy, and our positioning as professionals in a digital world. I believe this approach resulted in rich material that adds a real-world context to our studies.

You can find Tam Su on his LinkedIn profile at www.linkedin.com/in/tamsu/.

Question 1

With the launch of Studio TSU and your advanced view into product innovation, which will include user experience and even human behavioral studies, I am curious to ask you about the use of data from a broader perspective.

I have noticed that many of us might not be making the best use of data for different reasons. That can go from having a nontechnical background to being unfamiliar with the dynamics of user experience and human behavior in social media. I believe that maybe one aspect of the process that could be more explored in analysis is to go beyond the data itself.

With this context in mind, what are your thoughts into the use of data from a broader perspective? And going beyond data to find better results for analyses?

First and foremost, you're absolutely right about people not necessarily using data correctly. We've gone from big data being sort of a general buzzword to a much better general understanding, where people understand that data alone is useless. You can have all the data in the world, and if you don't know how to interpret it, if you're reading the wrong facet of it, it's going to lie to you. Then applying that to brand strategy, I think of the old adage with statistics, which is, "You can make numbers tell you any story you want."

Social data could be similarly misused, and we can use it to argue pretty much anything one way or another. And that's the dangerous path for a lot of companies, for a lot of businesses. As an example, I see huge retail brand names make very fundamental basic mistakes because someone has an opinion, and they're just shoving it down everyone's throats without understanding that they're essentially engaging in confirmation bias at that point, and they want the numbers to tell their story.

This becomes relevant to the product innovation side of things, and one of the big reasons why I've decided to launch the studio is to help people get through the fog of war and to get people past their own confirmation biases and past a lot of the vanity metrics.

Engagement, for example, fundamentally, can be a useless number. It doesn't matter how engaged people are if you don't understand the story behind it. They could be engaged for all the wrong reasons. They can be engaged because they hate you. They can be engaged because they don't like your sweepstakes; they can be engaged because their mom told them to be engaged. There is any number of probabilities why people are engaged.

A big core philosophy of what I'm taking into this new venture is this idea of deeply understanding customers, understanding human beings. We deal with complex product innovation and product design processes under such philosophy. We wrap everything first and foremost in the idea of jobs to be done, meaning that every human being is engaged with something because they're trying to accomplish something else. You pick up the iPhone because you want to check your Twitter feed. You don't just pick it up, just to look at the phone. It's beautiful, but more often than not you're not just doing that.

And then from there we try to understand the user's journey, the actual process to which you accomplish that job that you set out to do. "I'm trying to check my Twitter feed, this is why I wanted to check it, this is the process, and this is the end goal that will accomplish why I do that." We then break that further down into use cases. For example, picking up the phone is a distinct use case. Putting the phone down is a distinct use case, and each requires specific actions by you, the user. Then we break that down even further into very specific micro moments.

For example, what was the first thought that popped into your head to say, *Hey, I need to go pick up my phone and check Twitter?* Whatever that urging thought was is actually critical to the success of this entire process. It is the base of this entire action. We can see from a pretty simple example that something as simple as *I'm just picking up my phone/I've been checking Twitter* could be broken down into very specific and somewhat complicated and very in-depth user actions and behaviors. That's what we're trying to apply to everything we do because we understand that vanity metrics are a really dangerous thing.

And when it gets to that level of depth and color understanding, you're not just looking at a number like engagement anymore. You're not just looking at the number of likes, the number of issues. We're actually looking at very real human behaviors that have real implications on how much they actually engage with you and the brand.

Question 2

Relating to the collection and distribution of data, with your experience in working with different types of data and facing different kinds of limitations in areas that go from data privacy to technology and data strategy of social networks, what can you share on specifics of such challenging environments? How do you see social networks opening or limiting access to more of their data as we move forward? Would there be a winning strategy for networks, analytics companies, and businesses working with them?

There are two ways of looking at data. One is that data is very much the new gold. Data is very much the new oil and it is to be hoarded, it is to be protected, and it is to be leveraged within a "walled garden scenario." You see major players, such as Facebook with its own ecosystem with Instagram and WhatsApp, and so forth, very much playing aggressively in that strategy. In some ways, one can argue that even Google is like that—even though they're obviously a lot more open than Facebook is.

That is one way of looking at it. The other philosophy, when you see the Twitters, the Tumblers of the world being more engaged in that fashion, is that data is very much a resource. It is very much the oil and gold analogy so to speak, but it's also to be shared because theoretically, that derives exponential value. Within both of those core philosophies, it's going to be hard to say which side wins and which approach ultimately is best for technology as a whole. Moreover, beyond the technology, what's best for human beings? What's best for business? It remains to be seen how exactly all of this plays out.

Everyone has their day, and I've been here long enough to know that everything comes and goes and things crumble. I worked at MySpace back in the day, and back in those days that was the "hot stuff." MySpace thought that they could do no wrong, that they were the pinnacle of social networks. And obviously that was not true. So let's see how well the walled garden strategy plays out. We know that Facebook is obviously very capable of adapting to different strategies, as we've seen the case with it aggressively copying Snapchat's mechanisms.

Within that context, technology needs to embrace potentially both approaches until one or the other wins out. Crimson Hexagon, for example, is taking the neutral approach. On one hand, Crimson is now one of the few with full and historic access to everything that has ever been on Twitter. I believe it's now down to one of maybe two analytics companies that have that. That's pretty impressive—clearly embracing the open data strategy in the sense that Twitter is making all that data openly available.

At the same time, Crimson is not shying away from working with Facebook and Instagram directly within that walled ecosystem, and exploring the boundaries of what could be a concern within those walls, following Facebook's rules, following their dry lines. Obviously, with full respect to privacy of course, but still trying to figure out how they can deliver business value. Ultimately, as I mentioned earlier, the question is, what's going to be best for businesses beyond Facebook?

Facebook is ultimately an ads platform, in the sense that they are here in service of other businesses that need to sell products and services. What is best for both businesses? And ultimately, what's best for every individual user? The people that pop up all over the place? We keep seeing how everything pans out, and theoretically, a company like Crimson, with its fairly neutral stance, can make a difference in terms of helping both types of ecosystems move forward.

Question 3

Following this line of thought and thinking about ways that listening and analytics providers will enrich the data with different processes, such as machine learning, to work around certain data limitations, how do you see the enrichment happening today, and how do you see it evolving? Do you think that the networks will eventually share more or that the analytics companies will have to evolve in that kind of intelligence? How will the walled garden vs. open data evolve?

The enrichment aspect is obviously paramount. Basic stats are not terribly useful to anybody. Data, in general, becomes exponentially useful when you apply meaning to it, and you apply meaning by making connections. Ultimately, what we're talking about is an approach from a very classic science perspective. We're talking about the main metrics that connect various rows and columns that individually may be pretty straightforward, but when combined have exponentially more meaning, exponentially more value.

Now, how that then plays out in terms of the walled garden vs. the open networks is interesting and remains to be seen. For example, Facebook is actually hanging onto a lot of the data behind the scenes. They're doing a lot of enrichment by themselves before ever releasing data to a company like Crimson. That's a double-edged sword.

On one hand, obviously, they're very concerned about privacy issues, and that's great, and everyone's on board with that. But they're very much in their own echo chamber, and they're talking only to themselves. Are they able to make the right connections that the greater advertising ecosystem needs? We don't know. It's night and day.

On the other hand, by not releasing the data they are able to then say, "Hey, we know how to work with all the privacy restraints, and this way we are theoretically able to give you more than we would."

There are then two sides to the argument, and again, very much a double-edged sword in terms of whether or not one side or the other can be genuinely helpful and useful to the advertising ecosystem.

Fundamentally, Facebook is obviously under very high pressure to demonstrate value. You can't just continue to charge essentially the highest advertising rates and say, "Trust us." That was TV back in the 1950s. That was radio back in the 1940s. It doesn't work anymore in this day and age. The advertisers are obviously a lot more sophisticated, a lot smarter. They're a lot less trusting for a number of reasons. This scenario will continue to play out in the coming years.

I do not see this as a battle that's going away anytime soon. Back in college, my major was essentially around media studies, and the idea of mutually exclusive spheres, like walled gardens, is as old as human time. The Cold War, for example, was a huge and very clear demonstration of that general philosophy, and the Internet was born out of that general paranoia.

The Web, in general, has its roots in the concept of having walled gardens that are mutually exclusive. Obviously, there has very much been an opposite movement saying the Internet should be free. It's the place where anyone can do anything, and so forth, and so on. That struggle, that tug-of-war, is not going away anytime soon. With the advertising data collection in mind, the entire ecosystem will continue to face down this question for many, many years to come.

Question 4

Talking now about a different subject and a practical approach to being data driven, what are your thoughts on the importance of being data driven as a company and as an individual? How can we take a practical approach on being prepared to work with data and to use social media data specifically?

I was listening to an old episode of *Freakonomics Radio*. I'm a huge podcast person in general. I binge on series, and recently it's been months now that I am caught on the *Freakonomics* series. They were telling a story about how one of them went out as a consultant to a major retailer who is used to placing ads in newspapers all across the United States. They did a little experiment where they demonstrated that newspaper inserts were not at all effective. Over the course of ten years, or something like that, the company had been looking at the wrong numbers. The company has literally spent billions of dollars paying for these ads that didn't do anything. That's the bottom line. In that story, nobody was willing to speak up in that organization because everyone had the very firm belief that "this is the way we've always done things, this is how it works, if we don't do it this way, somebody is going to get fired." So they continued to pour money down the drain.

The reason I tell this story is it's a perfect example, and one that I've seen countless times throughout my career, where smart teams and smart organizations have not embraced the idea of being data driven, of being highly experimental, and being very, very iterative.

If you look at the success of Toyota as company, it happens because they fully embrace iterative improvements in their entire production process. They're still doing that, to the point where pretty much every other car company now has gone to do the same thing, and our cars today, for example, do not rust as cars used to back in the day. When I was growing up, the cars became rusted, and no one liked that. Countless other examples can be given, where successful teams, successful businesses across entire industries have learned to embrace the importance of data-driven iterations.

If you're stuck on a team where people don't understand that concept fundamentally, walk away. There is no point in staying, it's a sinking ship, you're arranging deck chairs on the *Titanic*, walk away. Go somewhere where people do embrace numbers. In that new context, you can then actually have a constructive conversation about whether or not social data is important. That becomes a much more meaningful conversation as opposed to *We don't care about analytics*. Then, within the data-driven environment, issues become more relevant, such as whether or not our brand seriously has a presence on social and how much we should care about that.

Obviously, not every brand needs to be on social. If you're Lockheed Martin, you probably don't really care what people think about you building jets and bombs. So what if people don't like it that you are building jets and bombs? If, on the other hand, you are in Nike, or Adidas, or Reebok, social is very much a battleground, and all of those companies embrace that.

All of those companies spend a lot of time, money, and effort on being engaged on social, and not only from an overall customer perspective, going back to the beginning of this conversation, but also from a brand equity perspective. This is where people spend time now. This is where people are talking. This is where conversations happen. In a sense, this is not just social media anymore. What is the line between "social media" and just life in general? This is how people live. This is how people communicate. If you look at Facebook as an app, it's not Facebook anymore. Formally, it's a collection of communication mechanisms rolled into a platform. Years to come, we're going to see apps as a concept die. So in a way, aren't these simply communications mechanisms?

If I want to send a text, I have the choice of WhatsApp, Messenger, iMessage, or old-school text. Isn't it just about the most effective way of delivering my message to somebody? If I want to show video updates, do I share it on Instagram stories? Do I share it on my Facebook Livestream? It becomes then a choice of what is the most effective mechanism for my communication needs and not the use of an app platform necessarily. In that universe, which is coming soon, if you like, we're not looking at "social" anymore. We're not looking at "social media" as a discrete set of data.

We're literally being able to, in many ways for the first time since villagers had merchants that knew everyone who lived in the village, the ability to understand our audience in their day-to-day lives, and to be able to deliver to their needs on a very intimate level. Back in the day, if I were a blacksmith, I knew everyone who was my customer because they lived in my town, and I watched their horses go by. If I saw that their horse was limping a little bit, I knew that they were going to need new shoes soon, so I would have shoes ready.

Today, as Reebok or Nike, I have no idea when my customers might need new shoes. What if we get that level of intimacy back again? What if we're able to understand conversations that are happening and see those needs before they ever occur? What if, as a Nike brand manager, I can detect the trends that are going to come up in six months from now and be able to advance-order colors that match those trends because people are talking about that. And we know that in six months people are going to run out to stores and want to buy those colors, and so forth.

Again, the focus needs to be on *we are first and foremost a data-driven org.* and beyond that, do we care about being intimate with our customers? If so, then is social media the right channel for us to be in at this moment? Again, not every business cares because not everyone is going to be talking about Lockheed jets. But most other businesses do, and we will need to care.

Question 5

Looking at the need for integrating and making sense of all the available data... While you already briefly mentioned big data, do you also see, for example, artificial intelligence and even offers like IBM's Watson being the answer to the integration challenge? How would that compare to companies like Crimson? What is your take on a potential technology setup in this sense?

As we talked about earlier, big data alone is completely pointless without connections. Without enrichment, data is just a pile of numbers and not useful to anybody. Now, this might just be my own personal bias, but companies like Crimson are very much on the cutting edge, and Crimson, obviously, has competitors, so they're not alone in following this path. They're very much on the cutting edge of trying to draw the right connections between diverse sets of information, to then derive useful meaning, useful insights, and all of that.

Depending on who you talk to, Watson is or is not useful. Watson in itself is an interesting collection of analytics apps that you can apply to potentially any data set. Some users will find it restrictive, though, because the Watson apps don't necessarily provide a lot of data. Then the onus is entirely on the user or in paying IBM a lot of consulting dollars to try and draw those connections. Which if you are a huge company with a huge budget and an integrated corporate-wide effort to just throw $300 million at IBM, sure, good for you. For the rest of us, who live in the real world, and by that I mean for the most part clients of companies like Crimson, which are huge multinational companies but not about to spend $300 million on IBM, you can get a lot of value by essentially learning and knowing how to use the essentially off-the-shelf tools.

This works because companies like Crimson have already done a lot of that work for you. They have made a lot of connections behind the scenes, including a lot of advance work around artificial intelligence integration, around image analysis, around cross-network analysis, around the latest thing that we've been poking at, for example, which is personality analysis, looking at personality traits based on patterns of speech.

So IBM actually has that offering, but again, good luck trying to make that work for you. Whereas Crimson is supplying it in a very practical way so that you can get very immediate value. Crimson's new product is essentially a search bar tool where you can type in some keywords, or a string, and get results within the next two to five seconds. That's very powerful stuff considering is potentially ready right out of the box, and is just a "magically works" type of product.

A conclusion I would draw is that it kind of depends on what you're looking for. There is a market for both, obviously. I don't think Watson is going away anytime soon. But it's not necessarily terribly useful for your average brand, your average company.

Question 6

Last questions. Would you have a core message for readers regarding their preparation for the use of technologies related to analytics? And related to the future of analytics—what can we look for in that sense?

I feel like the big focus, if I have a core message for our readers, would be that over the course of the next three to five years, we're going to see the idea of social start to fade away and everything starts to be simply referred to as just "online" again. Social will become essentially part of the operating system to everything we do online. Everything has a social element. Everything is interconnected.

If you think about Web 1.0 or Web 2.0, we're talking about connecting machines. We're talking about connecting websites, individual servers, and that's all fine, well, and good, and the latest and greatest of what people are talking about and seeing is connecting a phone to a fridge, fine, we're just talking about the "thing." Ultimately, what we're talking about is connecting human beings to all the technology around them and to each other. In that sense, "social" is the fabric that enables that. The term will fade away just as we don't talk about the technology that's behind how the Web works. We don't talk about the IP being a big deal because it's there, and it works. And to me, social will very much meet a similar fate.

Artificial intelligence is interesting. I believe that to be a huge driver for the next wave of technological advancements. It is going to be the big revolution. It already is in many ways. It will be as big as the Web back in the 1990s, or be as big as social was in the early 2000s, and again, I ultimately see that taking a path in which it too will become ubiquitous at some point.

Any technology over time becomes ubiquitous and not talked about because it is everywhere. So AI, too, will fade away, but for the next ten to twenty years, it's going to bring about some amazing changes. Now, if you're a social media manager or a brand manager and you are reading that everything is going to fade, what does that mean? It means that you should actually learn all about it.

You should be out researching about it. You should understand what it is. You should start to use it and as much as possible. You should be talking about platforms like Crimson. Again, there are others. You should be very much "out in front" looking at these new topics. You should understand what's going on. You should understand how companies are applying this, and you should understand the difference between just a talk about it and the companies that are actually really doing this. You should understand that Facebook and Google both are integrating AI very deeply into their core because it is such a potential game changer. Not to say that you need to learn how to work with technical details of an API, you don't have to learn how to code, but you should understand what it means philosophically and be able to rationalize around it. And you should understand how that can help you grow your business.

The Analytics Process

The Analytics Process

Elements to Shape Data Insights

The use of analytics comes with its processes. We are still not quite at the point where we have access to all the actionable insights we need immediately with the press of a button. We can simplify our reports, have a number of basic metrics delivered automatically, and prepare ourselves to reach our strategic conclusions faster and easier, but we are still in a stage in which we need the figure of the analyst (even if not our job title). We still need our human intelligence to participate in many parts of the analytics process.

When it comes to paid promotion of digital content and ads, we have access to systems that can basically run on their own. Many systems figure out the best prices for exposure and also dynamically target the audience and deliver our promoted content or ads. But when we are working on a more complex brand strategy, when we are considering having a true community with us, we are still the ones to make it happen.

Considering, therefore, the human element into the analytics process, we commonly find that there is a need for clear planning and a structured approach in the use of analytics.

© April Ursula Fox 2022
A. U. Fox, *Social Media Analytics Strategy*,
https://doi.org/10.1007/978-1-4842-8306-6_9

When there is no such planning, and someone connects to an analytics tool to perform an unplanned analysis, or to "just to have a look," there will eventually be confusing elements that call for a more structured approach. This means that it will not always be instinctive to jump into an analytics tool and find all of the hidden gems or connect all of the significant metrics to a conclusion or an insight.

The first analyses we do will usually be the most time-consuming. After structuring the information, such as the metrics and time periods to look at, the process becomes much easier and faster and delivers better results.

In this chapter, we take a look at a few of these elements that are part of the process of analysis. From building blocks to tactics, we will open our view into the different parts of the puzzle. In the last chapters of the book, we go further into strategy and tactics, to put everything together and make sense of all the material we are looking at.

Analysis Is Comparison

All analyses are based on some form of comparison.

Even if we are looking at just one piece of information alone, such as *500 followers*, we are inevitably comparing that to what we already have in mind. We might have seen that another brand has 7000 followers, so we think 500 is low, or we live in a tiny community where only 20 people come into our door every day and 500 is almost everyone in the neighborhood.

If we have nothing in mind regarding such information, then we are establishing that what we see is the first piece of information we will use going forth. So information that comes without a reference point will be only part of the process and need the reference to show its value. At some point, it will have to connect with other information to become part of a conclusion or to reach the so-called insights.

Percentages are comparisons by nature, for example, but it is very important to highlight that a percentage alone can many times have no true meaning, give us a false impression, or require more context, and this can also happen with any other metric.

Take the example of a study on the growth of followers on social media channels. If we come across the information that a channel grew 10%, is that good or bad? Naturally, it depends.

Taking the example one step further, and adding a competitor page of the same exact size, where the competitor grew 7%. Easy. We grew more.

Going even further into a more common use case of pages with entirely different sizes. What would be the value of saying that one page grew 10%

against another that grew 7% if they have different audience sizes? In such cases, the absolute numbers work better as a comparison, since we may know that, for example, 10% means 2,000 followers for one channel, while 7% means 5,857 followers for another channel.

The percentage of growth, as a last note into this, can also give us a view of how fast a page is growing. If we periodically check for this, we will have a clear view of how fast we are growing compared to the past periods. Thinking of speed instead of volume can be very interesting for your strategy. Speed can better relate to goals and deadlines, for example, and can add a sense of movement to a planned strategy. Naturally, the same number is giving us speed and volume, so independent of how we look at it, it is still the same number. What we are doing here is just expanding the ways in which we can approach our analysis.

As channels grow, it is likely that percentages will become smaller and smaller, so comparing against previous periods and considering the larger page size into our interpretation is crucial to understanding if things are good, bad, better, or worse. We look at defining what good and bad means in an analytics process later in the book.

Comparison, therefore, is in the core of analytics. If we get stuck at any point during the process, we can rely on it or think of a new comparison to make as a next step. But comparison comes with its own challenges, such as our simple percentage example. The peculiarities of each comparison we make add a lot of value to our process of analysis.

Insight: A Broad and Open Term

Insight is a very open term in a world of structured processes and manipulation of information. The fascinating aspect of an insight is precisely the fact that it is open. It is open because we might not initially guess what it is, or where it comes from, but it is also open to any input that can help us reach it, meaning that experiments can pay off in the quest for insights.

The greater amount of knowledge and information we have about an object of analysis, the easier it will be to reach an insight. Knowing about the company, product, general marketing strategy, allied to the knowledge of analytics and tools will be greatly helpful.

Insights are usually referred to only as the final output of the process, a genius moment where the vision of a great path to success comes to mind. Truth is that insights will be found along the way as well and not only at a final moment of conclusion. So we have insights that lead us immediately to new questions and further analysis and other insights that lead us into actionable and strategic changes for our business.

Some people prefer to use the term *insight* only when reaching a final conclusion and adopt terms such as *signals, elements, signs,* and *findings* to the moments throughout the analysis process when we find material that adds to a major conclusion. Despite our take on how often we use the term, it is important to understand that an insight will usually not be the end of the line.

It is possible that in our early stages of using strategic analytics, everything being very new, we feel that all that we find is powerful information and leads to an insight. In time, once we understand how far we have to go to reach the actionable point, and the building blocks to reach our strategic end game, we will have a better view of what we can call an insight.

Investigation Beyond Social Analytics

When a social media channel of a brand sees unexpected spikes of traffic and new followers and has not done anything specific to promote that, analysts have the job of investigating the possible reasons behind the performance.

This investigative research goes beyond social and into internal and external sources to look for anything that can give meaning to what the numbers show. The market, political events, the weather, anything can be part of the cause of certain events.

Even if our core focus is social media, it can be part of our analysis process to integrate information from other sources. We will look more into this throughout the book. At this point, it is just good to know that this is under our belts.

Shaping a Method: The End Game for an Analyst

I constantly hear from analysts who I speak with about having their own preferred way of doing things. It is very interesting to hear from them on how the entire process of analysis and use of analytics will be shaped to their taste. To me, this feels like the ultimate goal or the "end game" of being an analyst.

These methods—and discussions about such methods and how they ended up being created—become great points for learning and evolving your own skills as an analyst.

Methods don't need to be complicated. This is a very important point. Methods can be as simple as a list of metrics distributed in a certain order or displayed side by side in a certain way. Whatever is our preferred "way of doing things" in analytics, that will be our method.

By having an initial method, we can expand into having more than one and make use of each in different situations, where we use different tools or tackle different objectives.

My intention is not to tell you what your method should be. I am not stealing the fun out of your evolution into being a better analyst. What I intend to do is only open your mind and give as much as I can to let you build your ideal methods for analysis and enjoy the processes of analysis while at it.

As a list of elements that can eventually become a cornerstone for our methods and make this concept of method less abstract, we can consider into our methods our preferences around the following:

- Tools
- Metrics
- Time periods (hour, day, week, month, quarter, etc.)
- Dashboard setup
- Reporting formats
- Internal sources: what to look for inside the organization being analyzed
- External sources: beyond the organization
- Order of steps to reach a final report

Each of these elements is explored throughout the book. By the end of the book, you will be ready to experiment and build your own methods of analysis. For now, consider the methodic mindset so that you understand that each element has its place under a final method or "way of doing things."

The Analysis Cycle: Time Periods As the First Key to Comparison

Even before we know exactly which metric or information we want to use as a key for our analysis, it is likely that we already have a certain period in mind.

When we ask ourselves if our channel performance "is better or worse," we not only have to point out in which aspect (specific metrics) but also in which period.

Even when we think that we are not looking at any period, and we just log in to our analytics tool and simply see a current number that interests us (for any reason), we still have a period in mind. If we are not comparing what we see to a specific period, the period is still there. It is, by default, "since the beginning of time."

Being so significant to an analysis, the time period takes a leading role. It can be the first trigger in the planning of a recurring process.

Comparisons, when done frequently, tell a much better story. Fewer details are lost, and more context can be brought into the timeline. When this frequency is set on similar periods, meaning a regular weekly report, for example, it can be even more interesting because we get used to understanding what happens during these periods of time.

What can happen in a social media channel in a week? Or in a month? How much time is available in that period for people to interact with that page and take action on whatever "call to action" is proposed by the content? How responsive is such a community to the specific types of content? Do they react faster because of certain elements?

Periodic analyses help us understand such things.

Finding a Good Cycle: Considering Community Activity, Resources, and Attention Span for Reports

Why choose a certain period for the analysis cycle? Which period is the best one? A case-by-case approach is the way to go.

By "cycle," you can read a repeatable period, or one "block" of time in the ongoing timeline of a channel.

The use of a cyclic process is intended to help everyone involved benefit from it. So when aiming for a certain cycle, consider everyone's agendas, including the people receiving the final reports.

We then consider the time needed to take action upon the reports. In analytics, we find that it is not enough to only reach the insights as the end of the process or goal. Despite the hard work to get there, many times, the real challenge is implementing the insights into a new strategy.

The following three elements can be helpful when choosing the ideal cycle:

- **Community activity**: What happens in the channels during such time?

- **Resources**: Can the analytics process be finished within this cycle?

- **Attention span for reports**: How much from the report can be absorbed by our team in the given time?

Community Activity: Following the Dynamics of a Brand on Social Media

A very busy channel can benefit from a shorter cycle. If not too much is happening in that channel, then a longer period is needed to look at the activity.

A short cycle is great for high volume and high dynamics, such as the activity in a busy Twitter account. Figure 9-1 shows the average interactions per tweet on a daily basis; despite the brand, notice the spikes going up to 700 average interactions for the posts on that day. A short-period analysis helps to understand such dynamic patterns.

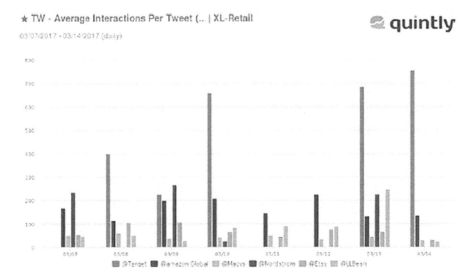

Figure 9-1. Average interactions per tweet

The analysis of a channel can also have more than one cycle going on at the same time. A very busy channel, in the example of the channels in Figure 9-1, can also have longer cycles of analysis running to display broader patterns and trends. Have one or more cycles that cover enough information to fulfill the needs of certain analysis. The activity can be related to the publishing calendar of the channel, to the reactions of the audience, or both.

If the proposition is to be reactive to what the audience responds over the content, then a short cycle is preferred. Crisis management, for example, is done best if done in real time.

Longer periods can serve a strategic high-level view of audience and channel activity, displaying eventual patterns that can then be a key to either enhancing or changing what the channel is doing with its content.

Figure 9-2 displays interactions over a twelve-month period, and this helps us understand if we are on a trend to have more or fewer interactions going forward. Note that for the longer period a line chart was chosen, instead of the column chart of Figure 9-2. Line charts can work very well for long-period trend analysis. In this example, independent of which brand it is, we see that the brand with the highest average is consistently dropping while other brands in the group are starting to show growth toward the end of the period. As a marketer in a leading brand, it could be interesting to go back a few months and understand what was driving such high engagement before. Many times, metrics such as those shown in Figure 9-2 trigger for us to dive into alternatives for research. Knowing in this case that a certain period was much better than others can help us focus on that, understand what was going on back then, and if we were doing something right, we can replicate it.

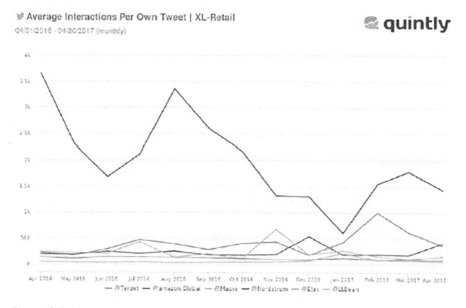

Figure 9-2. Average interactions per own tweet

Resources: Can the Team Deliver a Quality Analysis in Time?

Time-consuming tasks that are not directly related to the core business of an organization are usually not a priority. It often happens that the team assigned with the task of creating the analysis does not have the time to perform quality work in short cycles or in multiple cycles at the same time.

When this is the case, one way to deal with it is to choose a main working cycle, like one month, for example, and automate a few reports along the way.

A comprehensive report, which includes insights, suggestions for optimization, detailed benchmarking analysis, and so forth, can be created once per month. And once per week, for example, the stakeholders can receive automated reports from the tools, with less interpretation of the numbers, but enough to keep the flow of performance in sight.

Another option is a live dashboard with freshly updated numbers available at any time. For this, it is important that the team understands the metrics well and that they can take action if something peculiar is seen.

A more comprehensive report is recommended even if there is a live dashboard. This report can be the closing of a certain cycle, a moment to focus, dedicate time, and perform adjustments to the strategy before continuing. The choice of a good working period is key, in which the team can use the analytics to interfere positively on the planning of the next marketing or product cycle.

It is difficult to truly evolve our strategy without any such moments, without giving a greater focus into the strategy of what we are doing at certain points. Even if the actual work never stops, a strategic cycle of analysis can run in parallel, and implementation can then fit into the tactical and operational cycles of the company.

Attention Span: How Often Do People Want to See Reports?

It is better not to waste time with many reports but instead have only a very good one that everyone can dedicate time to and really make good use of it. There is no point in insisting on a short cycle if the team has no time to make good use of it. However, if the brand calls for a short cycle of analysis for strategic reasons, then the team will find the needed time.

As an analyst, many times, the decision of which cycle will not fall under our belt, but we can bring in such suggestions and questioning and help decision-makers to think strategically about the use of analytics. The objective is always to make the most out of our analyses.

The following are some important questions to ask when checking if people have enough time for a certain report cycle:

- What is your average number of meetings per day and per week?
- How many reports do you receive per day and per week?

- Which of your processes are affected by the analytics reports you receive? How often do they happen?

- How much time do you spend on an analytics report until you find a conclusion of what you see?

- How much do you enjoy looking at numbers and graphs on a scale of 1 to 10?

With these and other such questions, we can then suggest a cycle that will best fit into everyone's workflow. Questions can also indicate if the people involved will benefit from training in analytics. If we detect that the team is not getting what the reports show, a few sessions of group work can be helpful to generate more interest over the use of strategic analyses.

Learn more about the "analyst profile" of each team member. This profile comes as a result of questioning and indicates the preferences of each team member and how advanced they are in the use of analytics. If we find out that one of our team members does not enjoy too many details in reports and is really more interested in a high-level approach, we can expect lower performance from them when dealing with a very detailed analysis.

Dynamic Cycles: Keep at Least One Anchor Down

Many brands have multiple activities going on and sometimes even different teams leading these different initiatives. These could include work on different products, services, events, institutional communications, HR messages—you name it.

When we are working with or within such companies, we usually also have very dynamic cycles for our analytics processes. These cycles most likely follow each initiative and relate directly to the different periods established by them. So each team or department dictates the best cycle for its work.

Even if the resources are there, and the attention span is good, it is also recommended to keep at least one global cycle that brings everything together and serves as the main milestone for the entire company. This will be useful because despite independent efforts, a unified view is strategically important to the overall judgment of performance and offers a chance for unified strategies to happen.

Many companies have so much going on that they miss having a better performance because of the lack of synchronism between all the different initiatives. One anchor report can greatly help to enhance performance for the company overall.

The more we have going on, however, the higher the amount of resources will be needed to complete a well-rounded and insightful report. If this task is under one analyst, this analyst will have a lot of work to speak with everyone involved and reach conclusive views of objectives and performance to then be able to suggest improvements while pointing out the highlights. The challenge can be intense. It can be a busy task, and that is when our method and experience on the analysis process plays an important role.

By engaging with all the different teams and taking each of their different workflows into account, we can reach valuable insights. On top of that, everyone involved becomes very engaged and excited about what is being done. When analytics are well connected to someone's workflow, it naturally has a lot more significance to them.

It is a lot of work to deal with dynamic cycles, but when done right, it is worth it.

Short Periods: Ongoing KPIs, Buzz, and Crisis Management

Considering that short periods of analysis can be even daily or less, depending on the context of events, the elements under a short-period analysis will be best if kept brief and very clear to everyone involved.

A few KPIs (key performance indicators) can be set into an ongoing mode to quickly offer the monitoring of the performance to the team. This can be a live link to fresh information or daily reports, for example. Interactions, including mentions on Twitter, are very common ongoing KPIs. Conversions, such as link clicks, are also commonly followed in short periods.

These very short periods of analysis are a good option during campaigns that generate a lot of buzz, such as product launches, seasonal events, and political campaigns. Also, if there is any kind of crisis involving the brand, constant monitoring can be a good idea.

For weekly periods, which are still considered short by most standards, the collection of metrics can then be expanded.

Metrics such as the top posts become interesting, as well as top followers interacting with the brand and response rates for questions (if it is something being worked on by the brand), but not too many others.

Essentially, the focus in gathering the interactions, eventually also conversions, and the basics of where they are coming from, can be enough for a short-period analysis. A major shift in brand strategy will likely not happen in short cycles; there is usually not enough evidence to support major decisions and not enough time for the team to review and create a new complex plan.

In time, with experiences of the specific brand strategy, and the context of the brand in the market and with its community, such short-cycle reports can become more meaningful and receive addition of more information, such as more details in demographics and more qualitative insights.

Long Periods: Goals and Greater Optimization

Longer periods give room for greater exploration.

With a long time between cycles, it is possible to build a comprehensive report and include all metrics necessary for strategic evaluation and adjustments. Long-cycle reports can be the key to greater optimization. With such a comprehensive view of details, and the correlation of the information from analytics to the higher goals of the company, a long-period cycle can be an excellent choice to bring all things together and prepare to make it better going forward.

While the choice of individual metrics is very open and includes anything useful and meaningful that we can get our hands on, some elements can be highlighted as most commonly present, as listed in the following:

- A full view of interactions and sources
- A full view of conversions and sources
- Rankings of content and possible reasons behind performance
- Timeline correlation to company events
- Timeline correlation to external events
- Changes in audience related to content and events
- Competitive benchmarking of KPIs within the timeline analysis
- Detailed content and audience performance of top competitors
- A detailed view of paid promotion performance
- A view of competitive paid promotion performance
- As much detail on audience as possible

Going from One Cycle to the Next

Changing our strategy is usually something that is easier said than done. The point of using analytics, however, is to be able to act over what the numbers are showing. If changes in our strategy are needed, we must be able to make it happen.

To be able to make the necessary changes, a good presentation of cause- and data-based suggestions for improvement goes a long way. Added to the gathering and presentation of convincing information, we can also include and consider planning around the time needed for the analysis to be performed by each stakeholder involved and then eventual action toward change. It can be important to think of this as early into the process as we can, to include into planning all the necessary time for an evaluation of reports and for implementing any necessary changes.

As an example of this kind of approach, some teams have the closing of their analysis cycle happen before the end of a campaign period or a regular calendar period in cases when the following period is a busy one. The report, in such cases, can be presented one week before the end of the period or campaign, and during that week, the team prepares any necessary changes to the following cycle starting early next period. So there is an overlap of one week where the campaign is still happening, but the team has enough time to implement necessary changes toward the next cycle. If something extraordinary happens during that final week, it can be added to the next cycle's reports.

Solutions on optimizing the analysis strategy can be essentially simple, such as a shift in the evaluation period or a better format for reporting. What matters most is to be able to effectively implement any changes needed. Transforming raw data from analytics into a thoughtful analysis and then into practice is a process that can fail to be completed if there isn't a well-organized "push" to go with it.

In some cases, the analyst also becomes a project manager to make sure that not only a good analysis is made but that insights are taken into consideration and necessary action is also taken toward the overall strategy.

The Analyst Mindset: Making the Right Questions and Running the Right Experiments

We are all analysts, whether we think of ourselves in that way or not. We have constant analysis processes running within our minds, even while taking the simplest decisions, or tapping into our emotional judgment. Most people, however, distance themselves from the word *analyst*, avoiding identifying themselves as such, and reacting badly when given a formal task of analysis. But why that reaction?

The simple answer was found after asking more than 300 marketers. Most of us relate the word *analyst* to very complicated mathematical formulas and statistical work. We relate the word *analysis* to processes that are far beyond our understanding, so we position ourselves as being too ignorant to perform an analysis or to be called analysts.

While many analysts and analyses will, in fact, work with very complicated technologies or calculations to offer results, the term itself can be related to very simple principles, which every single person can relate to.

This is not to undermine the value of the analyst profession, on the contrary, once we all understand more about data analysis, we value even more the work of a professional analyst. The professional analyst goes further and pushes the technology and the field of analysis into a brighter future for marketing and business in general.

The idea under the analyst mindset is that, just as we can perform well on several activities in our lives without being exclusively dedicated to them, we can also perform analyses and see ourselves as analysts. Once we break the mental barriers holding us back from further learning, our results from analytics improve quickly and our joy of the process as well.

The easiest way to do this, to create this bridge between the term analyst, analytics, analysis, and our non-analyst self, is to think of subjects that are very familiar to us, that are even part of our daily lives. When dealing with such things, aren't we all specialists? Can't we give very analytical opinions? Can't we make quick analyses that provide a substantial amount of information?

Yes, we can. Easily.

The Instinctive Analyst: Share the Joy

A very short example that I can share is about a friend of mine who does not admit it, but is the definition of a "foodie." She loves food in a way that most people I know do not. It is not only about eating with her. It's about where to find it, who cooks it, and the origins of it. She is greatly interested in all the details about the food that she loves and the places she goes to eat it.

When I speak with her about food, or when I am lucky to go out with her for food around the city, her insights into all of it become fascinating to me.

The interesting point is that, even though I love food, I never read any food blogs or restaurant reviews. I don't know who the chefs are. I am not curious enough to go after this information myself. But when she brings it out to me, I get totally into it, and the pleasure I have from the food after all the context is much greater.

I am sure that all of us have such friends or know such people. These are people that enhance a certain subject because they bring out so many aspects of it in a way that you can easily get into the context and start seeing things from a different perspective.

This is the essence of the analyst mindset: to go through details of a certain universe and bring out the context to an audience that will then easily be able to relate to it.

But to form this mindset consciously, since it is likely that naturally we may not be as excited about creating social media analyses and reports as we are about traveling, eating, playing sports, or watching movies, we can define a few fundamental elements to use as pillars.

The following are some of the pillars of the analyst's mindset:

- Find the joy
- Get into the context
- Understand our audience
- Keep the flame alive

Find the Joy

What is fun about analyzing marketing campaigns and, more specifically, social media channels? What is the best about having analytics and tools at our disposal? How does it affect our work or the projects we have at hand?

- Do we enjoy the time it saves? Can it maybe save even more time through automation of processes?

- Do we enjoy tracking the performance and being on top of our game? Are there more metrics that can reflect our performance?

- Do we enjoy the competitive aspect? How far can we go on benchmarking our competitors? What are they doing right that we could learn from and do even better?

- Do we enjoy the structured reporting capabilities? Can we add our insights into making reports more interesting? Maybe a storytelling approach or the use of different graphs? Maybe a live dashboard with constantly updated information?

When we find what is most significant for us, we find a greater drive to dedicate time and to learn more about the entire process.

We also find common interest points with other analysts and the marketing community, and that gives us material to develop our networking and knowledge exchange.

I am personally interested, for example, in understanding behavior, usage of network features, and also the future of social media. So when I look at social networks and work on projects using analytics, I try to keep an eye out for the evolution of networks, for brands that drive huge community engagement, for specific behavior, which the numbers have a hard time explaining, and for any glimpse into the future. Many times, the analytics work for me as a trigger into a broader research. It drives me to going beyond the numbers and to think about the user experience, language, culture, and other subjective human aspects related to engagement. But this is just me; each of us has a different interest driving us.

Get the Context: What Is Not Evident at First Glance?

Brands always have many aspects that position them in the market. Getting into the context of the brand we are working with helps us find connections between what we see from analytics and what happens beyond the channels that we are analyzing. Context helps us perform a better analysis in a shorter time. But what can we grasp as context? What can we look for when trying to dive into the context of a brand?

Some questions can give us direction:

- What is the offer of the brand to the market? Which products and services push the brand forward?

- Who is the consumer of that brand? What details can we learn about them?

- What is the perceived image of the brand? Is it a trendsetter? Luxury? High quality? Low price?

- What is the history of the brand? Any remarkable events?

- What are the brand's active marketing campaigns?

- Are there any important people related to the brand? Executives? Sponsored athletes? Artists?

By diving into the universe of the brand, we can find more material to add to the analysis. The output from the work with analytics is richer, and the reports connect much better with the stakeholders involved when we bring into the analysis more elements of the brand context.

Understand the Audience

It is very easy to become carried away in numbers on social media without having a focus on who exactly a channel is interacting with. While the view of audience information on social media is limited (remember the chapter on interests and demographics data sources), an understanding of the general audience of a brand and the intended audience for certain content is very helpful in the analysis of content performance.

It is possible to then relate content performance to audience, since content is usually created with a certain specific audience in mind.

If a brand is not having the best performance with the content that it has tailored to its intended core audience, maybe the brand is not reaching the right people through social media, or maybe it is gaining a different audience than the intended and could eventually be the time to adapt to it. It could be time to change.

Such possibilities can come into view when an analyst understands what the brand is trying to do in terms of its targeting. But more than an age and gender group, we can try to truly understand what drives the audience.

Many brands are very homogenous with their content. They create such a strong identity that many times, if we are not into that context, we may see the marketing initiatives as repetitive, boring, and all the same, really.

With context and the support of performance numbers, we might understand that the audience perceives the slightest details in the brand communication, and sometimes just a change of color on an image, or the presentation of an apparently small new feature can be enough to drive the audience into high engagement.

With this in mind, we can better picture the benefits of analyses made with a clear understanding of context and how it is also risky not to have such a context during our work. When we don't understand the audience well, not specifically the audience being reached by social media but the general and intended audience of the brand, we risk having our personal opinions influence our process of analysis. We might overlook something important or give importance to something that is not touching the audience at all.

A brand can be open to a process of discovery, but it is very likely that the intended audience is always a part of the strategy. The discovery process when it comes to audience can be based at the end of the shopping cart, meaning that the people who spend money on the brand have more value than those that interact a lot but never actually buy. When we see that the intended audience (those who likely buy) is not being reached by our message, we know that it is time to adapt our strategy to reach the correct audience and not assume that our brand is having a new appeal only based on the analysis of communication.

Business strategy is ultimately about growth, so the elements that directly relate to growth always have more importance, audience included. In many cases, as a result of our social media analysis, we have enough insights to compare our reach and engagement to our intended audience. We can check for the people who interact the most with our brand, and in some cases, we can even run certain promotions to motivate engagement and check if the audience we reach is the audience that we want to reach.

An insightful marketer once gave me an intriguing set of points to help me understand audience and intended audience; it was a lot about putting myself in the audience's shoes and considering the master plan behind the value proposition of the brand. These are a few such points:

- Age, gender, location, buying power
- Cultural background
- A day in the life
- Why are they the audience? Why do they purchase? Why do they influence? Why do they promote?
- Do they purchase for themselves or for others?
- How much would they be willing to spend on the brand?
- What aspects of the brand excite them the most?
- If something goes wrong, will they be forgiving?

Keep the Analyst Flame Alive: It Feels a Bit like Sherlock Holmes' Intuition

Having an analyst mindset is an ongoing exercise. The more we are perceptive about contextualization and correlation of what we find, the easier and faster it becomes for us to do it.

One great advantage we have on this is that we can practice with any context we like. We can choose our favorite topics and go for it, dive deeper into context, and then start analyzing aspects of them.

If we go for brands that we enjoy, we are likely to even be able to do a great competitive benchmarking of the brand positioning and audience without too much external data beyond what we already know. In many cases, we even know the stories of the founders behind such brands and key moments in the brand's history. We simply know it because we enjoy or admire the brand in a certain way. So we can then tap into understanding why we admire such brands. Is it their products? Their values? Their fierce competitiveness? Their community? This kind of conscious exercise with knowledge that we already have is great to keep our mind sharp for analysis of brands unknown to us.

This is what I mean by "keeping the flame alive." We are constantly giving space for our analyst mindset to get to work and bring out remarkable conclusions or insights.

When I watch Sherlock Holmes do "his thing," I always start imagining what it would be like to go out into the world with his level of "intuition" and start "guessing" everything right. By "his thing," for all of you unfamiliar with Sherlock Holmes, I mean to describe his advanced process of deduction, where he observes everything around him and makes connections that are very unexpected but extremely relevant. Sherlock Holmes will, for example, correctly deduct the amiable personality of a character by observing the marks of dog teeth on a walking stick. The marks, in this case, being plainly visible and on the middle of the stick, indicate that the owner would let the dog carry the stick, pointing to a close relationship between the owner and the dog. This level of deduction can only happen when the observer can think beyond the immediate object, and this is the point in this book.

I feel that a bit of what we do in analytics has that kind of investigative approach—an approach that is very much based on evidence (analytics), but that also benefits from our experience in other fields, and from what we can grasp of the context of our object of study.

Many of the most interesting conversations that I have ever had were with people that have that kind of active thinking about the world around them. Once I started noticing that this was a natural skill of every one of us, I started relating it to my work and also bringing this point up with friends in the field of marketing and beyond.

As counterintuitive as it seems, the level of joy and pleasure is always a major element in the progression into learning about anything and putting even the most exact, nonemotional sciences into practice.

As subjective as this chapter may have seemed in some areas, my objective is to open your mind to all possible paths surrounding you. I feel that there is never one path to knowledge, but many, and that is the beauty of it.

Key Takeaways

- Analysis is comparison.
- The process of analysis becomes faster as we finish our initial setup and as we apply methods of analysis into the work.
- An analyst, in time, will have his or her own way of doing things, a personal method, or methods for analysis. This helps in reaching insights faster and in delivering reports that are more relevant to brand strategists.

- Insights are not reached only at the end of an analysis; they are found along the way and lead an analyst to investigate different aspects of the data collected. Finding insights is a dynamic process.

- The period of time is important to the analytics process—not only the period of the data collected but the entire cycle, from planning to reporting and acting upon actionable insights delivered.

- Be honest about deadlines; plan very carefully the use of resources dedicated to the analysis and the attention span of stakeholders receiving the reports.

- In a dynamic environment, take the lead into speaking with everyone involved and finding out what works best for the group and the objectives of the company; we can use our knowledge of analysis to centralize part of the planning or all of the planning toward the best possible analytics cycle.

- When many activities are going on at once in the company, look at creating an anchor point, one report that brings everyone together and can synchronize the strategy of all the different teams and departments.

- Short periods of analysis benefit from fewer metrics and simple metrics.

- Long-cycle reports can be shaped into comprehensive reports, in which we can include all details necessary to reach very strategic insights.

- As we move from one cycle to the next, we must be brave enough to take action when needed. The reason why we use analytics and perform analyses in the first place is to be able to act upon them.

- When planning on the time we need to close our analysis cycle, we must consider the entire process, from gathering the data and creating reports to the time needed for stakeholders to read such reports and take action.

- We are all analysts, whether we think of ourselves in that way or not. Being analytical is an instinctive human trait.

- When we find joy in the process of analysis, or whatever parts of the process we may truly like, we deliver better analyses in less time.

- Context of the brands we analyze helps deliver more strategic insights and even suggest greater changes of strategy.

- One step further into the context of the brand, the understanding of its audience helps the analyst relate to content performance and deliver qualitative insights. By audience, we can think of the intended audience, the audience reached by communications, and the audience that actually spends money with the brand.

- Keep the analyst flame alive. We can recognize the moments when we are performing analyses of common topics of our daily lives and understand what makes an analysis interesting and what drives people to be interested in them as well. This kind of exercise keeps our mind sharp, much like Sherlock Holmes and his intuition.

Armando Terribili

Founder of Impariamo Consulting

Armando Terribili, PhD, PMP Black Belt, has an extensive curriculum in the areas of business administration and, to our specific interests in this book, project management. His career involves working with multinational companies in very practical, real-world projects and teaching university students about the science and practice of business.

He is the author of several books on project management, most of which have become key references for professionals. His publications cover all aspects of project management, from different approaches to resource management and negotiation techniques.

For this book, Professor Terribili discusses the need that we have, as analysts, to structure our work and our methodologies around analytics. We see throughout the book that during the course of our analytics career, we need to integrate not only raw data into metrics but also the people and processes that are connected to the analytics process and are responsible for driving business success.

© April Ursula Fox 2022
A. U. Fox, *Social Media Analytics Strategy*,
https://doi.org/10.1007/978-1-4842-8306-6_10

I met Professor Terribili during my business administration studies at FAAP University in São Paulo, Brazil. FAAP is a unique place to study business, because most students come from families of business owners and entrepreneurs, which is also my case. This means that the approach to business was always very practical, and the discussions I had with my colleagues related directly to real-world cases from their businesses, which are among the largest companies in Brazil in every different sector from farming to industry, services, and technology.

During those years, I was very excited about the projects that I worked on and I was eager to push out the best possible results. Professor Terribili was always there to give me advice on structure and discipline. His approach from the project management perspective—where a big part of success involves being disciplined and organized with tasks, resources, team management, and deadlines—was key to my maturity and success as a student. I received the prize of best student in class from FAAP and from the Business Administration Council of São Paulo.

Professor Terribili also mentored my studies and final thesis on social media and the hiring process, which received the second-best grades overall that year. His view on structure and discipline was applied from the moment when I was brainstorming about the best possible thesis I could manage related to social media, to all the work in making it happen.

From there, I kept what I learned very close to the chest and took it with me into all other aspects of my life. I think that this is what university is about— helping us shape the best version of ourselves. With this book, my intention is directly related to that. I wish that this material can help all of us shape the best possible version of our "analyst selves."

Going into the questions of this interview, my objective was to bring us a real- world view of elements from project management that can come into play during the process of working with analytics and when setting up an analytics strategy in a company.

You can find Armando Terribili directly via his LinkedIn profile at www. linkedin.com/in/armandoterribili/.

Question 1

For a team aiming to make the best out of a process of analysis and performing recurrent analyses, which principles would you highlight as useful from the project management perspective?

Through social media, individuals can have their own "voice," sharing their unique opinions, their positioning, and criticism. However, the analysis of data collected from social media must still contemplate, above all, the largest possible sample, under a broad and comprehensive approach. To do so, project indicators must be created to effectively carry out a continuous and monitored analysis based on results being obtained.

The definition of project indicators is of fundamental importance because it will involve costs, which in this case can mean the activities around creating such indicators, adjustments, and delivery of analysis results. A key point is also to be very careful not to create "white elephants," which are measurements of the obvious or that don't truly measure anything at all. In either case, it will represent a waste of resources for the organization.

The indicators must serve as the basis for diagnostics of normal or exceptional conditions. In the case of the exceptional, an analysis must be performed around the root cause of contributing (causal) factors which generated such conditions, to then address them effectively with corrective action. In this context, the PDCA tools (plan, do, check, and act), widely promoted by Deming over the last century, come into play.

In conclusion, we have project management present in two key moments:

- Creation and validation of indicators
- Dealings with corrective actions, which can unfold the creation of new projects of different complexity

Question 2

For the manager of a process of analysis, the principal analyst, or simply the person responsible for performing the analysis and delivering reports, which points are useful for this position specifically, based on your experience in the field of project management?

Processes and projects are distinct concepts. While a process is something continuous, recurrent in the organization, a project is transitory (has beginning and end) and singular (generates a unique output: product or service). What process and project have in common is that both are planned and executed involving resources from the organization. With this in mind, the analysis of process must be very detailed so that it can supply the manager with the necessary elements to be used to identify key points for incremental improvement or radical improvement (innovation) projects.

Xavier Ferrás, professor of Operations Management and Innovation at ESADE, Universidad Ramon Llull de Barcelona, in his book *Innovación 6.0: en fin de la estratégia* (Plataforma Editorial, 2010) mentions two variables to classify a project:

- Competitive advantage (differentiation)
- Degree of risk (entry barrier)

According to Ferrás, the projects qualified as being "of innovation" are those that have elevated risk and high competitive advantage, while projects qualified as being "of improvement" are those with minimal risk and low competitive advantage. In the case of projects "of improvement," the organization is essentially doing the same as it already did, but with economy of resources or better performance. Complementing his analysis, we are given the "hygienic" projects, which are related to "following" the market, and offer competitive advantage with minimal risk. And finally the projects without competitive advantages and with elevated risk, which Ferrás denominates as "stupid."

With this concept in mind, every time opportunities for improvement in processes being analyzed are identified, the potential projects must be selected according to the strategy of the organization and further variables, such as

- **Impact**: The ones providing the most meaningful results
- **Time**: The ones offering faster results
- **Costs**: The ones requiring less investment
- **Risks**: The ones with higher chance of success

And certainly the "stupid" projects must be ignored.

Question 3

Going further into this topic, how do you see the importance of the relationship of the manager with the people involved in every stage, from collecting the data and initial material to preparing presentations and reports and finally implementing the insights into the strategy of the business?

The importance of the relationship lies in obtaining commitment. A team who is committed and focused on results becomes objective and productive. Commitment generates "a sense of ownership" over the process, avoiding detachment and minimizing conflict. The sentiment of ownership makes everyone feel that "this is mine," "I am part of its construction."

However, it is key to point out that to obtain commitment, the management must have a democratic approach, an effective and open communication field with the team, stimulating the participation of everyone involved, giving value to the professionals.

Question 4

Negotiation is an element that usually comes up during the use and implementation of analytics. It can happen between a company and its client, between different teams within the company, or even within the same team. Using your book Negotiations in Projects *as a reference, would you point out any important elements of negotiation that can be considered when working with analyses or implementing analytics?*

In general, publications on the theme only approach "competitive negotiations," where each part is trying to take the highest advantage over the other. In the area of project management, negotiation is different because it is collaborative, where the objective is to reach the best results for all parties involved.

A simple yet good example happens when trying to sell a car. If the interested party is a stranger, the financial results will be prioritized, and the relationship effect will be ignored, since it is likely that the buyer will never be seen again. In a different scenario, if the interested party is your friend, you will still aim for good results, but will take into account the maintenance of the relationship, since you are willing to nurture the friendship. In a third scenario, if the interested party is your younger brother, recently graduated and still an intern in a company, you will likely offer a price below market average and facilitate his payment in 12-24 installments, because in this case your priority is the relationship, you want to help your brother.

In project management, the negotiation style is to obtain good results and also maintain the relationship, because after all, many further negotiations can happen under a same project or in future projects, being them with clients, suppliers, or internal teams and colleagues. The key, therefore, is to always use collaborative negotiations and avoid the competitive approach.

On a last note, when dealing with clients, it is key to understand that clients will have different levels of maturity when it comes to project and process management. This is a factor that must be considered within the relationship with clients and when presenting proposals that may lead into negotiations. Therefore, the team or company taking the role of consultant, proposing or offering the service, must stimulate the development of their clients, but first perform realistic diagnostics so that actions may have at least a minimum level of adherence with the culture and organizational values of the client.

Question 5

Which final points can we keep in mind when bringing elements of project management into the use and implementation of analytics?

Periodic measurements using the right indicators will be key to success. The recurring measurement is critical for the evaluation of potential progress or decline in the process. It will eventually enable, in some cases, to create projections from results. However, the following three aspects must be always taken into account when working with indicators:

- **Applicability**: A measure what is intended to be measured

- **Independence**: A level of noncorrelation with other indicators and variables

- **Provability**: Proof that the indicator affects and/or is affected by the results of analysis

Author's note: *Project management is an area in which vast knowledge has been developed throughout the years. The goal of this interview is to spark interest on our side on researching further into methods and principles validated by project managers to help drive strategy around analytics and truly affect the business in a positive way. Throughout the book, we come across many elements that go beyond analytics specifically and add into our need for broader knowledge, so that we can become better analysts and implement analytics into companies successfully.*

In cases where we are building a new team or require assistance in our process, a good project manager can play a key role in establishing processes around analytics and implementing analytics in a company.

Metrics, Dashboards, and Reports

Metrics

The Basis for Analysis

Metrics are the basis for analysis. When raw information is gathered into an analytics system, it is transformed into a metric for user interaction, dashboard display, and reporting.

A quick example is the key metrics table in Figure 11-1. The table displays a collection of important metrics put together, making it easy for us to have a basic understanding about the activity on a social channel and compare it to other channels, which in this case are competitor brands.

Key Metrics Table | Fast-Food

02/01/2017 - 02/28/2017 (total)

quintly

Name	Fans	+/-	Posts	Reactions	Commen...	Shares	User Pos...	I Rate	Respons...
Taco Bell	10,449,422	8,988	11	45,700	24,231	19,129	1,600	2.9854%	4.9%
Burger King	7,957,600	25,929	13	249,623	24,693	20,996	0	5.2877%	0.0%
Wendy's	7,405,184	28,526	16	213,190	19,676	11,129	0	3.2039%	3.0%
Chipotle Mexican Grill	3,047,017	16,197	8	11,764	20,676	3,377	3,122	5.1489%	31.5%
McDonald's	2,413,459	15,512	46	329,140	149,317	50,829	0	2.4545%	3.0%

Figure 11-1. *Key metrics table*

Metrics can be very simple and straightforward, such as the change in the number of fans on a social media profile over time, as shown in Figure 11-2.

A. U. Fox, *Social Media Analytics Strategy*,
https://doi.org/10.1007/978-1-4842-8306-6_11

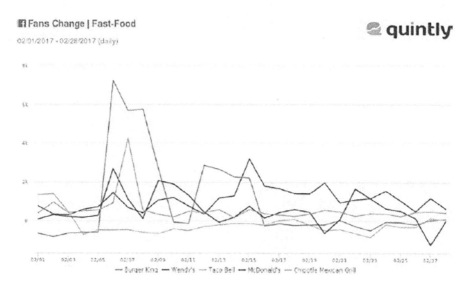

Figure 11-2. Fans change

Or they can be more complex and display the result of a formula, such as the interaction rate metric in Figure 11-3. Even with a line chart making it apparently simple, behind the results there is a calculation that needs to be considered when using this metric.

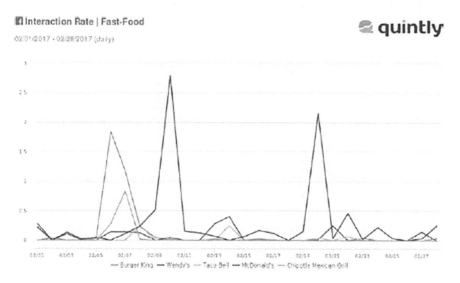

Figure 11-3. Interaction rate

This means that sometimes many metrics can be grouped into one, creating a new, unified version of what we had before. A calculation resulting in a simple line chart, such as the interaction rate example in Figure 11-3, is the result of interactions related to the fan base and will eventually have a specific use within the analytics process. There are different specific formulas for interaction rate, as we will see going ahead.

Metrics can become, in a sense, a living part of our analyst life (independent of our job title). Our familiarity with metrics grows in time and the relationship blossoms. This growing familiarity is extremely helpful for us to reach insights and conclusions faster. As we progress in learning and even creating more and more metrics, we are able to better prepare for common use cases and carry "decks" of metrics up our sleeve.

When we join discussions in groups of analysts over the Internet, or when we meet other analysts in conventions and events, we notice that metrics can become a fast-paced topic where each person enjoys bringing out the metrics that they are using. From there, a profitable exchange of knowledge begins within that group. It is very interesting to listen to other analysts and contribute to the conversation on different strategies. Metrics, being part of everyone's strategy, are a central part of the conversation.

This chapter covers several concepts behind the creation and use of metrics and briefly revisits a few points on data sources as we go along. The objective here is that we can feel confident to jump into the use of metrics and have them fulfill the needs of our projects, studies, investigations, or experiments.

Metrics Bring New Light to Events

A metric usually brings a different light to an event. What we are doing with metrics is creating a different angle of view of the facts happening in the world. Usually, this angle makes it easier for us to reach new ideas, opinions, or insights on the events or facts we are looking at.

A very interesting and unusual example of the effect of metrics on our perception of events is featured in the 2006 movie *Stranger than Fiction*.

In the opening scene, Will Ferrell's character is described by the narrator. The voice of the narrator tells us about his daily routine in a detailed way. As the narrator speaks, a series of metrics start showing up on the screen, illustrating what the narrator is saying, and what we are seeing the character do. These metrics are actual graphs showing up on the screen, as an extra graphic layer floating on top of the scene and the character.

The metrics in such case help the audience see the character as a very methodical person, possibly even boring, and as if such personality would indicate the cause to other aspects of his life, the methodic and metric-oriented personality suggests that he is a very lonely person. The graphs, in this case, reinforce the impact of the numbers in the mind of the audience. We now have a visual graph showing us the following:

- What time the character wakes up

- How many brush strokes he uses to brush his teeth

- How long he takes to do everything

- How repetitive he is in his daily routine

So what the metrics are doing to our minds is they are opening our rational and precision-oriented thinking over a scene that is really just about describing a human being. Since humans are not machines—not precise down to the last second and not so repetitive—we immediately see the character from a different angle and generate theories about his personality, which prove to be true or not throughout the movie. The use of metrics in that scene is a work of genius storytelling.

While this is a very unusual way to look at metrics, it can be quite interesting to approach metrics from such a perspective for once, only to "break the ice" on the apparently "boring" aspect that they inherently carry. Metrics change the way we see even the most common of things.

Metrics Help Us Remember Available Data

Metrics help us understand the data that is available out there. It is much easier for us to remember what we have seen within a metric than what we have read in a list of data sources or a blog post, a forum, and so forth.

One interesting idea is to build a collection of metrics and store them for our future reference. We can use an online spreadsheet for this and have it available anywhere or even share it with friends.

A Deck of Metrics

Since we can build with metrics what we need from the data, and metrics help us remember the availability of such data, we can then put together our ideal metrics into sets, collections, or decks to make it even easier to work with.

Some tools give us many dashboards to work with, and we can use them as our decks. In cases where we don't have such access, we can store metrics in online spreadsheets or any such dynamic medium.

A deck can be a good starting point for our work on any project. We can have themed decks, ready for high-level performance analysis with just a few KPIs, or detailed content investigation with content filtering and different views on interactions. A deck can become a live dashboard in one project or a linear storytelling report in another. The idea is that such decks can save us a lot of time, giving us a head start into new projects or goals.

Building and collecting metrics can become as exciting as collecting any of the common collectibles we have, in a social media analytics kind of context. Conversations on this topic are usually very interesting and become more so when we meet colleagues that are into customization of metrics and building new ways of approaching the use of certain data. This level of connection to metrics is easier to understand once we have experienced working with custom metrics and manipulating data sources toward the precise goals of our projects.

Default and Custom Metrics

Default metrics are the first sets of metrics we come across. These are the metrics that social media analytics tools set up even before we test the tool. They are the metrics that we have available to us before we decide to create our own.

While they come in all shapes and sizes, we find many similarities across different tools. Usually, an analyst quickly becomes familiar with the default metrics across the social media analytics landscape. The social media analytics market is not, by any means, fully standardized, but professionals everywhere try to make that happen as much as possible.

This means that the terms we see matter and the names of the metrics matter, but when going into certain formulas, such as *interaction rate* or *engagement rate*, it is always advised to take a quick look at the formula before assuming its meaning.

Going beyond default metrics, some tools give us the power to create our own metrics. This process is very simple with some tools, even with the help of their team. In other tools, it can be more complex, with the need for a special professional services team to be involved and extra fees added for the service. What matters is that it can be done, and we can take advantage of that. Many analysts say that we should.

Before jumping deeper into metrics, however, it is important to understand at least the basics about where the data is coming from in each of the metrics we find or try to build.

We don't have to stress ourselves about remembering every detail of every single data point, but knowing if we are dealing with public- or private-level data is an important first key.

This helps us not only prepare our strategy but also innovate what we wish to measure in different projects.

Private-Level Data

Private-level data is only available to users that have administrator access (admin access) to the social media channels. With the manager access a user can pull the private-level information into metrics.

Private-level metrics are defined by the networks as sensitive or carrying proprietary information. It is usually not visible from public access in any way. We don't have to worry about analytics tools using or selling our data when we unlock private access, that should not happen; but if it ever does, we have a winning lawsuit in our hands.

Examples of private-level metrics are reach, impressions, information on investment to promote content, and most demographics.

Public-Level Data

Available to everyone, as the name suggests. It is visible from public access into any social media network.

So if we are scrolling through our timeline on Facebook, and the post of a friend comes up, we usually can see how many interactions it has, the types of interactions, and the interactions themselves. This is public information, or public-level data. Eventually, certain networks will only deliver data on certain types of profiles, such as businesses and not individuals. Issues with privacy of individuals can also come into play.

Metric Categories: Divide and Conquer

How to turn something complex into something simple to understand and remember? Divide it into parts, and group those parts under categories. The term *analysis* comes from the process of dividing something into its parts to understand the details.

While separating the universe of metrics into categories, we find that most metrics fit well into a given category, which is extremely helpful for us to quickly find and remember them all. A few metrics, however, fall off from any category. These are usually metrics that involve formulas that mix many metrics together, or processes, such as machine learning, that mix many different sources.

The following are categories that we can often use to filter metrics:

- Audience
- Content
- Interactions
- Off-category

Within each of these categories, we then find collections of metrics, some available only in certain tools (analytics, listening, ads, etc.). Sometimes, metrics may be displayed in different variations of an original format, but essentially deal with the same information or data.

For example, when we find the metric "follower count over time" as a linear graph, we find that it can be displayed to us in different ways. It can have a month-to-month display, or a table with the key changes in fixed periods, or a per-network view showing us how each network has developed. It is still only showing us the same data: follower count over time.

Therefore, within each category, we have only a certain amount of data sources, and these data sources branch out into an array of different metrics. The number of metric formats grows even more when we start customizing metrics and manipulating data sources toward our needs.

The following are examples of metrics within each category:

Audience

- Follower count over time
- Influencers within our audience
- Location, gender, age, interests

Content

- Text analysis of the content
- Number of posts over time
- Type of posts over time
- Sponsored post distribution

Interactions

- Interaction count by content and over time
- Types of interactions by content and over time

- Comments and text analysis on comments
- Mentions and text analysis on mentions
- Questions and responses

Off-category

- Interaction or engagement rate
- Posts/interactions comparison
- Key metrics table
- Off-audience influencers
- Impressions and reach

Off-category metrics usually favor a certain category more than another; it may be found under that category within tools. Some tools even skip the use of categories; nevertheless, it is still a helpful principle we can connect with and keep in mind.

The idea on the use of categories is, again, to help us understand what is available and help us remember a broad list of metrics very easily. This separation in categories helps us to move forward together with the innovations from analytics tools. Once they launch a new metric, and we know in which category it is, we have a much easier time working and remembering that it is there.

Graph Types: Data Is There, but Does It Look Good?

Graph types can make or break a metric. The best data displayed in a bad way will not help our process.

This is a very important point that is often overlooked. Many analysts (independent of job title) tend to accept and try to work with the graphs that a certain tool gives them, and don't know that they can change the display to better fit their needs and enhance their analytics process in many ways.

In some cases, this comes down to personal preference, but in general, we can look for a few key elements when deciding if a certain graph type fits well with a certain metric.

The following are key elements that can shape an effective metric:

- Uncluttered information
- Quick reading
- Easy interaction
- Easy interpretation

The following are elements that can interfere with the effectiveness of a chart type:

- Period of analysis
- The number of channels or sources in display
- The number of metrics displayed in multidimensional graphs
- The size of the display surface (some metrics look good on huge screens but not on a standard screen or on a mobile device)

Example 1: A Simple Change in Chart Type

Compare a line chart (see Figure 11-4) against a bar chart option (see Figure 11-5), showing a weekly progress over a three-month period.

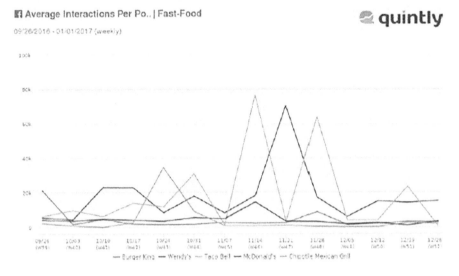

Figure 11-4. Average interactions per post (line)

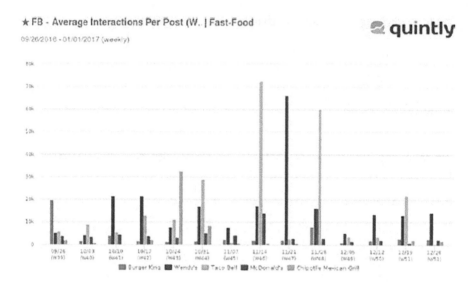

Figure 11-5. Average interactions per post (bar)

The bar chart (see Figure 11-5), in this case, arguably gives us better insights into the weekly progress of the average interactions per post metric that we see.

The reason is that we can better compare the performance of each brand during each week and better understand the scale even when some brands are close to disappearing from our eyes due to low comparative performance.

Example 2: Adding an Extra Dimension to a New Chart Type

When changing chart types, it is possible to add extra dimensions to the same chart. Figure 11-6 is a bar chart that tells us how many of the posts of brands are potentially sponsored. I decided that I wanted to see this data displayed in a bubble chart instead of columns, and that gave me the option to add new data into the mix.

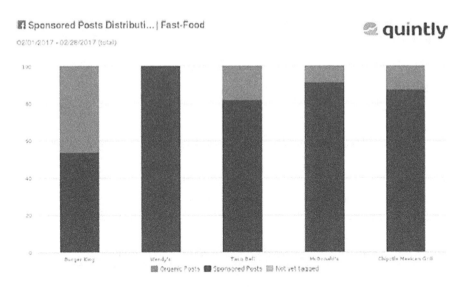

Figure 11-6. Sponsored post distribution

My reasoning came from the need for further information when I look at the default metric. I immediately know that I need to compare it to other metrics to start getting closer to insights. One way to do that is to build a dashboard and have that metric next to other metrics for ease of correlation. But instead I chose to add a second dimension into the same metric with a new graph type. I added interactions and have then more of the story told to me in one graph (see Figure 11-7).

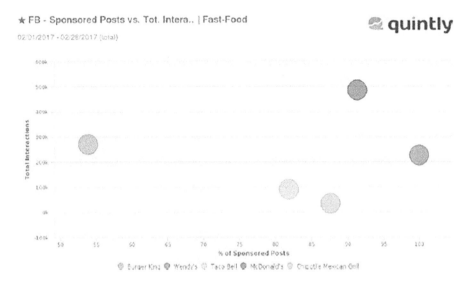

Figure 11-7. Sponsored posts vs. total interactions

With the extra dimension of interactions added to the graph, I can now understand if the brands sponsoring the most are also the ones reaching the highest amount of interactions in my competitive group. It is one possible first step into understanding the effectiveness of a sponsored strategy on a competitive level.

This gives me a better sense of the effects of promotion behind each brand and starts pointing me in the direction of the brands that I should investigate first if I am working on a competitive benchmark analysis.

While we can carry on and explore even more examples of interesting uses of chart types, the idea for now is just to have a quick example of how we can manipulate a metric to give us a better view of reaching insights.

Default and Custom Metrics Capabilities

When preparing to put metrics into work, we have two options available to us. One is to make use of the default metrics of our tool, and the other is to shape our ideal metrics, customizing them toward our needs.

Default Metrics

What do we already have out of the box from a tool? What can we look for in tools? A tool tries to cover as much as it can under the default section. If it is not a very comprehensive analytics tool, it tries to cover enough to answer for the concept behind the tool.

We can expect that if it is a publishing tool, with some analytics to cover the publishing, they have enough default metrics to help the user see how the posts are performing.

If it is a listening or an analytics tool, the main objective is to deliver relevant metrics, so usually they offer many metrics, and the best tools offer the greatest amount of metrics.

Although having more metrics or fewer metrics in a tool is a value that depends upon our needs, it is likely that if the investment is about the same, having more metrics is a safer bet when choosing a tool. Often, the needs of a project change, and being familiar with a tool that offers more options is a better investment in the long term.

As a note, focusing on the concept of the tool is the way to go when giving it a final judgment; an excellent publishing tool can have limited analytics and still be the best in its class of publishing tools. Having in mind our list of needs based on our marketing objectives and relating that to the three topics we have seen previously—private/public data, categories, and graph types—we should be well on our way into finding if the default section of a tool covers our needs well.

Beyond the default set, some tools offer custom metrics, which means that the amount of metrics within such tools is virtually unlimited. If the investment is in the same price range, a tool with such capability is likely a better way to go.

Custom Metrics Capabilities

Flexibility is important in the ever-changing world of digital marketing. No one really knows about the next trend. No one really knows about what is going to work next. No one knew social media would be as huge as it is. No one really knows how it will evolve.

As social media networks evolve, more features are added to them, more ways people can interact, more data. New data sources are eventually shaped by analytics platforms into default metrics at some point, but they are available to be used in custom metrics well before that.

Besides new data, customization makes currently available data much more useful. It is very rare that default metrics will cover the needs of a project in a perfect manner. Maybe with default metrics we can get close to what we need, and maybe we can even have all the data we are looking for, but chances are that some metrics will not display the best graphs.

The value of custom metrics is also something that grows as we go deeper into analytics. As we become more experienced, and we learn of what data is available, we begin to have new ideas into metrics we want to use and even experiment with.

There is a trend in customization all around the digital world. Even beyond social media data, new platforms are coming out to connect any data source into metrics.

If through social media analytics we have our first contact with custom metrics, it is likely that we will continue to use this knowledge in projects involving other digital data.

Along with all the practical value that custom metrics can bring, it is also fun to have the ability to test theories that we have or that we come across.

An Interesting and Simple Example

Once upon a time, a trend of blog posts throughout the Internet indicated that Instagram performance needed at least ten hashtags per post for it to work, and I started doubting that such a number could be a rule. Why would ten hashtags be a need? Could that be true?

Taking into account different brands, profiles, audiences, and all the different dynamics on different content, my doubt only grew even further. I then set out to prove this theory with the use of data.

I personally enjoy having data-based proof against rumors, and the Internet has many specialists sharing particular experiences in the form of a general guidance, which may be a very specific use case they had and is then seen and spread by other people as a general fact, or even worse, a rule. So I created a custom metric to look at that. My goal was not to create another rule; on the contrary, it was just to be free of such a rule and open my mind to different factors when it comes to the use of hashtags.

The metric was average interactions per post by average hashtags per post (see Figure 11-8).

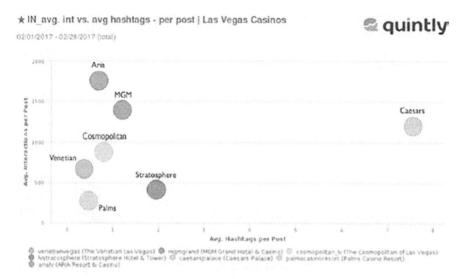

Figure 11-8. Average interactions vs. average hashtags per post

I wanted to understand if a higher amount of hashtags would in fact bring more interactions to a post. I could do an analysis on a post-by-post approach, but I went for a competitive benchmark instead, because I thought it would be more fun, and I would cover more brands in less time. Figure 11-8 is one example of the metric.

I passed over 400 brand profiles through this metric—from global pages to small and local ones.

The custom metric proved that posts had very rarely been using ten or more hashtags and that in many cases the brand with the lowest average hashtags had the highest average interactions.

Figure 11-8 shows a few of the Las Vegas casino brands. We see that most brands are far below ten hashtags, using about one on average, and that Caesars Palace has been using much more, around eight on average. Caesars, however, even while ranking in the top three for the month, is an outlier and not enough to prove that more hashtags would result in more interactions.

This kind of pattern was found throughout the entire study, where data did not support the idea that more hashtags equal more interactions. The graphs were never even close to being linear from a higher to lower average hashtags relating to equivalent interactions.

Maybe the key is to use the right hashtags, the trending hashtags, and go for quality instead of quantity in this case. We could also look at hashtags per post instead of average and see if, even being less than ten, more hashtags mean more interactions. My study did not go that far, however, but I would go in that direction if my objective would be to ultimately decipher the best use of hashtags within an industry or competitive group.

Another Interesting Example

An expansion of the famous engagement rate metric (also called interaction rate).

While the engagement rate is a metric that suffers from much debate on it, this example focuses on the use of a custom metric to clarify the reading of engagement rate. I will not address all aspects of the metric, which means that we will avoid the debate for now.

When doing a competitive benchmark, a common formula for this metric is *interactions on a page divided by the audience size.*

Competitively, we are bound to using public data, so we do not have elements such as reach, impressions, and so forth. The next best element we have, which is available via public data, is the audience. For our own channels and private-level data, reach and impressions can be a much better way to go.

This relationship between audience and interactions was more relevant in the early years of social media, before so much content promotion was going on, when a brand did have exposure to its entire audience, and content frequency limited the exposure a lot more.

The engagement rate, during that time, was an interesting way to directly compare different brands, with different audience sizes, and see if they kept a good amount of interactions against their audience size as they grew. *Could they still engage all their audience as they grew?*

In later times and today, with promotion of social media content reaching people outside of the brand's acquired audience, this comparison is still possible and can eventually be useful in some cases, but is much less relevant than it once was.

On a first approach to better interpret engagement rate (a.k.a. interaction rate), one element we can add is a longer period of analysis. When we have a view of the progression of engagement rate over time, it is much easier to understand where the changing points are and if there is an increasing or decreasing trend.

So a line chart for engagement rate over a longer period of time is one good way to start understanding what that metric is trying to show us, as we see in Figure 11-9.

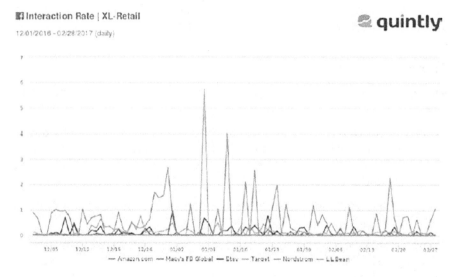

Figure 11-9. Interaction rate (a.k.a. engagement rate)

In Figure 11-9, we can see that one brand in that group had a good period of growth and then fell, another had just one big spike, and most are lower and lower as time goes by. The reasons behind this progression, however, are not clear in this graph. We don't know if the engagement rate changed because they gained or lost audience or because they gained or lost interactions, hence our need to separate the elements that are part of this formula to understand what is going on. These two elements are *interactions* and *audience*.

Did interactions grow because the audience grew? Did the interactions start growing before the audience and are part of the reason behind audience growth? Such questions cannot be answered by engagement rate alone.

One first version of this metric separation is competitive (see Figure 11-10), where we position the brands comparatively against interactions and audience in one chart.

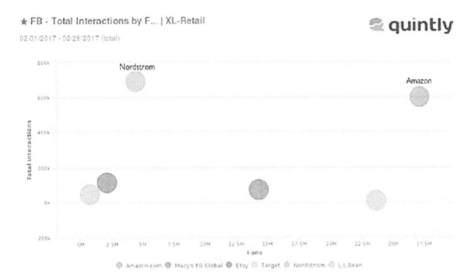

Figure 11-10. Total interactions by fans

With this graph, we can immediately understand the relationship between interactions and fans, which is really what the competitive engagement rate is all about.

This specific group of brands we are looking at also has a very peculiar pattern, where the two top brands in total interactions are on opposite sides of the audience spectrum. If you are a manager of social media in any of the brands in the group, it is worth looking into what both of these brands are doing.

A second version would be noncompetitive, in which we look at the evolution of interactions and audience in line charts over time.

Let's take a look at each of the top interaction brands in our group, which are Nordstrom and Amazon. Nordstrom is displayed in Figure 11-11 and Amazon is shown in Figure 11-12.

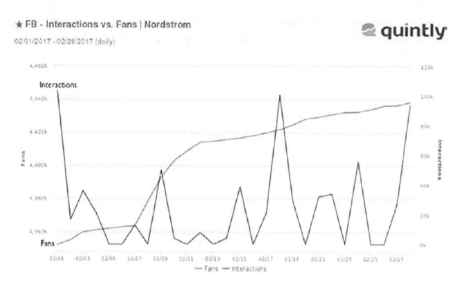

Figure 11-11. Interactions vs. fans: Nordstrom

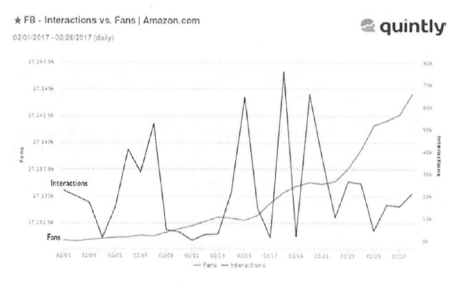

Figure 11-12. Interactions vs. fans: Amazon

The preceding graphs are an open view of the competitive interaction rate formula (a.k.a. engagement rate). With such a view, we don't need to crunch engagement rate into one number anymore when we want to quickly understand this relationship.

I am personally not a fan of having one unique number to display the result of this competitive engagement rate formula and would rather have an open graph such as the examples that we have seen to give me insight into the relationship between interactions and audience.

In Figures 11-11 and 11-12, I can easily understand if interactions are growing while fans are growing, or if there is no correlation between the two metrics. I can then keep pushing into such investigations.

A Third and Final Example (for Now)

A case of many metrics coming together to compose a *success rate*.

One main reason for customization of metrics is to save time, to use our time in a better way, so that we have better results in less time. Analytics is by default already a huge time-saver, but we can save even more time with customization.

Time is precious; life is all about time well spent. Optimizing a process with time savings as a main goal is usually worth it, especially when we are even enhancing the process on top of that. The key, therefore, is also to think about the manner in which we find ways to save time. This is also part of the fun, to cleverly improve our processes while saving time.

In this next example, we have a case that does exactly that kind of process improvement plus time saving at the same time.

It starts with the simple need to understand if the brand is doing good or bad. Good and bad are then translated into a more technical and objective approach: above or below a certain threshold, or a goal.

So if a metric is at or above a goal, it is considered good. If it is below the goal, it is bad. A goal can also be a range, and naturally there are different degrees of good and bad along the way.

Then the second challenge: dealing with many metrics at the same time. Since what we really want is to know if the brand is doing good or bad overall, we need to consider a collection of results, we must put together into one metric an entire process of analysis. The interpretation side of analysis is skipped. We will likely have mainly a set of relevant triggers that can then push us into action toward specific problems. Nevertheless, if we set our triggers correctly, the analytics tool can point us into the right direction and let us save a lot of time. Figure 11-13 is a view of the success rate next to all the metrics that compose it.

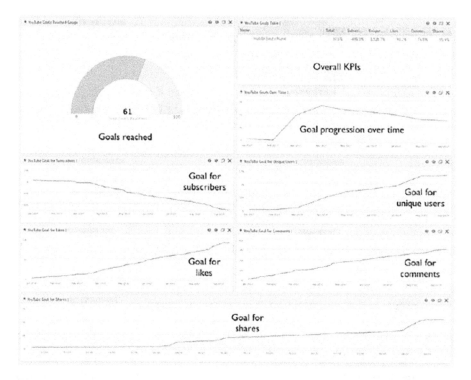

Figure 11-13. Success rate

What the success rate does is bring together all of the metrics selected for the project and then check for the goals of each metric. Each metric has a different weight to the formula, and they will translate into a certain level of success to the overall success rate. So the success rate can then translate how "good" or "bad" the brand is doing overall, from a quantitative standpoint.

What we see in Figure 11-13 is that the brand is reaching 61% of its success rate for the period. The metrics displayed around the main gauge then give us more information on what exactly is going right or wrong.

This success rate approach is particularly useful when there are many social channels to manage, when the time to analyze is short, or even when we just want to have a clear starting point for our analysis. If we see a 95% success rate, we approach the analysis differently than if we see 12% success or a negative number.

This is a simple yet good example of where the world of analytics is heading. The future of analytics is interpretation and prescription. We start by having one or more insights at hand and only then go into the details of any aspects we wish to look further.

Custom Metrics in Paid vs. Organic Analyses

Paid vs. organic strategy and performance is an ongoing debate in social media. During my career and research, I have met with strategists that were all about using social media as a very direct paid-to-conversions channel. They mentioned that this is what really mattered to them; all the rest was irrelevant if they didn't have the conversions they needed. So they looked only at investment against conversions.

While this is a valid argument for some strategies, and a very practical approach as well, in many cases, the focus on conversions alone can blur our vision from the bigger picture. It can also diminish our sense of community when looking at social media and leave us with nothing more than cold commercial-only channels inside social networks, channels in which we are actually not being social at all.

Even when we focus mainly on conversions because our project needs us to do so, we can still keep a view of the organic effects to understand if there is any correlation, if paid is being worth it, and if we could benefit from being a little more "social in social" in case we are not.

Paid vs. Organic Tables

The table in Figure 11-14 is interesting because we can compare the performance of paid and organic content side by side. It is easy to have an initial view over the effectiveness of each type of content in the period with a snapshot of what happened. The table shows first the total posts and interactions and then separates the data into what was organic and paid. This is a variation of what was initially a default metric, showing only the count of potentially sponsored posts.

★ FB - Paid vs. Organic Table | XL-Retail

quintly

02/01/2017 - 02/28/2017 (total)

			PAID			ORGANIC			
Name	Posts	Interactions	Sponsored...	Share of S...	Interaction...	Organic Po...	Share of o...	Interaction...	Undetecte...
Amazon.com	105	611,025	64	60.38%	463,254	42	39.62%	147,771	0
Etsy	74	113,851	12	16.22%	53,779	62	83.78%	60,072	0
L.L.Bean	53	43,896	13	24.53%	14,459	40	75.47%	29,437	0
Levi's	16	650	3	18.75%	393	12	75%	245	1
Macy's FB Global	24	71,627	17	70.83%	61,346	7	29.17%	10,281	0
Nordstrom	23	697,022	23	100%	697,022	0	0%	0	0
Target	9	8,955	9	100%	8,955	0	0%	2	0

Figure 11-14. Paid vs. organic table

We can further explore the use of tables and have an expanded view of just the paid content or just the organic. With dedicated tables, we can then, for example, look at types of interactions, questions received, and other information on paid vs. organic to help us evaluate results.

The Use of Machine Learning

It is important to highlight that we are looking at a competitive benchmarking approach in Figure 11-14, an external analysis. This means we are comparing the results of pages that do not belong to us, that we do not manage. These results are obtained by a machine learning process, which analyzes each post to see if it shows signs of being promoted or not. If detected as a promotion, it is added to the list of paid posts and all the interactions from it are added there as well. So what we are looking at in Figure 11-14 is an estimate of what is potentially paid. This is still very useful, because machine learning processes can reach high accuracy rates. The result is still an estimate, so we can ponder our analyses and data-based decisions.

Interactions vs. Paid Posts Graphs

The interesting aspect of using graphs in this example is to explore different chart types that can help us to quickly position brands against each other in a more visual way than a table. These charts are easier and quicker to grasp if more sponsored posts resulted in more sponsored or total interactions. We also don't know how much each brand invests per post, so if we see a brand with fewer sponsored posts but huge amount of interactions from them, for example, we can adequately expect that they invested more on a per-post level. It is one insight, or trigger, that can lead us to invest our time and further investigate into that brand.

Impressions and reach are also private metrics, so the only available reference for us during an external analysis is interactions. For our own channels, we naturally have a more detailed and precise view, but the choice of being competitive in this example is to explore how we can still work with possibilities even under limited conditions.

Figure 11-15 shows sponsored posts vs. total interactions. Figure 11-16 shows sponsored posts vs. sponsored interactions.

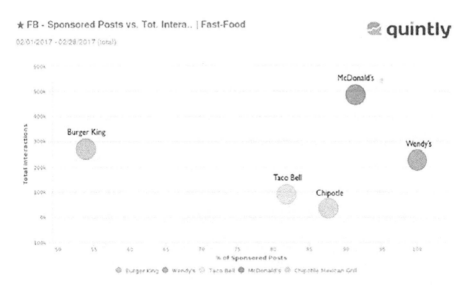

Figure 11-15. Sponsored posts vs. total interactions

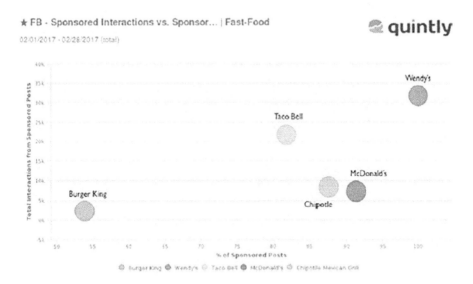

Figure 11-16. Sponsored posts vs. sponsored interactions

The terms *sponsored* and *paid* refer to the same metric throughout social analytics. Different social networks and analytics tools might use different terms. It is interesting, therefore, that we can become familiar with the use of both terms and that they mean the same thing.

Figure 11-16, sponsored posts by sponsored interactions, will be expected to display a somewhat linear distribution when dealing with brands or channels that have similar strategy and volume. The higher quantity of sponsored posts likely relates to a higher amount of sponsored interactions. When we see channels breaking that pattern, it can eventually indicate a significant difference in the investment per post.

Since this is a complex problem with missing data and many variables to consider, we are not certain whether there is more or less investment by using this one metric. Results can come simply from a higher general interest of the audience, or that difference in audience size is affecting the performance. Once we investigate, we can better understand how much the audience is truly interested in the content and the brand, how much the brand engages back, and increase our level of certainty regarding potential investment.

These signals that we see from metrics such as Figures 11-15 and 11-16 can trigger our analysis into further investigation of the most relevant brands. In analytics, we constantly become exposed to triggers that point us in the right direction. So in many cases, certain metrics indicate what is valuable for us to then go ahead and invest our time into further research. Like a prospector, we detect that there is gold there, but still have the work of digging deeper until we find it.

When it comes to competitive analysis, it is common to question the need for external investigation. Why not just look at our own channels? The keyword here is *reference*. By tracking external channels, we gather many interesting insights that can be applied into our strategies. In the examples within this section, we can then push farther and learn more information about the effectiveness of paid content for brands in our industry and even brands in different markets.

In the digital communications world, we are actually competing for the time and attention of people. So we do, in fact, compete with any brand that is exposed to the same people we are.

As overwhelming as this can be, it is still the "naked truth," and competitive or external analysis plays an important role in our process of dealing with it.

Linear View of Paid vs. Organic Posts and Interactions

This is an interesting approach when looking at just one brand at a time. We can check if individual paid or organic posts are generating more interactions, check for variation on interactions, and also if a high interaction on a paid post can be influencing interactions on the following organic posts or vice versa. Figure 11-17 explores an example of such metric.

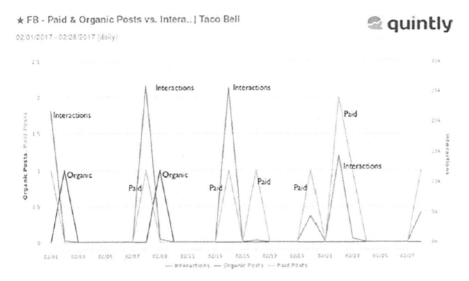

Figure 11-17. Paid and organic posts vs. interactions

We are seeing in Figure 11-17 that organic is not performing anywhere near paid (invisible in the scale) and that interactions still have a high variation, even between paid posts. A graphic or visual approach, when compared to a table, can quickly open our minds to further investigation into the content details in relevant posts.

Such metrics (see Figures 11-14, 11-15, 11-16, and 11-17) are interesting examples of custom metrics being shaped toward specific objectives. They are mainly working as triggers to expose relevant brands, channels, periods, or specific posts. Social media analytics is a dynamic activity; it is likely that we are shaping new metrics as communication concepts and technology evolve. Therefore, this chapter is a guide to empower us to do that during our own projects.

Metrics and Strategy: Selecting the Best Metrics for the Job

It is common to approach a project with goals that are initially too broad for an immediate specification of which metrics we should choose.

Requests that are somewhat vague from the analytics standpoint may come up during our work and include the following:

- Who is my audience?
- Am I doing better than my competitors?

- What are people saying about my brand?

- When is the best time to publish?

- Which content does my audience enjoy the most?

- Which social network is the best for my brand?

- How can I have a better performance on social media?

Such questions require us to choose metrics to help answer them, but they do not quite indicate which metrics. On top of that, what will really "bake our noodles" later is learning that there are always different ways to answer such questions. So what can we look at when we move from project requirements to metrics?

Focus on Being Actionable, at Some Point

The goal of metrics is that they can be actionable or as actionable as possible. If a metric does not drive us to take action, either it is because we are high above our goals (and might need new goals), because we are not using the best metric, or because we are not using enough metrics.

So being actionable remains the focus, but maybe "actionable at some point" describes the journey through analytics a little better.

What this means is that in some cases, we need more than one metric to reach the actionable point. So one metric may lead us to the next, then to the next, but at some point, we reach an insight that leads us to take action. This is perfectly normal and a regular part of any analytics process.

In time, the tendency is that we become faster in reaching actionable insights. However, having a fast process doesn't always come down to our experience alone. It relates to the nature of each project and the demands we have as analysts, or in other words, the questions being asked.

Some questions in project requirements, client briefings, and general brainstorming are very straightforward. They usually lead directly to the metrics we need to answer them. Other questions can be more complex, however, inviting us to perform initial work on giving meaning to certain parameters and goals before we can start finding the metrics that will answer them.

Dealing with Straightforward Questions

Some questions or project requirements are straightforward and lead directly to the metrics needed to answer them. When is the best time to publish? That is one example.

Immediately, we think of a metric that deals with performance per time of the day and per day of the week. In Figure 11-18, we look at one example of a metric that works toward answering such question.

Figure 11-18. Posts/interactions comparison

Figure 11-18 shows the time of day and days of the week when there are posts (light circles) and interactions (dark circles). Technically, the interactions in this specific case are represented by an interaction rate value, which is the default for this metric in quintly analytics. We can, however, keep in mind that we could also just use the total interactions. This also does not change the concept and objective of such metric. We see large dark circles on the days and times with the highest number of interactions.

Some social networks might give an estimate of the time when our audience is online, so there can be more metrics to add to our study of the best time to publish. However, even with the information on the potential time when our audience is online, if we see that the engagement is actually happening at a different time and not matching the estimated time for the audience to be online, we trust actual interactions more than the estimate.

This is one of the keys to data-based decisions: We have to trust the most reliable data. So even if a social network tells us that our audience is online mostly at 2 p.m., and our best performance is consistently gained at 4 p.m., which information will we use?

This leads us to think about estimated metrics against metrics that actually capture interactions. It is interesting to bring estimates as part of our studies (impressions, views, reach, time when audience is online, etc.), but interactions generate the ultimate reference to the final evaluation of performance.

Which type of content does the audience enjoy the most? This is another very straightforward question, which can later be expanded into a more detailed analysis.

Potential metrics fall into the categories covered next.

Content Ranking Tables

By ranking the content in Figure 11-19, we can understand which piece of content specifically drove more interactions and more of each type of interactions. The own posts table immediately leads us to the best and worst performing posts and gives us a detailed approach to answering the question.

Figure 11-19. Own posts table

Interactions by Content Type

In many cases, we might not have time to work on too many details at first, so we can approach the problem from different angles, such as a broader view of performance by content type and interaction type.

It is also interesting that many of these metrics can be extremely useful when we decide to experiment with our strategy. Sometimes there is an unlikely element inside a metric that can give us ideas to explore, such as the cover photo. Not many channels change it very often, but it is interesting to experiment on its exposure. I have seen many cases where it had huge engagement, so I would recommend trying it out specifically. It is, however, unexplored in Figure 11-20. Also, Figure 11-20 shows interaction rate instead of total interactions as a base value. This is default in quintly so that many brands can fit into the same graph scale. It will not change the concept or effect of the metric in this case.

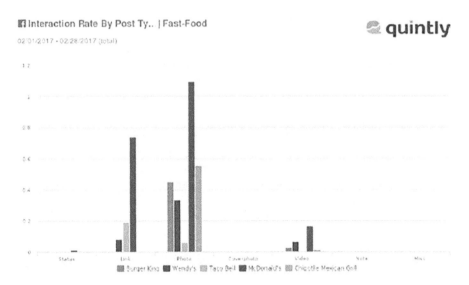

Figure 11-20. Interaction rate by post type

Types of Interaction

Figure 11-21 shows the types of interactions, which can provide a good trigger to help us prioritize which competitor we can pay more attention to if our goal is to learn and grow a certain type of interactions. If we are looking only at our own brand, the unified view adds speed to our overall analysis.

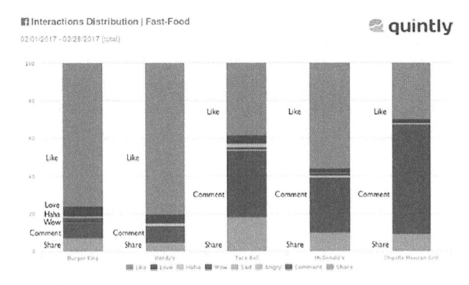

Figure 11-21. Interactions distribution

Different types of interactions can work as different indicators of which brands or channels we can further research into. Comments are a good example, since we don't know what is behind a comment, and shares, when we want to understand what is driving people to endorse that content within their timelines.

Interactions Distribution by Post Type

Figure 11-22 shows which type of interaction is driven by which type of post, which can help us choose the post type we need to boost the interactions we want. In our example, videos are driving a higher percentage of shares, so we can look at videos if we wish to drive even more shares. Because the scale is in percentage, though, it is interesting to have the absolute numbers in view before taking final decisions. Depending on the amount of interactions, a higher percentage of shares for videos can be a smaller absolute number when compared to photos or links, which can be dealing with a higher amount of total interactions. Adding the total interactions to Figure 11-22, which is a view of a per-post level, helps us in this case.

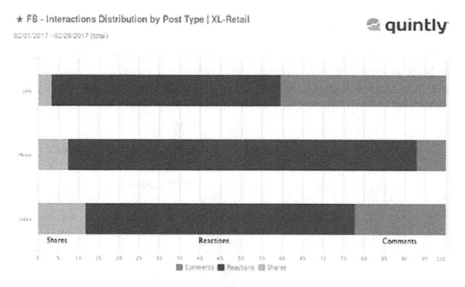

Figure 11-22. Interactions distribution by post type

Going beyond these initial metric examples, we can approach this question from a more topic-related perspective, with metrics such as word clouds, and filters of hashtags and keywords, which can show engagement by specific topics or themes of our content. Some metrics focus on a detailed analysis, while others have a broad approach and save time if we do not need a detailed view. These filtering metrics are also useful for answering more complex questions, as we will see.

In this example, notice how the analysis of even the very straightforward questions can be expanded into more and more details. We also have a practical example here of how, in analytics, one question usually leads to another. This is a natural part of the process, much like the investigation work of a detective in a certain case, where one clue leads to the next.

Dealing with Complex or Subjective Questions

These questions may lack a clear view of the practical use of analytics or may require that a new combination of data, a custom metric, or a dashboard be created to answer it.

The following are some examples:

- Am I doing better than my competitors?

- What does my audience enjoy the most about my content? What is it that gets them engaged?

- What do I need to do to grow my audience and boost my engagement?

Time is likely one of the major challenges that we will face in such analyses, mainly because the process requires the initial step of structuring what we need from the data to perform the analysis. We need time to translate the subjective information of the briefing into practical analysis points and then go through the list of best potential metrics to finally build our case.

After the first steps, we can then get the team together and discuss initial results, to then adjust what we are doing and finally reach a model that works for the analysis up to its completion. If we are working alone on the project, we can consult with all stakeholders once we have a clear plan so that our effort is not in vain, and we are delivering results that are relevant to everyone.

A *model* in this case can be any combination of metrics or dashboards that we use. A model is likely to be used again and again in different projects. This model can start very simple in some cases, just as one custom metric, and then become as complex as we need it, becoming a collection of metrics grouped into one dashboard or report, displaying all the different parts of a bigger story.

A good point to start the approach into complex or subjective tasks is to clarify the meaning behind each question, objective, or goal we are given. We can then start by asking the questions more questions.

Step One: A Simple Example

Let's look at other questions that we can make when the brief includes "Am I doing better than my competitors?"

- Do you have a list of your competitors?
- "Better" in which aspect?
- Overall interactions? Conversions?
- Audience growth?
- Over which period of time?
- By product line? By theme?
- By questions answered? The use of a two-way channel?
- By sentiment, despite head-to-head interaction comparison?

The list of questions can keep going, until we feel that we have enough information to move forward, and everyone involved is happy with the direction of the project.

Step Two: Building a Story

From there, with a list of interesting metrics to use, the next step can be to start finding a good order of metrics to make up a storyline.

We will look at the details of building dashboards and reports in later chapters of the book, but a good point to mention is that whether we like it or not, we are always working with some kind of story in analytics. After all, events are linear no matter what. A story can also be applied to the way we present the data, so that people understand the events they see.

A simple example of this is thinking of posts generating interactions. We can then approach our collection of metrics by looking first into posts, understanding what the posts are talking about, their frequency and timing, and then jump into interactions to start correlating types of interactions with types of posts, and the timing of the campaign. We then go back and conclude the story with insights from the results. Different approaches can be taken, depending on our objectives, as we will see in the dashboard and reporting chapters.

Some insights come to mind after exploring linearity, following a line of thought such as "if this, then that," which means that once we find out about one event, we look for a correlation of that event with other events in a timeline. The sense of linearity can make the analysis process much easier to perform. Building a linear line of analysis, however, requires a setup process; hence, time is a primary resource in our work.

The specific choice of display type can be significant to our workflow as well. If we are dealing with a graph that is confusing to us, and if we need to correlate such graph with other graphs in a dashboard or sequence of slides, the analysis is even more tiresome and time-consuming.

Ideal metrics are found with experimentation, trial and error, and looking at different charts until we find the best ones. At some point, we will have enough experience to choose metrics very quickly, even without having to open a tool to do so.

Our objective is, in essence, to look for the fastest way to reach an insight. An insight, in this case, can be the final answer to one of our complex questions. This means that even though we have clear principles to work with, such as linearity and clarity of data, when choosing the ideal setup, all we have are guidelines instead of definitive rules. Guidelines mean that it will come down to personal choice if we decide to start from this or that point in a timeline and take a linear approach from there. We can even have a random approach and focus initially on the metrics we suspect bring us insights. In the very end, however, linearity plays a definitive role in giving us the final answers we are looking for.

Estimated Metrics: Avoiding Bad Decisions

Many times, we come across metrics that have an unclear meaning or that don't represent facts but estimates instead. While there are good uses for estimated metrics, it is great to be standing on solid ground when working with them.

Estimated metrics can eventually even be disguised as true performance metrics, making them even more dangerous if they are presented in such a way. They can lead us to think we have great performance, and this illusion will not help us to truly work on improving our strategy.

It is important to keep causality in mind when working with estimates. Causality is vital to analytics in general. We are constantly looking for the causes behind performance and their further effects. The focus on causality, as simple and somewhat obvious as it seems, can then help us to fit estimated metrics into our thought processes. Once we come across an estimated metric, we then ask ourselves clear questions. Is it adding information to the cause of certain performance? Is it estimating the effects based on given causes? Is it doing both?

What Are Estimated Metrics Exactly?

In short, these metrics take into account potential facts. They are not able to prove such facts; the truth is that they do not intend to prove these facts in the first place.

Once we get to know them better, we can then find good uses for them, but it is likely that they can become much less important than they seem at first, or just have an entirely different value to us.

There are two main categories of estimated metrics:

- Given by the social networks
- Calculated by third-party technology

Given by the Social Networks

True reach and true impressions fall into this category. With such metrics, social networks are indicating to us how far our content has gone within the network. This does not mean, however, that they had a positive effect into our marketing strategy just because of that. A content that passes through someone's timeline can very easily pass without being noticed.

What is most valuable is to be sure that the content was noticed, and these metrics don't tell us that, and don't aim to tell us that. The aim of such metrics is to help us have an extra reference toward our true interactions. It helps us have an idea of the dimension of the network and of the distribution of our content within the network.

Sometimes these metrics can help understand the effectiveness of good copy—good text that is well written and uses the best keywords for the topic. Good copy can expand the reach of a content piece within a certain network just by the natural correlation of the words to what is being searched and suggested by the network to its members.

Audience insights are also often estimated, even by the social networks themselves. Part of the reason is related to privacy, and part is related to missing data. Most people do not answer all the little details about themselves on social media profiles.

Calculated by Third-Party Technology

Potential reach and potential impressions are included here. Different from true reach and true impressions, these metrics are calculated by third-party technology and not from the networks directly.

This is where we can be as careful as possible before including such metrics in our dashboards and reports. The first step is to have a clear view of what exactly is the formula behind such metrics.

A common approach for potential reach, for example, is to calculate the amount of followers of our followers. So followers that interact with our content have their networks counted as being potentially reached by our content. Other metrics might only take followers into account and create an estimate based on that. Again, the aim of such metrics is only to give us an extra reference; by no means do these metrics aim to be our top key performance indicators.

Calculations are usually necessary when a social network does not provide a key metric directly. So it is common to see analytics platforms creating such calculations, and we will see more of that with machine learning and artificial intelligence in the future.

Other calculated metrics involve detecting if particular content has been sponsored or not, predicting the outcome of certain posts based on its content or targeting, and audience sentiment. Notice that all of these are useful metrics that make it into our analytics setup in one project or the next. The key is not to dismiss them, but to understand what exactly they measure and how to make better use of them.

Making Good Use of Estimated Metrics

Once we understand what is behind an estimated metric, being it a formula, hidden data sources, or a machine learning process, we can then safely place such metrics into our strategy and make very good use of them.

The following two points are common applications of estimated metrics:

- Patterns and correlation between estimate and true performance
- Supporting metrics: from substitutes for missing data to predictive and prescriptive analytics

A very common use, for example, is to look for any correlation between reach and impressions to interactions and conversions. When we have higher reach, do we also have higher interactions?

What is the use in reporting "we had a reach of 10,000," if in the end, we earned maybe 100 interactions or less in total? Should we be happy about the big estimated number? Or concerned about the small number of interactions?

So the idea is not to have reach and impressions as a final number to report performance, but instead use them as a reference. This reference fits well as part of a train of thought and part of an analysis to find any valuable correlation. To perform such analysis, we can then build metrics to check into such correlations.

The example shown in Figure 11-23 brings together impressions and total interactions, so that we can follow the trend easily, detect key events, and better understand if there is any correlation.

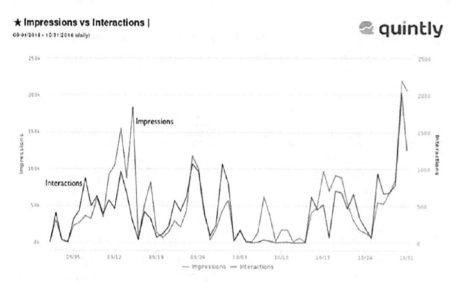

Figure 11-23. Impressions vs. interactions

The reasons for peaks in interactions would then have to be further investigated. It could be that the content was more relevant to the audience— that it reached the right people at the right time, and so forth. These are all possibilities for us to look further into with our analyses.

Figure 11-23 shows how interesting it is to relate an estimated metric to actual interactions. There is usually a correlation between the spikes of both metrics, but against all expectations, sometimes we even have more interactions at a point when we have a comparatively lower amount of impressions. So more impressions does not mean we have more interactions in this example.

It is at first surprising, but once we think about it, there are many possible causes behind this. One possibility is that sometimes the same people generate more than one interaction. They like, comment, and share a piece of content, leading to three interactions from one person in the same post. It could also be that we were just lucky to have reached the right people at the right time, or that our content connected better to the audience, and so forth. Note that more impressions do not necessarily lead to more interactions.

This relationship is essential to understand and keep an eye on while we are using estimated metrics. We are always looking at actual interactions at some point, so we might as well put estimates and facts together in the same graph when possible. The key here is to understand that in most cases, estimates need the support of descriptive or factual information, even if they are based on such information to begin with.

Metrics and Tactics

The essence of metrics is to have a revealing view of the facts. Metrics then become part of tactics, where we apply them toward strategic goals and learn how to repeat such tactics when successful. The tactical use of metrics gives us experience, and initially much of it is done with experimentation. While in time we will not need as much experimentation to reach our goals, it is very likely that we enjoy being open-minded and continue to experiment with metrics independent of being master analysts.

Tactics are approached later in the book, when we will look at more information on metric correlation and a few more examples of tactics that have worked in given cases.

The most important aspect regarding metrics, however, is that we can understand the nature of metrics and have a flexible approach in dealing with them. So while it is great to have a playbook of tactics to work with, and we inevitably have one of our own as we work with analytics, by keeping an open mind about the nature of metrics and the problems we are solving, we are able to adapt our metrics and tactics to higher success rates for reaching our goals.

Key Takeaways

- Metrics can be very simple or very complex. It all depends on the amount of data each metric is dealing with and the way that it is displayed.

- Metrics change the way we see the events and facts that happen around us. They translate events into a format that enables us to reach strategic insights faster by using them.

- Metrics help us remember the available data we have. It is easier to remember data we have seen within a metric than in a list of data sources.

- Metrics are flexible in nature. We can build any metric we need to display and work with data in the best way for our specific needs.

- Default metrics are a great starting point. They often have industry standard names and formulas, which help us jump from one tool to another with ease if we have to.

- The default metrics of any tool should cover the concept behind such tool. A good publishing tool doesn't need to have the best analytics, but usually cover enough to help publishers understand the basic performance of their posts.

- Custom metrics give freedom to analysts who wish to go further in the use of data or even just simply adjust a platform to their taste.

- Custom metrics are giving the first step into the future of analytics. By creating custom metrics that calculate better results in less time, analysts are preparing the foundations for the intelligent analytics machines of the future.

- Metrics can be shaped to offer a view of the correlation of paid and organic content performance. They help us navigate through the changes in our own community behavior and in the technology and algorithms behind the social media networks themselves.

- Most projects start with goals too broad and unspecified; we are the ones who clarify goals until we can point to which metrics to use.

- To be actionable is always what we are looking for, even if we only reach an actionable insight after looking at a series of metrics.

- Estimated metrics need support from factual metrics to show their worth.

- When choosing the ideal graph type, remember four essential traits: non-cluttered information, quick reading, easy interaction, and easy interpretation.

- Metrics are part of our tactics to reach strategic goals. Despite building a tactical playbook along the way, we can always keep an open mind about metrics related to our objectives.

Dashboards

More Than a Collection of Metrics

Dashboards are everywhere. The more digital the world becomes, the more likely some form of dashboard will become part of our daily lives. Even beyond their use for companies and business, we may bump into personal dashboards that display information about our bank accounts or the status of our home appliances. Social media analytics are highly connected to the use of dashboards, so it is worthwhile to explore more information about them.

While some of us are very comfortable with the concept, many of us have a hard time fully making use of a dashboard and an even harder time creating one ourselves.

A very simple and initial example on how our relationship with dashboards can sometimes be less than optimal, or just different from what we think, happens with the dashboard of a car.

I went out to test a theory and asked more than 100 people driving their cars, "What is the ideal temperature mark on your dashboard display?" They rarely gave me a precise answer and usually told me something along the lines of: "As long as it doesn't get too high or too hot, it's okay." Most were not able to tell what is too high, or hot, and gave an answer that in reality represents a problem beyond fixing. They perceive the signal of "being too hot" when there is nothing they can do about it anymore. This was just one test done for fun, but I do have the habit of asking people about peculiar information in

© April Ursula Fox 2022
A. U. Fox, *Social Media Analytics Strategy*,
https://doi.org/10.1007/978-1-4842-8306-6_12

dashboards they are using. My point is that I am always curious on how much of a dashboard people actually understand and use and how much they don't perceive or don't care about.

In our example, such lack of overall perception can likely happen because our focus is on the speed of the car, the most actionable of the metrics in front of us when we are driving. We tend to focus on the main metric, and if we never need anything else, we will likely never bother to learn about the details.

This kind of limited focus on our perception of a dashboard can be okay when we have little information to work with and also when we are driving a car and don't want to cause an accident because we are distracted looking at different points of the dashboard. There are times to learn and times to act.

In dashboards that are very actionable, such as in a car, we usually see a very small amount of metrics on display. The more actionable we need to be, and the faster we need to act, the fewer metrics we have to look at.

This kind of inversely proportional ratio between the number of key metrics and the speed in which we have to act upon them is present throughout our creation of dashboards and reports on social media as well.

It is a general principle that we can even take beyond social and into marketing and business analytics. The faster we need to act, the less metrics we can have.

With these initial ideas in mind, and being it a main element of social media analytics, we can then dive into concepts and principles around dashboard creation and use, so that we feel secure in working with them and also in building new ones ourselves.

Dashboard Purpose

The best way to start building a dashboard, or to choose the best one when a tool offers that option, is to have a clear objective before we start. What is the main need around such a dashboard?

This process is similar to choosing metrics; only here we are ultimately selecting several metrics based on a common purpose and based on the group of metrics working well together. So a dashboard is effectively more than a collection of metrics because there is a purpose behind it.

When defining the purpose for a dashboard, in many cases, we have to go from a broad objective and into more specific needs, so that we can then decide on the details of the overall dashboard size, positioning of metrics, and range of content. As you may notice, this initial step of preparation is present throughout many parts of the analytics process.

Defining Dashboard Objectives

To help us define the objective for our dashboard, we can take the following elements into consideration:

- The time available for analysis
- The level of detail we are looking for
- The range of areas of analysis
- The period of analysis
- The frequency of analysis

The better we can answer these five points, the easier it is to build or choose the ideal dashboard for our specific case.

A Quick Example

A broad dashboard objective is given to us:

I wish to have a view of our Facebook and Twitter performance.

- **Time**: little time available for each analysis (e.g., 10 minutes)
- **Level of detail**: maximum amount of information
- **Range of areas**: audience growth, content performance, competitive benchmarking
- **Period**: 7 days
- **Frequency**: weekly

Attending to the little time available for analysis, the dashboard can have few metrics, and metrics that are very clear, which can offer a quick view of the major points.

The "*maximum* amount of information" is a common request when we ask clients what they want to see, but it creates an opposing need. It calls for more information and possibly more metrics.

The main point in such cases is the choice of metrics. We can find or create metrics that show more information within them, such as tables or graphs with more than one area of analysis grouped together.

Dashboard Suggestion

This request can have, for example, only seven metrics per network to keep it a simple and fast read and still cover the main project requests. The following graphs are for Facebook, so we need to add the equivalent Twitter metrics to the same dashboard.

Key Metrics Table

The key metrics table offers a quick overview of the performance and offers easy benchmarking (see Figure 12-1). If we have the capability to customize our key metrics table, we can explore it even further and really focus on having only the most meaningful metrics for our given case.

Figure 12-1. Key metrics table

Content Table

All content from the competitive group of channels regardless of brand, so that benchmarking can still be done in a more detailed content comparison (see Figure 12-2). If the post table can be customized, we can explore it further and add or remove columns or even show more or less of the content itself. These metrics give us the option to spend more or less time with them, depending on the level of detail we are looking for.

🔲 Own Posts Table | XL-Retail

03/15/2017 - 03/22/2017 (total)

Post	Total In...	Reactio...	Comme...	Shares	hRate	Type	Sponso...
Nordstrom - 03/16/2017 09:43:36 Set out on new adventures. Shop spring looks for the little ones. http://bit.ly/2rwODY	33,446	32,463	261	722	8.7442%	Photo	Highly Likely
Nordstrom - 03/17/2017 12:01:19 Happy St. Patrick's Day! — Products shown: Women's Adidas stan Smith Sneaker	32,465	31,607	459	649	8.7197%	Photo	Highly Likely
Nordstrom - 03/20/2017 11:17:17 Introducing: Lingerie by Madewell. http://bit.ly/2mfvd4ZQ	29,703	28,973	372	353	6.6366%	Photo	Highly Likely
Nordstrom - 03/15/2017 16:25:59 We've made essentials for the well-dressed man. http://bit.ly/2ndU8Vg	18,183	17,871	109	143	8.4042%	Photo	Highly Likely
Amazon.com - 03/20/2017 15:25:03 For when the starry night turns into a party one. — http://amzn.to/2rdMX2w	15,021	12,391	817	1,413	6.9573%	Photo	Highly Likely

Figure 12-2. *Own posts table*

Audience Change by Weekday

This is an interesting choice because of the seven-day period request. It can be related to the posts by weekday (see Figure 12-3) and the total interactions by weekday (see Figure 12-4) and give us a parameter for our campaigns and the timing of audience reaction (see Figure 12-5).

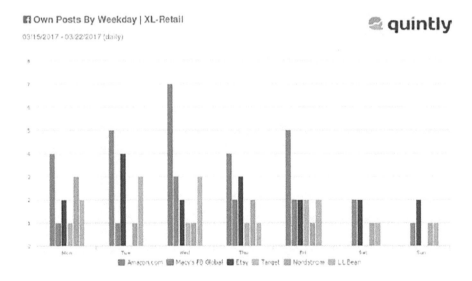

Figure 12-3. *Posts by weekday*

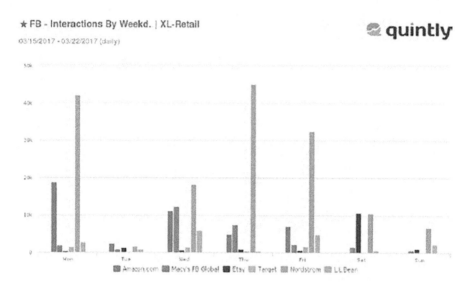

Figure 12-4. Interactions by weekday

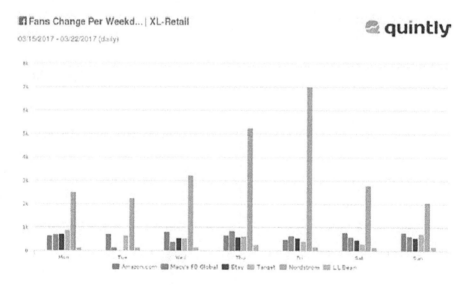

Figure 12-5. Fans change per weekday

Interactions vs. Posts

This chart offers a quick glimpse of the relationship between the number of posts and total interactions (see Figure 12-6).

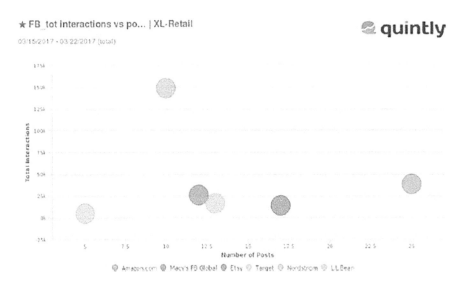

Figure 12-6. Total interactions vs. posts

In competitive analyses of similar brands with similar volume, we may find a pattern where the more a channel posts, the more interactions it gets overall, which seems like an obvious outcome but does not always happen. Some social networks, such as Twitter and Instagram, often display such patterns, but in networks like Facebook, it is usually not like that. One reason can be the well-adopted concept of investing in posts on Facebook. Currently, Facebook is among the most sophisticated social networks when it comes to investment in content promotion. When a network reaches such a level of sophistication with paid promotion, patterns of engagement against activity become less and less obvious.

Independent of expected patterns, when we see any slight pattern and one channel breaking out from the group, we can give it a bit of attention. In Figure 12-6, it could mean that a certain brand has a very different investment pattern, or that certain specific content was huge with the audience, or that there is a general love for the brand no matter what, and so forth. The goal is to follow these triggers to find out what exactly is different about that channel. In our example dashboard, we have other metrics that add to our view of the brands and help us answer some of the triggered questions without the need for additional metrics.

Interactions Distribution

This chart brings types of interactions per channel in the period (see Figure 12-7). The important thing here is to have a glimpse of the quality of engagement without going too far into details. Shares are evidently very valuable, likes are much less, and comments do not necessarily give us their value under such a chart, but indicate that there is interest in the topics, independent of whether the actual comments are positive or negative.

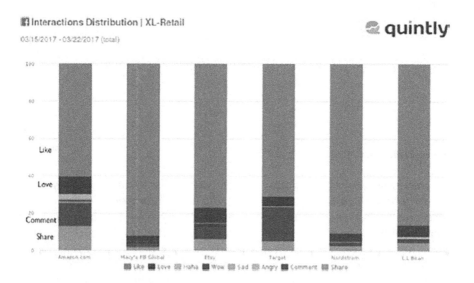

Figure 12-7. Interactions distribution

To attend to our example demand, this dashboard can be a good start. It gives us a good enough view of performance and brings enough triggers and indicators of what we can focus next for a more detailed analysis. Many times this is what we are looking for.

It can be complicated to cover absolutely everything in detail within one dashboard, so compromises have to be made. We can then think of how far we are covering basic core aspects and how many triggers or indicators we are bringing in.

If we are building a series of dashboards, something like a deck with templates of different dashboards based on what most of our projects demand, we can prepare such dashboards by the level of detail we need. So we can start with a dashboard such as this example and then have another, more detailed, ready to be used after we understand our focus points. In this example, we detected one brand that is an outlier in terms of performance and, if we wish to improve our strategy, a close benchmark of what they do is a great next step into our process.

A Final Layout for the Dashboard

We built a dashboard from scratch for this example (see Figure 12-8), which is usually what we want to do once we become more familiar with the universe of metrics and data sources available. Many tools offer premade and default dashboards that require you to adapt to the manufacturer's concept of what is most interesting and/or necessary. With the dynamics of different projects, teams, goals, and devices that we use for our work, I am an advocate of building dashboards ourselves whenever possible.

Figure 12-8. Dashboard layout, seven-metric performance overview

Default vs. Custom Dashboards

Different tools bring different levels of depth and detail to the data they can offer and to the interface users have to work with such data. Some tools are very complex and full of options, add-ons, and integrations, where the more time we put into them, the more we eventually are able to pull from such tools, but the learning curve is steep. Some tools even have special learning courses, with detailed stages of learning and tests to go with each stage.

I personally believe that complexity in analytics is only a need while we don't develop a better interface to our data. Once we have smarter systems in place, analytics will move toward being extremely simple to access and use. There are challenges in this sense, but simplicity in access to analytics is an inevitable goal.

In the meantime, before we get to that level of overall simplicity, the simple first step into each analytics tool is usually the default section. If we are new to a certain tool, once we are familiar with their default section, we likely feel more comfortable with moving ahead to a custom setup.

The custom side, while seemingly complex at first, lets us create a setup that streamlines our processes. The objective of customization is to optimize our experience and use of tools. So it is possible that after a custom creation of a dashboard, for example, we end up having a much more simple way of looking at that data. To start, however, the default section of a tool is usually our best approach.

Default Dashboards: More than a First Step

The default metrics and dashboards are the chance that the developers behind each tool have to welcome new users into what they have created. They are also the chance to keep users happy with the tool and quickly show the innovations which are added to a tool through time.

Default dashboards are usually connected to the specific objective of the tool (the concept of it) and to other vital functionalities within the tool, such as reporting, navigation to find specific metrics, or tutorials and templates. Depending on the concept of a tool, the default dashboards have more or less to show on the analytics side.

A publishing tool likely has basic analytics pointing out to elements that help with publishing, but not on the performance analysis overall, and not on benchmarking or listening.

It is also likely that default dashboards aim to be as simple and as straightforward as possible, so that a user can focus on the insights right from the start.

While the default dashboards can be a great first insight into a tool, some tools still have the best offerings set on the custom side, so we can keep an eye out for that when a tool offers any kind of customization.

Custom Dashboards: Building the Ideal Setup

The use cases that a custom dashboard handles can be as diverse as we can think of. Customization has been a complicated task in the past, but as we move forward with technology, the process is becoming very simplified.

Most companies that offer custom dashboards also have a team to help create them. This makes things as easy as they get at this point in time. Some tools offer this service as part of a given plan, or do not charge a lot, while others charge more. So here is a point to keep an eye out for. It is likely, however, that we will not need the help of a team to build our dashboards. It is more a matter of choosing and positioning the metrics we want into the right place, as we will see going forward.

A few companies go as far as creating a custom graphic design for the dashboard, transforming it into a beautiful visual display of the data while delivering the crucial information to reach insights. Such dashboards can even resemble animated infographics and even become an interesting display for events.

Regardless of an elaborate design, a dashboard must be true to its objective. What matters is that we can customize the dashboard to work even better than a standardized view of the data.

Improvement is the keyword when working on custom solutions.

Key Points to Shaping an Ideal Dashboard

A few key points can give us direction on shaping an ideal dashboard, independent of the final objectives we have in hand:

- Linearity and order of metrics
- Metric positioning and correlation
- Layout
- Graphic design

Linearity and Order of Metrics

There is always a story behind the data—a reason for the numbers to be what they are. There are different ways to approach the story, but in the end every story is linear, no matter what. One fact leads to the next and then to the next after that. Causality plays a big role in analytics, and the cause naturally always comes before the effect.

The catch here is that we don't always know exactly where the causes are at first. Sometimes we think that our content is performing well because we gained more followers, but at the same time we might also wonder if the new followers came because of the content in the first place. We can use analytics to approach and answer such problems.

In digital marketing, finding the causes for performance is a major challenge. Initiatives and campaigns are usually very spread out through many channels, and on top of that, there are offline effects coming into play, so marketers today have a very hard time proving what exactly is causing certain effects.

Despite the challenges, when working with dashboards, we are bravely looking for causes, or in the worst-case scenario, for a "picture" of what happened in the period, and the possible causes.

Linearity applied to analytics also helps us understand and remember all of the data so that we can take action by the end of the analysis. It helps us understand, for example, if there is a chain of events going on.

Even beyond the use of analytics tools, setting events in a linear manner can help us understand and remember significant moments along the way and relate such moments to broader aspects of company strategy or to external influences.

I worked with an analyst once who created a separate timeline of events during her analyses. She added to that timeline the information she found from the analytics tools, plus the information from other company sources, and even external information from the market. With that timeline approach, she had a much easier time to correlate events and find potential causes. Her reports were very well received and the positive feedback mentioned that "it was very easy to understand."

The approach to linearity relates each one of us personally to the way we think about problems and the way we build our knowledge. Some people need less structure to grasp what is going on, but most benefit from a more linear approach—an approach that reveals what happened first in the line of events and the effects spreading out from there.

Order of Metrics

When it comes to dashboards, some analysts work on having a template of the broad structure that they prefer to use when going through data, an order of which areas of the data to approach first.

Templates and structure give us a head start on building ideal dashboards for diverse projects. We can look at areas of analysis that resonate the most with our sense of linearity and relevance toward final insights. If certain pieces of information are easier for us to fixate on and work with as a basis, we can start with them.

Going into a simple example of a template structure, we can choose to look at the different areas of social performance in this order:

- Audience change and total overall numbers

- Content: quantitative

- Interactions: quantitative

- Content: qualitative

- Interactions: qualitative

Such example structure can be interesting because we can first understand quantitative performance numbers and correlate audience change with the strategy behind content planning and interactions.

Then, at a second stage, we can dive into the qualitative information with the overall performance numbers already in mind.

As an example, we would first know that our audience grew by a certain amount, that we are sharing a certain number of posts, and the number of interactions with these posts. Then, we jump into which posts are performing best (or worse), what kind of interactions they drive, and the details of such interactions (which can include sentiment). From there, we can push further into the main aspects of what we find.

In other cases, however, if everyone involved in the analysis is familiar with the events, and our project only needs a view of the high-level performance, we can approach things very differently. The start can be a highlight of the top content, then overall key metrics, a broad view of interactions, and the changes in audience as a final metric. This setup will not tell as much of the story, but can eventually be all the information we need to complete a story that we already know.

Remember that having a concept and sense of linearity at some point in the analysis can greatly help with reaching an insight. Even if we don't have it as a layout of our dashboard or report, and even if we don't feel that we need to follow a linear-oriented concept with our dashboard, linearity is still an underlying element to the information we are accessing.

It comes down to personal choice on how much we embrace linearity when setting up our views of our data, but inevitably, we are working with it in our analyses.

Metric Positioning and Correlation

In a dashboard, we can have a good view of more than one metric at once and grasp possibilities of correlations between them. With this aspect, it is a good idea to closely position metrics that have high correlation to each other or that complete each other in a certain way.

By making it easy for us to navigate around the dashboard with our eyes and our thoughts, we speed up the process of analysis and make it less cumbersome. A lesser need to scroll or click on an interface opens more space for thinking and finding what is interesting about the data we are working with.

A Simple Example: From a Long Period into Weekdays and Hours

A chart of an entire month next to the change by weekday can be an interesting view to build. Taking audience as an example, one metric shows the variation over a long period of time (see Figure 12-9), with its peaks and low points, while the other tells us if there is a specific weekday when we gained or lost most of our audience in the period (see Figure 12-10).

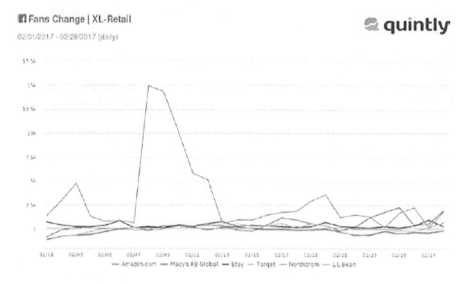

Figure 12-9. Fans change

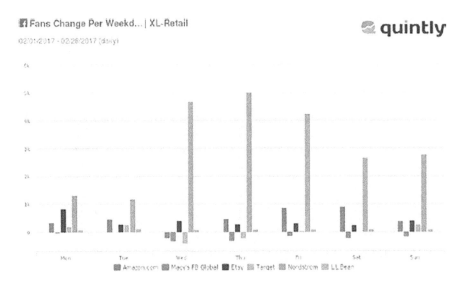

Figure 12-10. Fans change per weekday

An interesting addition in this case is to have a snapshot of our top day for gain in audience, to confirm if our unique top day falls into our top peak of the month and weekday. The top day, or top 5 days of the month, can add insights into potential further analyses.

If we enjoy this view of a long period next to the weekdays, then we can add metrics following the same logic, under categories such as posts and interactions.

We can then go slightly beyond this initial view and check the details of specific days to understand if we are looking at a pattern or if, for example, one Wednesday in the month created a peak, but not every Wednesday is good. We can then repeat this analysis for different months to check if there is a monthly pattern.

When a campaign is very dynamic, it can be interesting to go into an even more granular view than weekdays and look at specific hours, amount of posts by day, and the timing between posts. Even if the goal is to have high exposure and a high amount of total interactions despite the amount of posts, by performing the analysis, we can detect which are the premium spots of our day. So even if the publishing is very busy anyway, the choice of which content is posted at which time can be affected by an analysis of engagement by time and day.

Interlude: The Revealing Case of the Busy Nightclub Manager

Working with a massive and very busy nightclub, it was noticed, with a similar dashboard approach, that the strongest weekdays on social media were weekends and the days when they opened a VIP list. While this was expected, it was also noticed that every month the first two weeks were stronger. Speaking to the marketing manager, she mentioned that it could be an effect of customers being paid their salaries and having money to spend early in the month. She mentioned that the pattern would also happen in the attendance to the club and that the first two weeks of every month were more crowded. The analysis went naturally into a lot more detail, and the project evolved into the club strongly promoting the big parties of the next month during these last two weeks, with part of that promotion involving social buzz and the attendance to the club during the less busy days and weeks.

This is a very simple but interesting example of a social media analysis going beyond social channels and finding correlation with the everyday activities of an offline business. The report then pushed the very busy marketing manager into action. Maybe she just needed the final push to go out and make it happen. What I enjoyed the most about this case was that after our work, she continued using analytics to make data-based decisions. She became very comfortable working with data and convinced her management to start adding more data-based systems related to loyalty programs, digital purchases, and so forth. The lesson I took was that even simple studies can push positive change when stakeholders are willing.

A Second Simple Example: Positioning Toward Content Overview

A simple dashboard focused only on content can include a ranked content table next to a hashtag performance filter, and eventually a word cloud of the comments from the audience, with an extended view of interaction distribution and engagement by content type. It can give us a good initial view of the content using very few metrics. The metrics correlate well with each other, so they can fit well into a dashboard layout (see Figure 12-11).

Figure 12-11. Content dashboard layout example

While these are just very simple examples, the main concept to remember is that when we set up metrics in such a way that our eyes and mind can easily navigate from one metric to the next very quickly, and correlate them to each other, our reading of the full set is highly enhanced. This seems very obvious, but will likely be overlooked by many of us, and even with advanced knowledge of metrics and strategy, we just spend an unnecessary longer time on dashboards that have a random layout.

Metric and Dashboard Layout

Some graphs need to be expanded in shape and size to be able to show the details of what they bring.

Many dashboards that I have seen display, by default, all the metrics in the same size, even when the tool behind it lets us design with different graph sizes later. This can happen for technical reasons, or simply because the developers behind the platform prefer to give us a standard starting point on something custom based.

Insights are the goal/correlation/causality—so design can play an important role to help us get there.

Even line charts, apparently very simple and clean, sometimes become cluttered when we add too many lines into them. A competitive benchmark of five brand pages inside one line chart can get confusing, depending on the size of the chart.

It is perfectly fine to have metrics with different sizes sitting next to each other and different shapes as well. This is a simple element, but a very important one nevertheless.

Figure 12-12 gives an example of a simple adjustment in size of certain metrics to enhance our reading and interaction with a dashboard.

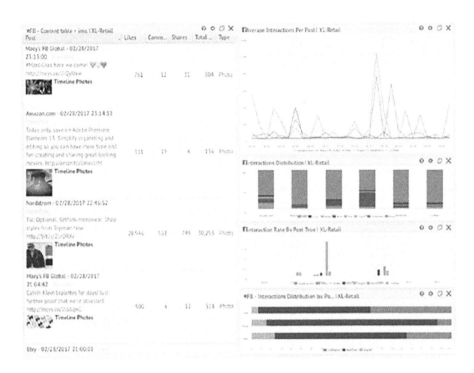

Figure 12-12. Dashboard example with different chart sizes

On the example of Figure 12-12, we stretched the content table vertically, so we can see more posts at once, and we have the line chart showing the average interactions per post expanded as well, to let us quickly perceive the performance of more of the brands in the group.

While the example here is quite simple, the objective is only to highlight how we can adjust the layout to a better workflow even with very simple resources.

Metric and Dashboard Graphic Design

Most dashboard tools have limited design features. Usually, we have a default base design in which all we can do is add or remove metrics, change graph types and sizes, or in some rare cases be able to choose from a few different colors and eventually invert from a white to a black background.

Some companies, however, offer a full design of a dashboard, and even if we are working with a company that doesn't, we can always have a separate designer hired to work on a custom design for us if we like.

With this level of customization at hand, if we are building a dashboard that is not only meant to be beautiful and visually attractive but also functional and improving our analyses, it becomes even more important to remember the principles of the three previous points: linearity, positioning, and layout.

Another reason to be thoughtful with heavily graphic-designed projects is that it is likely that once such complex designs are created, it costs time and resources to change things if we need to.

On the good side, having this level of freedom in design truly opens limitless possibilities for us, and we can then have the dashboard of our dreams (yes, we can dream of dashboards, sometimes).

The open design also gives us the chance to create animations and moving elements that can help to highlight certain points.

Design is a very visual element to work with. We can use the design to truly highlight the main points of interest coming from the data.

In a practical sense, creating such customization is a balance between the level of complexity of our design and the resources we have. If we have amazing designers, enough time, and a clear idea of the metrics we wish to work with, we can go very far with a custom design.

Data Integration Dashboards

When diving into a custom setup, we come across the possibility of working with companies that are specialists in integrating data and go far beyond social media data.

This option is highly recommended independently of also having dedicated social, web, and business analytics active in parallel. With such solutions, we can bring together important metrics from any source and build a view of the broader story, getting closer to insights that can be very strategic to the core business of the company. While the data in these dashboards can be very diverse, the principles follow the key elements we are studying in this chapter, so the essence of what makes a good dashboard remains.

Social Media Command Centers

A social media command center is a dedicated physical space that is optimized for a social media team to push out the best content and pull in the best insights.

This space includes one or more dashboards displayed in a way that the entire team can make use of them at any time. Because of specific characteristics of the physical space layout, in some cases, we see a series of screens with only one huge metric in each, instead of a dashboard. In these cases, the space conceptually becomes one huge dashboard.

Depending on the extent of the activity of the social media team, the command center can include a dedicated space for social media customer support, so that they are closer to the social team than to the main support hub of the company.

I came across such a command center in a very large retailer and ecommerce operation. By having the social support inside the command center, they leveraged their contacts and detected major customers and vital influencers to introduce to other programs of the company. They also started featuring clients within their content, and they mentioned that many times the people that approached them initially with a complaint became huge advocates for them after experiencing how closely they took care of the case.

Another strong point for them was crisis management. They mentioned that they had managed to detect a fabrication problem with one of the products and stop production before having to recall a huge amount of sold products. The main point in this case is that they sent preorders out before producing the main lot that would hit the stores, and one person who preordered mentioned the problem on Twitter. They stopped the operation in less than 40 minutes after the tweet came out. For the massive scale of production they deal with, and the huge amount of employees and hierarchy they have in the company, this was an epic feat.

Independent of scale, a command center can be a good option when working with social media analytics. Naturally, people can access analytics from anywhere, but if the company is not yet moving into a remotely based operation and requires people to be present in the same physical space anyway, giving focus with strategic dashboards in a dedicated space can be a game changer.

The Essence of a Good Dashboard

If we have a hard time remembering what we read in our dashboards, if our thoughts freeze when searching for insights or building our story, we can come back into our design and reshape the dashboard until it works for us. The process of reshaping the dashboard already helps us gain experience with interpretation and analysis.

With experience, it becomes easier to read graphs, navigate through dashboards, and reach insights. We perform analyses faster and catch the meaning of graphs with a glimpse; however, there is one key element in our journey that we must keep in mind before beginning the creation of a dashboard: *don't get too good.*

"Don't Get Too Good"

The famous jazz drummer Louie Bellson once told me at one of his gigs at the Blue Note in NYC, "don't get too good, never get too good." He saw me sitting there, very young at the time, tapping along all of his tunes during his show. Then afterward, when I went up to shake his hand and have a chat, he asked me if I was a drummer, which I am, so he gives me that one piece of advice: "Don't get too good."

What he meant (and it stuck with me forever since then) is that no matter what we do, and no matter how good we become at it, we don't want our experience to get in the way of enjoying what we are doing now and going deeper into it to learn more. Louie had been drumming all his life and was still learning as he went along.

By "not being too good" at analytics, we want to avoid assuming that we know something without checking further into it. Especially with promoted content, people tend to immediately assume that high performance comes from a higher investment, the pay-to-play curse that is affecting us all.

In many cases, however, the brand with high performance is doing much more than just paying for exposure. They may be interacting with the community within the comments of a post. They may have amazing content in which, even if not a potential client, we want to share. They may have a good alignment between their offline presence and social media. Many factors can justify good performance. So again, "don't get too good."

So… The Essence…

With this in mind, the essence of a good dashboard is a setup that enables us to use our experience in our process of analysis, that enhances the results of our analysis and values what we have learned along the way, but leaves space for discovery and learning. We are looking at spending the least possible time to reach as many possible insights as we can. We are also looking to keep an open mind and be able to access information that can lead us to unexpected insights.

One example is to have metrics next to each other that are apparently always correlating in the same way, such as the number of posts and the average interactions per post. Naturally, we expect that the more we post, the lower average interactions we have; but in some cases, we run into a brand that breaks that rule, which is the brand that we can take a closer look at and learn from. Figures 12-13 and 12-14 illustrate this example very well.

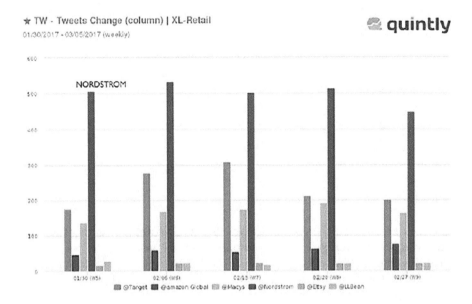

Figure 12-13. Tweets change

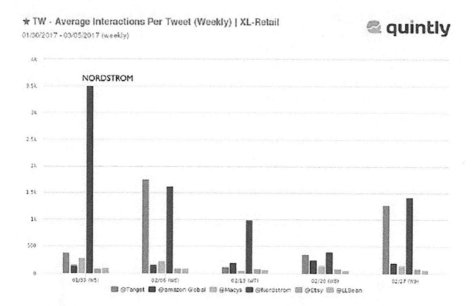

Figure 12-14. Average interactions per tweet

In Figures 12-13 and 12-14, the same brand (Nordstrom) is tweeting the most and having higher average interactions per tweet. If I were in their competitive space, I would look at what they are doing. If I am not a direct competitor, I can look at them for inspiration and insight. As a note, this is a group of similar pages with similar volume.

When we find such metrics that work well together and still give us room for surprises, we have great material for a good dashboard.

The essence is to spend the least amount of time to reach the highest amount of insights, and for that, we need room for discovery. As an open-ended theme for ideas and discussion, we try to discover different ways of reaching more insights in less time throughout our life as an analyst (despite our job title).

Key Takeaways

- Dashboards are everywhere around us; we usually pay less attention to them than we think we do.

- The faster we need to react using a dashboard, the less and more actionable metrics it can contain.

- Having a clear objective is the best start when building a dashboard. As simple as this seems, we many times forget about it when working with dashboards.

- If we can answer these five points, we can start to build or select a good dashboard: time available for analysis; level of detail we are looking for; range of areas of analysis; period of analysis; frequency of analysis.

- Default dashboards are most likely part of our first steps into a tool. They are a good way to learn about such tool and are usually focused on our success with that tool and on fulfilling its concept.

- Custom dashboards give us the flexibility we need to work on more complex projects or to have a setup that is best to our way of working.

- When building custom dashboards, we can keep four key points in mind as a guideline: linearity and order of metrics, metric positioning and correlation, layout, and graphic design.

- A good dashboard allows us to spend the least amount of time on reaching the highest number of insights.

- "Don't get too good." Keep an open mind about learning and discovering more about the data. We can leave space for discovery when building our dashboards.

Reports

The Key to Analytics Success

Reporting effectively is often the ultimate goal of analytics. Despite our quality as analysts or how experienced we are, if the reports cannot deliver the actionable insights hidden in the data, the cycle of analysis is not properly complete.

Many analytics tools offer automated reports. Some of these reports are only a collection of metrics; others bring descriptive text and highlight significant events of the period. Most tools also offer custom reports, which gives us the freedom to choose metrics and add some of our thoughts in the form of text. Custom reports can sometimes be sourced on custom dashboards, so as we customize dashboards, we are also customizing our reports.

Despite specific resources from analytics tools, reports have to go beyond the medium and technology used to compose them. An effective report needs to truly get the message across from the sender to the audience. Going even beyond the message, with good reporting, we can motivate people to take action and effectively apply the insights from analytics into strategy. Good reporting can be a driver and a key to analytics success.

© April Ursula Fox 2022
A. U. Fox, *Social Media Analytics Strategy*,
https://doi.org/10.1007/978-1-4842-8306-6_13

Elements of Reporting

The elements of reporting closely follow the principles of communication itself. We have five main elements we can work with, which must succeed in their tasks individually so that the entire process succeeds:

- **Sender**: Must be prepared to compose the message

- **Message**: Must carry the correct information and be prepared to travel through the chosen medium

- **Medium**: Must be suitable to carry the message and reach the receiver without loss of content

- **Receiver**: Must be prepared to interpret the message and generate feedback

- **Feedback**: Must reach the sender with all qualities of message and medium

Good Qualities for Each Element of Reporting

Each element has a few important qualities that we can look for when preparing or evaluating a reporting workflow.

A *sender* has the following qualities:

- Good understanding of the brand strategy

- Familiarity with the social networks' details

- Understanding of the analysis process

- Knowledge of the tools being used

- Experience with the chosen medium

- Previous experience handling/working on the entire reporting process

- Clear understanding of the objectives of the message

A *message* (includes format, resolution, and overall quality) has the following qualities:

- Clarity of content

- Attractive images/graphs

- Relevance: only information significant to the objective of the report or message

- Brevity: keep text to a minimum
- Best possible quality
- Best format for the transferring or display on chosen medium

A *medium* (includes storage, transferring, and display) has the following qualities:

- Enough support for the quality of the message
- Enough speed for delivery (includes streaming)
- Accessible by sender and receiver

A *receiver* has the following qualities:

- As many of the qualities listed for the sender
- Critical view of the process for potential improvements
- Practical and objective approach into generating feedback

Feedback has the following qualities:

- Nonpersonal approach
- Focus on the objectives (short and long term)
- Scalable (teams and large organizations)
- Succinct

Elements in Chain

As simple as this concept may seem, many times, we catch ourselves thinking about why a certain report failed to produce the necessary results. We can then go back into each of these elements and find out where is the point in need for improvement.

The main idea, as we will see going further, is that the report can successfully close its cycle and drive necessary changes for the improvement of our strategy and ultimate success of our projects.

In many cases, a single report will not immediately drive change; we could have an uncommonly bad performance and decide that our current strategy should be pushed further. But if the reports start to consistently show that something is not working, we must be able to detect what it is and change that.

A Case of an Unstructured Approach to Reporting

When it comes to social media analytics, many businesses tend to overlook the reports as a centerpiece for the evolution of strategy.

I have worked with teams that produced reports but did not focus as a team over such reports. Each team member was also generating individual reports on the side, and some were accessing analytics tools directly and getting bits and pieces of insight here and there. This was a workflow that did not help them move forward. They got stuck on the same issues over and over again. Partly because each team member was looking only at a certain aspect of the strategy, and no one had the big picture, and partly because there was no collective effort, since everyone was "doing their part," even if it was not truly enough. They were suffering from a lack of interest in social media in general because they never took time to work on the strategy together.

When we are facing such situations, it is always recommended to check if our reporting is playing its part. In many cases, an adjustment to the reporting workflow can put the strategy back into an improvement cycle.

There are many different approaches to reporting. We can create new ones as we become more experienced and familiar with our specific context. In this chapter, we explore a few fundamental approaches and further concepts as a guideline to structure our reporting process.

Reporting Approaches

What matters in reporting is to get the message across. As simple as this seems, this process usually brings an array of elements that either help or hinder the reception by the audience. These elements can be technical and relatively simple to fix and improve, or very subjective, related to the perception of the audience and somewhat unclear reasons to why it may or may not be working well.

Subjectivity is in the core of human nature; some say that it is the very *thing* that makes us humans. Therefore, under such variety of opinions and points of view, it falls upon us to make sure that our message is understood as we intend it to be.

While reporting and getting a message across is quite an open topic, and also a topic that changes through time as we evolve our way of thinking, our languages, mediums, and technologies, it is still possible for us to find and apply certain methods that fit perfectly into specific needs.

Here, we look at five approaches and concepts. The idea is to explore potential situations in which we have specific objectives related to our reports.

The following are interesting reporting approaches to explore:

- Highlights
- Full KPIs
- Goal oriented
- 360 overview
- Storytelling

Each approach is more or less friendly to certain formats and mediums. The choice of format or medium depends on the context of the content, period, audience, available presentation resources, and such details around our reports. Each approach fits well in a different objective.

A Note on Reporting Formats

With the evolution of technology, new reporting formats come up. They come up because it becomes possible to use them effectively, such as with live dashboards, video, augmented reality (AR), and virtual reality (VR). They also come up because people become tired of certain formats, such as the well-known presentation slides and simple document exports.

The essence of reporting, however, will not change. The objective is that a certain message can be delivered properly and action can be taken accordingly when needed.

When working with dynamic formats, such as live dashboards, video, AR, and VR, it is important that we take into account the perception of the audience and their possibilities to work with such formats and provide feedback or take action.

A certain audience may need a certain specific format, independent if they are not impressed by the format. It will likely be more effective to innovate on the way we present the message and tell the story behind the report than on the format. When reporting, it is usually better to be safe than sorry.

During our feedback sessions, we can include questions about the format and double-check with the audience if the chosen format is working well for everyone.

Back into reporting approaches, it is good to note that even simple reports such as the highlights and full KPIs can eventually require some level of context added for the receiver to better understand the message. Some level of explanation regarding the reasons for the results to be what they are can be highly effective.

The numbers alone will not reveal information external to what the analytics can capture and display. Interactions can be high because of an offline campaign or because of a specific incident around a certain piece of content, among so many other points. Even within the analytics platform, there may be a correlation of events that we can point out.

In cases when everyone involved is familiar with events in the period and with whatever is behind the numbers, less context can be given and correlations can be pointed out very briefly.

Visual Resources Available on Pinterest

To add to our studies, I have created a Pinterest board with visual examples of all the types of reporting we are investigating here as ideas to what can be done with social media analytics and beyond. The interesting aspect about the board is that it is updated through time, so as I come across relevant new visuals, I will add them there.

Please access the following address on the Analyst.Life Pinterest board: www. pinterest.com/analystlife/reports-infographics/.

Highlights

> **Formats**: one page, slides, spreadsheet, infographic, live dashboard
>
> **Time involved**: minimum
>
> **Automation**: recommended
>
> **Period cycle**: short, real time, daily, weekly
>
> **Graph types**: tables, highly numeric, very simple graphic charts

Highlights can be great for short periods of analysis such as daily and weekly. We can cover only specific areas of a campaign and even focus only on what is worthy of mention. Our final report can be as short and succinct as possible.

The objective is to point out, or highlight, results that are above or below a certain goal or acceptable range. For that, however, it is important that the audience understands what the goals or parameters are. A short guide can be added to establish the goals or standards.

Automation works very well with this approach. We can build a dashboard with custom metrics that include the goal limits and display results next to the goals, giving us the highlights directly. To better focus only on what is important, we can add to the automation an initial summary with metric names and their relation to the goals.

When the receivers already understand the context behind the numbers, this format can be fully automated. Otherwise, it can be a good idea to add a minimum of context to clarify the details and potential insights.

Full KPIs

Formats: one page, slides, spreadsheet, live dashboard

Time involved: minimum

Automation: recommended

Period cycle: any

Graph types: tables, highly numeric, choice of graphs with reference to previous period, goals, or competitive benchmark

A full report on the *key performance indicators* (KPIs) provides a more comprehensive version of the highlights. After carefully choosing the best metrics and setting KPIs, the entire report can be automated.

This approach is useful even without specific goals for each metric. It can be closer to a descriptive report where we leave much of the work of interpretation to the audience. When possible, however, using goals can add useful reference and save time.

As in all formats, the amount of additional context that we may need to add to a report is proportional to the lack of understanding that the audience has about what is being presented.

Goal Oriented

Formats: one page, slides, spreadsheet, live dashboard, mixed

Time involved: depends on final scope and application

Automation: partial, depending on final scope and application

Period cycle: any

> **Graph types**: tables, highly numeric, choice of graphs with reference to previous period, goals, or competitive benchmark

The goal-oriented approach can be explored as an element of any other approach. It does not have to be a stand-alone approach per se.

The main difference is that in this case we can take the concept of being goal oriented as far as we can. We include specific goals for metrics, but we also look at higher-level company goals and keep track of our progress toward all possible goals related to our strategy.

Under this approach, we can study different ways to measure our progress toward goals and to create calculations toward a unified view of our progress. Being goal oriented leads us to further investigate our readings from each metric and sharpen our judgment of results.

As a simple example of this effect, we can take the reading of percentages missing the numeric value and being unclear.

In many cases, percentages alone do not help us understand the impact behind certain information. While we can detect this at any time during our analyst life, being goal oriented pushes us into detecting such aspects faster.

If one goal is to have 15% more total interactions than the previous period, it is helpful to see the goal next to the numeric value: 15%; 250 interactions.

Then, if we pass the goal and see that we are at 29%, we can see that it translates to 35 extra interactions in this example.

This helps us understand the dimension of what we are working with. Staying only within percentages can give us an illusion that we are doing better or worse than we truly are.

The true dimension of our results helps us build our strategy around whatever we do. It is one thing to think of an initiative to generate 100 interactions and a very different thing to generate 5,000.

When setting goals, we can be progressive and go beyond the short term, to medium- and long-term objectives. As we aim higher, we prepare our strategy to reach such objectives in time and monitor our progress along the way.

This aspect of a goal-oriented approach is enhanced as predictive and prescriptive analytics technologies evolve. Such technologies calculate the chances we have to reach a goal, the time it may take to reach it, suggest the best way to get there, and even suggest the goals themselves.

In the meantime, before we have access to such technologies, we can run a few manual exercises with our goal-oriented approach.

One exercise is to generate predictions ourselves, despite our desired goals. So we ignore the desired goal for this exercise and try our best to be as realistic and precise as possible. This helps us check how well we understand the market, our company, and the dynamics of digital marketing. Insights from this exercise eventually circle back to planning stages, which helps us to better allocate resources.

One way of generating a first set of predictions is to take a simple approach and base the future numbers on the averages we currently have. On the following cycles, we can add more variables and relevant information and insights. This generates a prediction along the lines of *if we continue with this strategy, we will reach…*

When we have close alignment with the content planning strategy for the future period and understand the context of what is coming up, we can then use that information to better estimate results. We can add all the knowledge we gather from the market, from seasonal events, internal company events, external competitors, and so forth.

This predictive approach does not have to be a priority by any means; it is just one more approach we can take to better understand our strategy and the market. It is more of an exercise than anything else.

Having the predictive aspect in mind, one point of goals in analytics is that we are also testing ourselves, we are putting ourselves and our expertise on the line. This will likely help us grow into a more detailed understanding of social media, of the connection of social to other areas of the company, and of the broader strategy and objectives of the organization as a whole.

If we decide to create a unified view of our performance, such as a success rate, exercises around creating goals and realistic possibilities to reach such goals are very helpful. We will look further into the use of goals and success rates when we look at tactics in the next chapters.

360 Overview

Formats: slides, spreadsheet, live dashboard, video, mixed

Time involved: medium to long

Automation: partial

Period cycle: medium to long—bimonthly, monthly, quarterly

Graph types: any

The 360 approach aims to give maximum context to the performance of the period. All relevant events are mentioned, including offline initiatives. The main idea is to relate what happened on social media to the company, brand, or organization as a whole. We can be as goal oriented as we like in this approach.

The 360 report can be of any length. It can be partially automated, lacking only the information out of the reach of the analytics platforms.

When we depend on other teams to give us such information, it's a good idea to have an early deadline, so that there is enough time to work on fixing things in case something goes wrong.

The following are a few areas that can be added to a 360 report:

- Web analytics
- Digital ads performance
- Digital marketing campaigns
- Offline marketing campaigns
- Full social media overview: social ads, publishing information and strategy, listening, and analytics
- Sales performance
- External events relevant during the period

A 360 approach can be built into a dashboard as well. It will likely be a busy dashboard or a series of dashboards showing the full picture.

When researching the possibilities of creating such a report, you find that data integration companies can offer the option to connect any sources of data on the same dashboard. These are the companies that can help us if we are looking to automate a 360 report. The integrated automation can be useful even if we still have to input some information manually, which happens when we are adding offline activities. It saves precious time to automate what we can.

An interesting addition to this report is a timeline view. We can add to such timeline all the events we find within the analytics, including those from external sources. This view can help the audience connect events and better understand the efforts and results of our activity.

The timeline view, as with many other concepts we are looking at in this chapter, can be added to any reporting approach we choose. The objective is not to create rules, but to study examples that can open our minds into finding the ideal approach for each of our future projects.

Storytelling

Formats: slides, infographic, dashboard, video, mixed

Time involved: long

Automation: partial

Period cycle: medium, long, or very long, monthly, quarterly, yearly, plus

Graph types: any

Storytelling tries to build a sense of meaning to the report while also creating rapport with the audience.

Many times, it introduces to the audience a series of apparently irrelevant events that reveal themselves as a hidden story behind the strategy and the results of the period.

It could be anything, from whatever caused a burst of creativity on the content manager and a viral idea came to be, to how much the company has worked on a certain aspect of its culture until it reached the current success.

Humans are a story-driven species. We connect to a timeline where characters are facing conflicts and maybe winning over some while losing against others.

Conflict is the basis of a story. It is precisely the conflict that keeps us interested in a story and makes our minds work on figuring out what will happen next. The expectations build up and the story reaches its high points as each conflict is faced.

We must not underestimate the audience's capacity to grasp the underlying points and generate all the possible outcomes in their minds.

We do not have to overexplain the points we are making; we do not have to treat our audience as if they have a hard time to understand what we are talking about. As long as our material is clear, they will understand.

Storytelling is somewhat new to the business and analytics world, but not to marketing, and much less to screenplay writing.

With screenplays, a technique that is commonly applied is the *method of the two climax points*.

The first climax comes early in the story, setting the scene for the main conflict of the story. The second climax comes in the very end, when the conflict is dealt with and the story flows into its resolution.

In other words, we would have the following structure:

- Introduction
- Climax point 1
- Development
- Climax point 2
- End

Most Hollywood movies follow this method; it is surprisingly useful for business, and in our specific case, social media analytics reports.

A Simple Example of a Storytelling Report

This follows the structure mentioned earlier.

- **Introduction**
  - Who we are
  - What we are all about
  - A hint about what the story is about

- **Climax 1**: A major goal as the first climax point
  - How did we choose such goal?
  - What challenges are involved in reaching such goal? How hard will it be to beat the goal? Why?
  - What are we doing to get there?
  - What are the chances of success?

- **Development**
  - Speaks of our process

Displays the results of each main point we selected to then move to and reach the second climax.

- **Climax 2**: The match against our goal, do we win or lose?
  - Displays our results and all the details against the challenges we faced, even if such challenges are a comparison to a previous period, for example.
- **End**: The conclusion of the process and what is done next

Animation and Effects in Reporting

When used wisely, animation and effects can highlight reports and presentations. More often than not, however, they are unnecessary.

One common mistake when using such "tricks" is to use them around elements that are not so important or that have nothing to do with the essence of the message being told.

The audience also has a different time to absorb the information displayed, so if we are hiding a certain point until a moment when we finally show it, for example, we need to remember to give the audience enough time to perceive it.

It is good to create an "awe" effect, but we must be careful not to focus too much on the effect, to the point where it isn't so significant to the main message anymore and even hurts the communication process.

Focus is an important element in reports: focus on the objective, the audience, and the information shared.

Images, Graphs, Numbers, or Text?

Sometimes a big number is better than any graph, image, or text. A big number will do nicely if the question is simply, *How many new fans we had from this campaign?* If we are looking at evolution over a period of time, or a more detailed comparison, then other options can come into play.

Graphs can also work well, and much better than text, but keep in mind that they work at their best when they are easily understood. Graphs work even better when the audience is closely following the report and the specific graph falls into place within the narrative, when it is somewhat expected.

As an example, if we first mention that the best time of the day for engagement is 2 p.m. and that Thursday is the best day, when they open a graph with a view of the performance across days of the week and times of day, the audience will likely find the graph easy to understand.

Images and illustrations can be very powerful if used well. They can even be the very best choice to enhance a certain message and help the audience remember the report or presentation.

A simple example happens in the financial market, using bulls and bears to represent the two different layers of investors. The bulls positioning their investment in a lower layer in the trend, hitting everyone else above them with their horns, against the bears on an upper layer, smashing everyone below with their paws. One is interested in seeing the prices rise; the other wishes the prices to go down. When we start learning about the financial markets, and we are told the story of bulls and bears, we never forget it.

Text is an element that is usually best kept to a minimum. Unless we are educating the audience in a complex issue or absolutely need a more detailed explanation of any aspect in our report, we can hold back from too much text in our reports.

Critical thinking on the use of images and text is essential. What matters is that the audience captures the message in the best possible way. When in doubt, we can use a test audience to validate the effectiveness of what we are trying to do.

Stakeholders and Feedback

Feedback is the last point on our communication chain. It connects all of the work done to a new beginning, a new cycle, which is improved upon the last one. Without good feedback, we cannot properly improve on our strategy, and even before that, on our reports. The reports themselves may need improvement before an ideal setup can impact the strategy.

Stakeholders need to have enough time to send feedback on the reports received. Feedback, in some ways, also includes discussions on the changes in strategy that eventually an analysis may propose. When the team gets together to discuss the reports, it counts as a feedback session as well. All of what is done after the report was created, sent, and received can be part of the feedback process.

In the position of analyst, we can prepare the workflow for receiving all the possible feedback, either individually or as a team in feedback sessions. For that, we have to establish the workflow with our stakeholders first, meaning we have to adapt to their context as much as we can. The idea in the end is to have the most efficient process for feedback.

If we feel that we can educate our audience to better understand our reports, we can do so. However, keep in mind that even more time is required during the process, so we can instead have educational material set up beforehand, and such material can be as to the point as possible. In many cases, a simple and short guide within the report can be enough as educational material.

Defining Stakeholders: What Matters to Each One? And Who Matters Most to the Project?

A stakeholder is simply *a person with interest in the matter*. Different stakeholders, meaning people with different interests, likely enjoy a different report from a certain analysis.

People that are not directly involved with the social media activity, but still wish to keep track of what is going on, might prefer to see a very simple-to-understand report and only a very high-level performance instead of all possible details.

Analytics tools can have multiple different reports being sent to different stakeholders, so we can make use of that when working with such tools.

Depending on the scope of the project, it can be a good idea to contact stakeholders individually, during different stages of the process, to understand what they are looking for and how the process is working for each of them.

Also, it can be a good idea to separate stakeholders by their responsibilities. Those who have the most responsibility over the specific project or area being analyzed can have a stronger voice regarding the information in a report being shared.

The reason for this is that people connect better to reports when they enjoy them, when they are involved, when it has been tailored for them. If we are not the key decision-makers, working with people to have a perfect setup for them is part of our job.

Reporting with Teams

Sometimes it is hard to get the team together around a certain project. Usually, when a project is not a major priority to everyone involved, finding a time slot that is good for everyone is a challenge.

On top of that, leaving individual tasks for the team to perform at their leisure can compromise our deadlines.

Working with a team on reporting, analysis, and feedback is therefore somewhat tricky. We can cover a few points with the team to have everyone perform a better work together:

- Education
- Clear tasks
- Honest deadlines
- Feedback sessions

Education

When everyone is up to date on the contents being discussed, the results are greatly improved. Metrics and analytics are fields that include very specific terms and knowledge; it is not as instinctive as we may think, and it is very easy for people in a group to have a very different view of the process (or not understand the process at all).

One way to deal with this is to have a series of articles or materials created for the group. Each group member gives a check once each material is read, and we know how far the group has gone into the subject. It can be called a *ready check*.

Clear Tasks

Usually, in team meetings, some tasks and next steps are assigned very quickly. This can lead people to be unclear about what they need to do next. A second *ready check* can be good during the acceptance of tasks. Check if everyone understands all the information about what is planned and what each person in the team is doing.

Honest Deadlines

Deadlines must be taken seriously. When we know we have a chance of not making it, go for a safer date. Teams tend to agree on deadlines without giving it too much thought. It is highly important to think about the details of our tasks and to figure out the time we need to produce or review certain reports. We can stick to being honest; it pays off in the end, even if at the planning stage, the project seems that it will take longer.

Feedback Sessions

Be sure to have good and honest feedback from the team, only then will the project move forward.

It is terrible to hear that someone "didn't really like this or that" (in the past tense) when the project has been going on for a while—even worse, when we hear that people "never liked this or that."

We are better off if we are brave enough and humble enough to be criticized if we are the analyst or the project leader. People share more when they feel that we enjoy their ideas and feedback.

The Report As a Key to Success

In conclusion, what matters the most in reporting is that it can be a driver toward success. Despite specific tactics or techniques, what truly matters is that we are successful and use our reporting strategically toward our goals. The final thought is to make the best possible use of reporting, since in most cases, we need to have it in place anyway. Don't let the chance of having a good report go to waste; let's make it a key to success.

Success *(noun)*

> *The favorable or prosperous termination of attempts or endeavors; the accomplishment of one's goals.*

—Dictionary.com

Key Takeaways

- Reporting effectively is often the ultimate analytics goal.

- A good report can motivate people to take action.

- Principles of reporting follow the principles of communication itself, a cyclic chain of five primary elements: sender, message, medium, receiver, and feedback.

- If one of the main elements fails, the chain fails, and the report risks not being an entire success.

- What matters in reporting is to get the message across.

- Under the subjective human nature, it falls upon us to make sure that our message is understood as we intend it to be.

- Reporting can make use of different conceptual templates, or reporting approaches, where a specific approach can fit best into a specific context, case, or situation.

- The amount of additional context that an analyst may need to add to a report is proportional to the lack of understanding that the audience has about what is being presented. When everyone involved understands the context already, not much context needs to be present in the report.

- Goals and goal-oriented approaches and measurements can be great assets to add to any report.

- Humans are a story-driven species, so a storytelling approach will likely be the best choice when we wish to really connect to the audience.

- Animations and effects in reports are only useful if they enhance the main focal point for the audience.

- Sometimes one big number is all we need.

- A cleverly chosen image can promote long-lasting memories of the report.

- Without good feedback, we are not able to improve. We must be open to feedback even if it criticizes our work.

- Education of our audience is time-consuming; approach it wisely.

- Find ways to build a report that the entire team is happy with; it will pay off in the end, since people become more involved with what they like.

- Sometimes we need different reports sent to different people. Sometimes there is no middle ground on a truly best option for everyone. When prioritizing, value the people with higher responsibility.

- If we have teamwork to build our reports, we must be clear and honest and have everyone at the same level of basic knowledge to make it work.

Milan Veverka

Building Data Partnerships, Integration, and Solutions at Keboola

Milan Veverka is the person we look for when it comes to data integration and custom solutions. His more than 20 years of experience with technology projects, working directly with clients and also in the development process, gives him a unique perspective into finding the best solution for any given case.

His work with companies of every size in every industry sector has led him to deal with any kind of data problem we can think of—from integrating different systems and huge legacy databanks to developing new solutions on top of newly integrated data, and also to work on the integration of very new technologies as they come out. This is the case with social media, which is constantly renewing itself and releasing more features, more systems, and more data into the world. This is also why it is great to have Milan as a guest in this book.

My first contact with Milan happened when a partnership came up with Keboola, a highly innovative company in the areas of data integration and custom solutions. The project was about integrating different kinds of data to a client of Keboola, and I came in from the social media analytics side. During that project, I had the chance to speak with Milan about his views on data integration, on how the landscape was changing in that sense, and how

© April Ursula Fox 2022
A. U. Fox, *Social Media Analytics Strategy*,
https://doi.org/10.1007/978-1-4842-8306-6_14

important it would be for companies to use integration technologies and services such as Keboola to become truly data driven. Being data driven is not an option anymore; it becomes a requirement in the digital world, and integrating data is a big part of that.

I later found out that Milan and I also had a few friends in common, from the years when I was living in Prague, which is a great place for technology development. This connection, and my admiration for the work being done by Milan and Keboola, led me to invite him to share his knowledge with us in this book. It is great to have him with us.

Going into the questions, my intention was to reveal details of data integration related to social media and beyond. I also approached topics about strategy and our roles as professionals in the digital age. The interview took a conversational tone, where we could navigate through subjects that will add important value to our studies.

You can find Milan Veverka directly through his LinkedIn profile at www. linkedin.com/in/milanveverka/.

Question 1

With the very diversified technology landscape of the world, and the need for integrating all of these technologies to become data driven and truly make sense of the data we have access to, keeping social media in mind as a focus point, how do you see the importance of data integration? Why would we need to go beyond social media data?

Social media technologies, or however you want to call them, have been around for ten-plus years in various forms. There are many companies that do nothing else but show you data from within your Twitter or your Facebook account. Frankly, the business cases around those products have been suffering.

A few good companies have survived, but ultimately, what does it mean for the business that we have X followers? Or what does it mean that there is so much happening on that particular page? The value of the social data or the data from social media interactions grows exponentially once you put it in context with some of your business data.

I think that there are two main aspects to consider, both requiring integration.

One is the marketing impact of social media, which is basically what is coming to you as a business from social media, and can be seen as a very strong case in ecommerce. There is a link on the Facebook page and clicks on a call to action, which leads to the website and creates new customers.

Another aspect is the way I use social media to maintain my community of customers and whether or not their activity within the platform or within that ecosystem in any way correlates or determines their lifetime value for me as a business.

These aspects bring very clear use cases, and obviously, you need more data and to bring everything together, right?

You need to know if a certain person on Twitter or on Facebook happens to be a certain customer. You then need to know what they're doing, what they're reacting to, the content they're consuming, and finally what they buy, how they interact, how they further promote you, and how they influence others. Influence on social media is a big deal as well.

On the second use case more specifically, an interest that is only becoming mainstream rather recently is to learn details of what people are actually talking about. This interest is leading us beyond simple metrics, very often called *vanity metrics*. How many likes do we have? How many dislikes? Where are they coming from? This shift is very good. I have come across marketers with businesses built on increasing those numbers without ever actually bothering to validate whether or not such numbers have an impact on the business whatsoever.

I think what is really important on social media is that people are sharing thoughts and people are expressing their thoughts. People are using social media as a communication channel, and whether it is one-to-one or public venting, it is important for things like brand image and perception. We see the use of social media changing a lot from what it was five years ago. Companies also follow each other on new trends. One company starts using social media in customer service, as a customer service channel, and suddenly everyone else is doing it. Close monitoring of competitors' profiles and activities thereon is also becoming commonplace.

On the data and technology side, social media monitoring is becoming more and more important, especially with the onset of more affordable and easier to use natural language processing systems and algorithms. It is easier to run processes in customer analysis, anomaly detection, and we're talking about anomaly detection within the text, which will show us that people are suddenly talking about particular topics. You can then be monitoring multiple channels at the same time and realize that, *Hey, here's an important topic, there's something happening in my business.* Such "chatter" can be a very strong indicator of a problem or an opportunity.

Question 1 (Interlude)

I read about a recent use case of Keboola with an airline company, where you found major problems in specific parts of the client's processes. What I thought was most interesting was how you showed that sometimes the strongest "buzz" might not be the most important. We have to go deeper into the data, because sometimes the important element is not as "popular" in a sense. Not everyone is saying the bad things, naturally. Otherwise, a business would fail—that is, if most people hated them. But I saw that type of anomaly detection analysis you mentioned, and just wanted to reinforce how interesting it is…

Yes, that was a great use case, and I can give you an even better one. We ran a test of the same application on a completely different data set. We went into the hospitality sector. We are talking here about mostly very rich data, from channels such as TripAdvisor, Facebook, Twitter, company internal channels, their own complaint lines, and their own communications. In this particular scenario, we put about seven different data sources together, which for this particular customer represented, on a weekly basis, roughly 5,000 text entries, or 5,000 pieces of communication, 5,000 verbatims, as we call them. So nobody in their right mind reads all of those things, and even if they do, they monitor just one slice of it, just one channel. Maybe someone is responsible for the Facebook page and for responding to that, and there might be an entire team doing it, right? Some companies make their business on managing this type of communication for customers.

What happened then was that within these 5,000 texts every week, there were five pieces of text from different data sources where people complained about the behavior of a particular manager of a particular location of a restaurant chain. A very important finding, right?

The low volume, the fact that it's not a trending topic, makes it something that you would not see on any kind of leader board. You need a sophisticated machine learning algorithm to go in there and say,

Hey, this looks important! I'm not entirely sure why because I am just a machine and I don't know everything yet, but it is statistically significant enough to offer it as one of the things I want you, the human user, to take a look at and tell me whether or not this makes sense.

Something like that has a massive business impact. I don't know if they fired the guy yet or not, but this is a great example of an actionable insight, if I've ever seen one. There is also the bigger concern there that if five people complained, there were probably one hundred more who noticed and didn't complain, right?

Question 2

Following on that line of thought, thinking now of a practical case where someone would knock on your door and ask how they could apply such data integration to their business cases. Can you share a practical view of the process and the possibilities of data integration?

Yes, this is precisely the kind of work we do. The use of social media data and even the text analytics example are just a few of the many applications for integration. For us, it is all about operationalizing the data. How do you make the data a part of the way you're running business? How do you leverage data to the maximal point? We provide the tools for that, and both the aggregation of data and integration with analytics are the "Lego blocks" used to put everything together.

Typical use cases for us will start with collecting the data, which in this last example it was great because most data sources and integrations were available out of the box. When this happens, it is very easy to put things together without the companies being involved, since their primary business is to run ecommerce, or run a hospital, or whatever it is. Their core business is not to work on data integrations. They have us to do that for them.

Question 3

Regarding the investment and effort around integration, some people I speak with are often scared of data integration projects. They don't understand the potential costs and further resources that they might need to spend on the process, such as time. This can lead to the assumption that integration can be complicated and not worth it. To help bring down this "myth," what can you share with us in this sense?

I feel we are touching several good points with this question, so I try to look at each point at a time to better reveal the entire picture.

A lot of software and a lot of technology out there are very inexpensive or even free, but it's free only if your own time is worthless, right? Meaning that if you can spend the time to learn it, to do it, to develop the capabilities, then you don't actually pay for the technology.

Then you have technologies that are trying to do a lot for you, but you're paying for it because you're saving the time. These technologies go through a much more complex development stage because they are trying to "think in advance" for all those things that you might want to do later as a user. The complexity then grows exponentially with the variables here.

Our job as a company is then to make the technology available to our clients, that's part of our core value. The example of our text analysis of the "chatter" within certain communication channels is something that NSA has been doing for decades, but they spent an ungodly amount of money because the technology wasn't there at the time. What is happening now and going forward, which is something that happens with all technologies, is that it is becoming much more accessible for significantly smaller companies.

The issue then becomes the availability of skills to work with such technologies. If you are working, for example, for very large enterprises, you can find teams that will have the capabilities necessary, but you will pay them, again, a huge amount of money because they are very rare on the market. That will be harder and harder to do for smaller and smaller players. If the technology in place is requiring, or the solution is requiring, that you have all these skills, it becomes a barrier on its own.

So if I'm running a restaurant chain, chances are I don't have a data scientist on staff. And if I do, I'm either really big and really sophisticated or really inefficient in what it is that I am doing because that's not my core business. I don't understand it. I don't know how to hire those people properly. So, that's where partnerships start kicking in. Who is out there? Whose primary business is this? And who can help me do that? And whether it can be done in a consultative basis, or on a type of OEM, which then becomes a part of the product offering, will be part of the different business decisions that come into play, and they are very specific for each customer. There is no "one size fits all."

What we've done with the approach that we have at Keboola is take all those pieces that everybody needs, such as the database behind the scenes, and the API layer for the integration—like the API integration we have with quintly, which makes it easy to get data from there—and then provide this as building blocks, or a "Lego set" to clients. From there, we can either train the client or we can seriously lower the amount of skills and time required to put these solutions together.

We also do that without being bound by the limitations of one technology product. When you have one specific analytics solution, it will give you, for example, "these five data sources, and then run this type of data analytics on top of it, give you this type of dashboard," and so forth. The flexibility we offer is great for our customers because they can choose the data sources and workaround issues with any data sources that are missing. We use this logic of the "Lego blocks" to be able to put the necessary pieces together to build what it is that the client is trying to do. The "Lego blocks" analogy is also a good one because, just as in playing with real Lego blocks, with a little bit of training "anybody" can do that. Now, keep in mind that there are big quotation marks on both sides of the word "anybody."

The skill requirements are dropping dramatically, though. So you don't need an architect type of person; you need people who understand what is it that you are trying to do with the data and have the basic tools at their disposal to put it together, because all that complexity is already hidden from them.

One simple example of this effect happens in voice over the Internet. You can very easily send voice over the Internet, right? But it's actually a very complex task. You can do it because you have an app that is doing it for you. It was not built by you, it was built by someone else, but it brought the task to a level in which you can do that without having to know how to do it. The skills required were reduced to pushing a button. And that's exactly the same principle.

Question 4

Thinking about the role of marketers facing the use of such technology and considering that most marketers do not come from a very technical development background, how do you see them dealing with such challenges, and maybe taking the role of a strategist, understanding enough from the technical side to still be able to put things to work under the demand for technical solutions?

Don't you take that role of strategist for any other aspect of your business that you're not personally specialized in? You will figure out, *I need this skill set to achieve this goal, I don't know it myself, so I'll hire someone.* Then you can think later on, *Do I have enough of that skill in my team to hire someone internally? Or is it too specific?*

We can take a very simple example and look at the most basic infrastructure of business, which is accounting. You obviously need it to run your business. You, as a businessperson and not being an accountant, have a rough idea of what you need from it to run your business. You then think in details. Do I need an in-house bookkeeper? Am I going to hire an accounting company? Do I need a CFO? There are multiple ways of solving the problem depending on what type of organization you are and how you will satisfy this particular need.

And frankly, data is becoming an asset that flows through the company in a very similar way to money, so you need to be managing it in the same way. You must understand enough details to be able to judge if the opportunity can be satisfied by an external organization, group, team, or advisor helping you, or if you need to internalize it. The internal elements will then branch out into multiple aspects, which are mostly different for every single company.

We call this the *soft data stack*, which is the people side of this process within the organization. You have the *soft system* and the *hard system*, terminologies from 20 years ago. I guess now I dated myself. But you have the same thing in data. You have the technology, but then you have the people. The people have different roles.

Some of the roles you might want to bring into the company. Some of them you might want to outsource. Some of them you might want to automate. It's exactly the same principle of what you're doing with financial management in the organization. Do I use an automatic billing system? Or do I have two people whose only job is to write invoices?

As a marketer, I would then be looking at it from the perspective of the usage of data. How to make sense of the data? How to draw the conclusions? Or how to draw the lines between what the data is telling me and what the business is? How do I leverage the data to make a better business decision? These are not technical questions. It doesn't require coding. That's not what you're doing. This is the human component of interpretation of the data.

Then there will be a lot of things happening behind the scenes, which will be allowing you to do what you need to do, which will be serving you the data and giving you ways to make use of it, and so forth. An intriguing point is that the technical knowledge required to be on the marketer side is decreasing, while such knowledge for the development and technical side is increasing.

So, the answer for someone coming from the marketing space and being asked to make data-driven decisions or make data-driven recommendations is that they have to understand the interpretation of the data and the impact of it to the business. They do not need to become data engineers, which is a role somewhat further down the stack. The data engineer will be making sure that the infrastructure is doing what is expected from it and that the updated data shows up the next morning, which is a totally different task from the marketer. The engineer will have a limited reach regarding an understanding of the ultimate use case of the application and if it is being used in marketing, ecommerce, or hospitality analytics. For the engineer, it is, in a sense, "all the same."

Question 5

As a last question, thinking about the diversified technology landscape we have and current need for integration, how would you see integration companies such as Keboola and the integration process itself in the future? Is it going to become more popular and less scary for people that don't work with it yet? How do you see the future in this sense?

The understanding that the data is an essential element, and that working with it properly is as crucial as managing cash within any organization, becomes a business reality. If your competition knows more about what your customer thinks about your product than you do, you are obviously at a huge disadvantage, going back into our example of text analysis. That means that the demand for this service is going to grow, which is going to drive the cost down, because the technologies are going to become more and more efficient.

A few years ago, we worked with a company that used humans to tag every single message coming through. They then had other solutions built on top of that enriched data. That is obviously expensive. Their customers still happily paid for it because they understood it was giving them the competitive advantage over smaller competitors who were not able to afford it. But guess what? Now, and going forward, that type of technology, together with machine learning, will make such tasks repeatable and affordable using the out-of-the-box solutions that are suddenly becoming available.

In conclusion, I believe we are going to see two things: the technologies making themselves more accessible and more data products—meaning that in situations where we are talking about something the company should build, there will be someone who will be selling it to them out of the box.

We will also see an expansion on availability of data. As an example, it can be difficult to get certain data from Yelp at this point. Why is it difficult? Well, because Yelp understands the value of their data. Sooner or later, however, they are going to come to the market with the idea that, *Hey, this is what people are trying to do with our data. Voilà! Let's sell it to them.* When they do that, suddenly anyone who is willing to spend a little bit of money to get some of that data toward their insights will do it. Data providers will also come into play, facilitating the process of data collection. So it makes sense for companies like Yelp to do this, because it adds more and more value to their business.

Add to that integration capabilities of the various technologies. A comment made by someone on public channel can directly trigger a process within the organization, customer's favorite conversation topics can be provided via the CRM system to sales staff, a chat can be triggered post-purchase to collect customer feedback via their preferred channel.

As a last thought, something that will not change is that *no data lives alone*, once you put it into context with other data sources, with other information, you will start to make sense of it, find insights, and see the broader picture.

Strategy and Tactics

Strategy

Applying Social Media Analytics Toward Business Success

Throughout this book, we have been looking at many different aspects of the social media analytics process and landscape. It is time we bring it all together and study the application of such knowledge into practical business cases.

A good connection point for all the different elements that we have been looking at is *strategy*. A study of strategy can help us fit every piece of the puzzle together so that we can make it all work toward a clear objective.

Because social media analytics directly affects the use of social media by the business and the impact of social to the overall business, many elements we see go slightly beyond analytics.

To start, we can briefly define what strategy is, then have a view of its elements, and finally look at the details on how to build a good analytics strategy.

Strategy in Social Analytics

Analytics is a process that runs on top of other processes. The activities that feed analytics will likely be more dynamic and significant to the business than analytics itself. Under the perception of having lower priority, analytics still

© April Ursula Fox 2022
A. U. Fox, *Social Media Analytics Strategy*,
https://doi.org/10.1007/978-1-4842-8306-6_15

has the objective of enhancing the processes being measured. The value of analytics is equivalent to how much these processes can make use of the analytics insights and improve themselves.

This means that there is an entangled relationship between analytics and the process or activity being measured. The understanding of this relationship is key to understand the concept of strategy related to analytics. It is therefore inevitable that we must consider certain aspects of the activities feeding analytics as part of the analytics strategy itself.

If we implement analytics but don't go beyond to make sure that it is generating a positive impact in the business, we are leaving the outcome of our analytics strategy to chance or luck. Whether we like it or not, when implementing analytics, we must ensure that all other processes related to it are well aligned with the analytics process. With this entangled relationship in mind, we can then better explore elements of strategy and its definition applied to social media analytics.

Strategy *(noun)*

> *A plan, method, or series of maneuvers or stratagems for obtaining a specific goal or result.*

> —Dictionary.com

Expanding on such definition, three main elements of strategy can guide us into further studies:

- **Planning**: The process of creating the strategy
- **Application**: The analytics in action under the strategic plan
- **Evaluation**: Understanding the overall impact of the strategy to the business and generating resources for improvement

Strategic Planning in Social Media Analytics

The planning stage is an essential part of the strategic process. If our planning is flawed, the application stage suffers, and we risk having to abort our implementation and return to the planning stage to start again. A good plan considers as many inconvenient events and changes to the environment as possible and offers enough resources to push implementation forward despite challenges, to complete the cycle or campaign successfully, or at least with minor losses.

It is in the planning stage that we can be very creative with minimum risks. We can bring in all the innovative ideas we have and work out the details to decide if they will be part of the strategy.

It is important to note that strategy can be applied at a campaign level, with relatively short cycles, and also at a global level, with long-term goals. So the elements we study here can become part of temporary projects as well as long-term and ongoing cycles of improvement.

Going into details, a few elements covered in the book up to this point can fit particularly well into this stage:

- **Data availability and data sources**: Be knowledgeable about the data available, which is important to effectively plan on how far you can go with your analytics process.

- **Knowledge beyond social media**: Know about the company—products, markets, and competitors. Have a global view of all marketing assets and strategies in place and even of a marketing road map if such knowledge is available.

- **Tools and technology preparation**: Be sure that you have all the necessary technology in place or at least ready to be activated. This includes eventual customization of metrics and dashboards and integration of data.

- **Team preparation**: Be sure that the team is ready to implement the strategy. Education and training can be added at this stage.

- **Goals and objectives**: Define the major goals and all intermediate objectives related to the strategy.

- **Reporting cycles**: Estimate the best possible cycles for reporting and improvement. Consider all variables for the completion of a cycle, including time to prepare reports, share with the team, analyze, generate feedback, and make any necessary changes in the strategy of social channels.

- **Timelines**: Prepare a clear and detailed timeline for implementation.

- **Contingency plans**: Plan what needs to be done if certain negative or excessively positive events occur along the way. What can we be prepared for? Here, we consider our reactions to the effects on the social media strategy itself, which are detected by analytics.

To better understand how such elements can be used within the planning stage, we can take a more detailed look at each of them. Under each of the elements, we explore general principles of strategy, which helps create a bridge between theory and practice.

Data Availability and Data Sources

In the planning stage, the approach to data can be very practical. If we start the planning stage without knowledge of which data sources are available, we can create a list of what we believe that we need based on our objectives, and from there seek the advice of the team within the analytics tools that we are working with, or of a colleague with such technical expertise. More than one source of information is always good in such cases. A second opinion can go a long way if we don't find all that we need straight away, since there may be different ways of gathering certain data and different approaches to objectives with the use of processes such as machine learning.

In cases when we are mining for rare resources, which can give us a competitive edge, that process in itself can become an independent project, and we can separate its details from our overall strategy. It is interesting that we don't mix two projects into one, even if they are closely related.

Rare resources, when it comes to data, can be related to exclusive access to certain systems or databanks and also to the output of calculations, programming, and advanced technology such as machine learning and artificial intelligence.

On a practical approach, if we are thinking about gathering rare resources, we can first consider our access to them. Unless we have the power to access such resources, being this power financial, based on our professional networking, or in an innovative team of developers and data scientists, we might as well focus on what we can afford to access and avoid wasting time toward an impossible or highly unlikely objective.

Speed is a major element in strategy. Even if the strategy calls for waiting, and taking action only in specific timing because a new technology is coming out, or a seasonal event is coming up, we must still have such waiting as part of our plan, and not let it happen because we are lost in planning stage, or even worse, lost in the application stage. The time we spend on planning ultimately adds to the cost of our strategy; so the faster we can get through planning and into implementation, the better.

It is important to note, however, that this does not relate to experimentation. If our objective is to experiment and learn before we are ready to implement a solid strategy, then by all means we should do that, and as much of it as we can. If we have time and resources to spend on experimentation and learning, we only gain from it.

When gathering data, certain data we need may not yet be available but will be soon. In such cases, we can include this possibility in our strategy and consider what the strategy can be if the data would actually become available. It is very important to keep track of the progress on such availability as we go, meaning we must follow up with the sources that gave us such promise. If our sources are unreliable, and we have no access to a follow-up and tracking of progress, then we can avoid including such possibility as an integral part of the strategy and have a minor set of guidelines and ideas of what to do in case such data comes out.

In the event that we plan to go beyond premade tools, and integrate different data sources through a third-party system, or to build a solution on top of certain data sources, we must not only check for availability but also on the formats of such availability. Depending on the way in which we can gather certain data, we may need to adapt our strategy accordingly or even abandon certain data that may be available but too complicated to work with.

Such compromises are also a crucial part of data strategy; it helps us know what we can leave aside for a faster, less complicated, and more effective process.

This is also an important point in any kind of strategy, as you will see throughout many chapters of this book. There will always be trade-offs that we need to consider and decide upon. Time, for example, plays a major role as a limited resource in our projects.

Knowledge Beyond Social Media

To build an ideal strategy, this aspect of the planning stage plays a key role. With such knowledge, we can be very specific about our analytics work and find objectives that truly relate to the overall strategy of the business.

In many cases, we may come across a generic approach to the use of analytics and to analysis itself. This can be done and can be useful to a certain extent, but with more specific knowledge of the business, we can go far beyond the results of a generic analysis.

How many times have we seen articles on the Internet that bring generic rules to certain content strategies and social media management practices? The best times and days to share content, the best frequency for content, the best demographics for certain content types or networks, the best metrics to use in analytics, the best ways to invest in promoting content, and the list goes on. It turns out that such studies can have very remarkable information in them and can give us ideas and even inspiration for our work, but when it comes to building a solid plan that can truly add to the growth of our business, specific context is crucial in defining solid objectives.

This point is where a lot of the knowledge on traditional competitive business intelligence comes into play. We can consider classic elements related to communication strategy, from branding to media planning and the generation of awareness on top of conversions and client touchpoints. We can investigate more production-oriented and administrative elements of the business, which helps us relate to stakeholders even if only in our reporting stage. We will find out, for example, if we can truly implement changes from the insights we have in social analytics, or if we are stuck within a small area of a nonintegrated company that rarely makes any changes based on feedback from the market. Such answers come from this broader analysis.

But why go so far if our focus is on social media analytics?

Alignment between social media and the overall business strategy is important. Measurement is important to this alignment, and hence, the importance of a solid strategy on measurement. External knowledge added to the planning of analytics enhances the impact of analytics in social channels, which then truly impacts the business.

A simple example comes from the debate on return on investment in social media—the famous *social media ROI*. Analytics and the knowledge of it plays a big role in creating a view of the return, or the R in ROI. The knowledge beyond social media, or the knowledge of the overall business itself, will play a big role in defining the investment, or the I in ROI. So we need to first define what the investment means to understand the return. Many times, we need to create a view of the context to be able to evaluate our results, and to create such context, we need to go beyond our immediate field.

This is also an interesting point for our overall analytics strategy. Many times, we need to create greater context about our activity so that we can truly understand the impact we generate and be innovative about our overall social media strategy. In some cases, for example, we may be dealing with very limited resources, such as a small team, zero budget for promotion, a product that does not appeal to a simple content strategy, and such elements must be taken into our final analysis of performance. Many of these elements are not detected by an analytics tool—they go beyond the use of analytics technology, but play a crucial role in the final evaluation, and even in reaching truly actionable insights.

The following are a few examples of areas beyond social analytics that we can consider:

- **Culture and history of the company brand and community**: Gives reference to results and indicates possibilities and limitations on suggestions made from analytics into the business strategy.

- **Competitive landscape**: Gives context on performance within the social channels, ideas, and possibilities on social strategy and elements for predictive analytics when disputing for audience time of a shared audience (such as best times to post, paid post analysis, etc.).

- **Market**: An extension of the competitive landscape, gives broader context of trends, demographics, effectiveness of partnerships, and networks.

- **Product**: Adds reference for analysis of product feedback from social media and adds context to suggestions from analytics to content strategy.

- **Global marketing assets and strategy**: Particularly helpful in larger organizations and when the social media team is separate from other marketing initiatives. Gives context to performance of specific content, adds context to cross-channel analyses, and adds to suggestions on improvements based on analytics insights. May indicate the need for data integration and creation of new measurement systems across different departments.

- **Activities of nonmarketing departments**: Particularly helpful when more departments of the company participate in social media activity and wish to gain from it. Human resources with recruiting initiatives, sales with networking and lead generation, customer support, events (when not under marketing). Knowledge of information in such departments adds to delivering useful analyses and suggestions on improvement in strategy. It also contributes to decisions on data integration and unified measurement systems. The analytics team can also, in many cases, suggest the implementation of new technologies related to social media into such departments and even train departments to become more data driven in their decisions.

- **Key company employees**: Particularly useful in cases when individual employees generate high engagement for the company through different means, such as social media, events, interviews, research, education, content streaming, and so forth. This knowledge can indicate potential influencers for enhancement of social strategy. It can indicate the need to add the channels of such employees to the analytics strategy, to be sure that they participate in the overall analyses. In many cases, such employees generate more engagement with the community than the company; many of us prefer being connected to another person than to an institutional channel of a company.

The use of knowledge beyond what happens within social media channels will likely be the key to insights that lead to innovation. When analytics refer to many different aspects of the business, not only will the interest in it grow, but the results serve many different areas and integrate into a global business strategy. In many cases, we may be constrained by limitations in time and other resources and will not be able research and apply such views into our strategy. Such limitations should never keep us from understanding the value of what may be available beyond our immediate reach.

The most interesting analyses are the ones that bring broader aspects into context to better justify conclusions and insights. The very direct and easy path of using a tool to export standard and default reports very rarely delivers the best possible analysis. While artificial intelligence cannot yet make sense of all that happens in the world and in human nature, the best analyses come from insightful analysts (despite the job title) who can correlate the broadest sets of objective and subjective information.

Tools and Technology Preparation

The research into analytics tools and any technology to support our measurement process can start even before the planning stage of our strategy. This aspect of our work will be, in fact, an ongoing process of learning new things. Updating ourselves on what is available will always be an interesting thing to do.

Whether or not you are familiar with analytics tools and technology, your approach here should be very practical and follow many of the principles covered under the topic of data availability and data sources. We do not wish to waste our time in browsing the market, so instead we can approach this by having our goals and objectives as clear as we can. From there, we can build a list of the primary features that we are looking for, independent of knowing if they already exist. With this concept in mind, we can go out into the market and be open to discovery, but still have a clear view of where we are heading.

We may discover in our research that there is no tool that delivers everything we need. In such cases, we can choose to work with a few different tools in parallel, and also to integrate such tools, even if only as a final dashboard.

The two main things to keep in mind when choosing tools and technology (besides having all needed features) are contract commitments and if the tools are useful in the long term. Naturally, if all we are doing is a brief and temporary project, none of this matters; but if we are preparing to implement and optimize a long-term strategy, it would be great if the tools we choose evolve and deliver more of what matters as we move forward.

It is common that technology companies ask for long-term contracts, some offer a short-term and no-commitment option, but usually, pricing is much more attractive in the long term. To work within such model, a good idea is to prepare to also store our data ourselves. We can pull our analytics data from our tools and choose a good format to store it in, just in case we need to change tools at any point in the future.

After having the best possible tools in place, we can then finish to optimize the tools for our specific work. This means that if we need to perform any kind of customization of dashboards or metrics, the planning stage is the best time to do so. Naturally, as we apply our strategy, the need for adjustments will come up, and we will perform such adjustments and move forward. However, the almost certain need for adjustments does not mean that we should skip the initial setup steps during planning stage. It is one type of process to adjust a previously planned setup and a very different process to perform the entire setup once we have the pressure of delivering results immediately.

In cases when there is absolutely no time to spend in planning and there is a need to jump immediately into work and perform the entire planning stage simultaneously to the application stage, we can expect and inform stakeholders that results from analytics will not be optimal for some time. The main risk of skipping the planning stage entirely and jumping into action immediately is that we will never have time to come back into planning and properly optimize our strategy. We may become stuck in a process that is not the most effective, spending higher resources and more of our time to collect very basic results that do not truly help us evolve or gain advantages toward our overall business strategy.

If we find ourselves stuck in a loop of high delivery pressures and below-optimal results, we can break out by having a dedicated team member drive a parallel planning stage and prepare for a shift in our analytics strategy. If we do not have people in our team with such time, an external consultant can play that role until we have the new strategy implemented.

Team Preparation

The team can eventually be the most important aspect of our strategy. Since the team plays a big role in applying the plan to make analytics work toward the business, if the team is not in tune, we risk failing at our strategy, even if we have a great plan, great tools, and a great brand to work with.

As much as you may feel that you are already familiar with all of this, and that you know how important the work of a team is, when the pressure kicks in, it is easy to forget that many team members may not be on the same page and are quietly struggling to deal with their specific challenges. It can be hard to help the team once the pressure to deliver fast results begins.

To keep the team on track, preparation is paramount. There is not enough we can say about that. The better prepared our team is, the higher chances we have to succeed in any strategy that we come up with.

Some team members only need a basic understanding of certain aspects of analytics. For many of them, we can often include broader descriptions of goals and context within reports and don't have to worry too much about initial training. Other team members work with the actual analytics; they are the ones we need to be more concerned about in terms of having as much understanding of the strategy and process as possible. Hopefully, they are insightful analysts (despite job title).

During planning stage, we can distribute the different tasks among team members. In such cases, different team members can be responsible for researching into knowledge beyond social media, or into tools, and even in putting together potential goals and objectives.

When it comes to training, an interesting system to apply can be based on education tracks and a check made by each team member once a certain track is completed. In practical terms, we have a series of topics in a logical sequence and each team member goes through each topic, leaving a check once the study of that topic is completed. This is also interesting because each team member can create a different track based on their expertise, or we can even separate the research process so that different people can study and dedicate themselves to different tracks. This also works as training for future team members.

The preparation of the team also promotes a better discussion during the analysis. It is not only about understanding what is going on but also about thinking ahead and coming up with innovative ideas and suggestions on the social, marketing, and business strategy itself.

Some kind of knowledge base setup, or even an internal wiki, would be an asset. These two links can illustrate examples of such knowledge base: www.mediawiki.org and www.atlassian.com. We usually have that for many aspects of our business, especially when we are part of a larger organization, but we rarely have such asset for a very specific field such as analytics and social media analytics. This is much easier to implement than it sounds. The software that Wikipedia uses, for example, is open source and free. It is very easy to use and has all the support material we need. The very interesting aspect here is that the entire team can collaborate into creating the knowledge base in a very dynamic way. This process helps to fixate what we learn, share knowledge with the team, and be prepared for growth and the arrival of new team members in the future. If we customize our analytics setup, it is worthwhile to have the information about our process registered and a clear reasoning why we worked on customizing our tools and workflow. Such assets help us adjust our strategy as we move forward.

One last suggestion is to have a monthly reunion of the team with a focus on education—a monthly update session where every team member brings in new points found during that time. Such sessions can be extremely helpful to bring everyone onto the same page and also push the team forward on their expertise. This session can be part of a longer session of discussion on analytics, results, and strategy. I have worked with teams that dedicate one full day, or half a day every month for such sessions. It is an interesting approach that can renew motivation toward the next month.

Goals and Objectives

Clarity is vital to setting up goals. The more specific we can be, the better. We can follow here the idea of transforming subjective goals into objective ones if we need to, so that we can track how far we get into reaching a goal.

We can explore calculations to give us an overview of what is happening to many metrics at once. Success rate is a good trigger for keeping track of our progress.

Examples of goals are

- 1,000 new followers per month
- More than 2% conversions to website
- More than 200 average interactions per post
- Double the reach interaction rate by end of year
- Drive 500 people to an event

. . . and so forth.

Such goals can then be related specifically to certain areas of the business, if needed. Salespeople can broaden the goal into conversion of leads. The human resources department can relate to the amount of new candidates. Customer support can relate to the amount of the tickets to resolve. The product team can tally the amount of feedback and even find potential beta testers. All stakeholders can add their specific goals into the list.

Discovery processes can also be present in social analytics and within the use of social media data. In many cases, we can run processes that don't have clear goals as an experimental way of reaching any potential insight. This is very interesting, but usually has a lower priority than the clear goals that are first established. In many cases, we run such discovery processes to help us reach a certain goal or even just break a certain growth plateau. When we run very detailed listening processes into the comments of people under our posts, for example, we may find surprising results and even the key to higher engagement and sales.

Such discovery processes can add to what we call *tactics*. So the strategy is a higher-level plan, while tactics are processes to help the strategy become successful. We will look at tactics later in the book.

Reporting Cycles and Timelines

The key here is to aim for perfect timing. The objective is to be able to effectively implement changes indicated by analytics. So if we can plan on a cycle that facilitates the application of insights from analytics, we have found the right timing.

This involves being in tune with stakeholder agendas and also with the company road map for campaigns, product release, and any activity within specific departments if these relate to social channels somehow.

We really want to avoid having a process where reports are lost, or no one reads them, and there is no continuous cycle of improvement. There is no point on running analytics if we are not going to make good use of it. We can always help the team get more involved with the process or we can adapt what we are doing to fit their needs. There is always a way to reach a good cycle of improvement.

No excuses. Make it happen.

Contingency Plans

The interesting point here is to be prepared for any unplanned situation, good or bad. Many times, an excessively positive effect can harm a strategy more than a bad one. Negative effects can escalate very quickly and become a crisis, which calls for a state of *crisis management* within social channels.

Analytics trigger such events, so we need to have a clear view of the threshold we are working with. When do we know we have a crisis at hand? When are we reaching an excessively positive effect that might break our workflow?

This is partially a connection to our goals, but goes one step beyond that in the sense that we plan a few possible actions to take in such cases. Actions can include, for example, shifting to shorter reporting cycles and more actionable metrics to manage a crisis. It can mean more work in filtering sentiment and comments and even the need to hire freelance analysts temporarily, so we want to make sure we have them close before we need them. An alignment with the public relations and marketing teams is essential here, so that everyone can share their plans from different angles into a cohesive final contingency plan.

Application of a Social Media Analytics Strategy

Pressure, deadlines, deliverables, stakeholders, changes in the content strategy that call for changes in metrics, changes in dashboards, new data formats, new social networks, data integration, communication with external parties—results, results, results.

The application of analytics is when our plans are put to the test, along with our ability to improvise and change when needed.

As simple as this may sound, many projects can become extremely delayed because of the lack of preparation to work with such a dynamic set of processes.

Especially in larger organizations, it is not uncommon that different team members become too busy with certain tasks and less dedicated to the process of analysis. This delays any necessary changes in the strategy, which can lead to a big drop in performance or a loss in momentum and loss of opportunity to really create a positive impact.

Ownership of the analytics process must go beyond the point where a report is delivered. It is important to close one cycle and cover the entire process of finding and applying insights to then measure the next improved cycle and keep moving forward.

If we have separate teams taking care of technology development, data generation assets, analytics, content strategy, content creation, and the overall business strategy, someone needs to have an overview of the entire process and make the connections between the separate teams.

This level of connection and feedback from every stakeholder making use of analytics helps the team push forward on delivering truly relevant insights and helps the company move toward having a true cycle of improvement.

If we take that role, of being the supervisor of the full cycle, we can look at resources in the area of project management to help us streamline the process. The Project Management Institute, or PMI, is a great starting point. Other than that, we can explore a few simple ideas to make things easy for everyone involved, for example

- A check system: stakeholders signal when receive and read reports.

- A timeline view pointing out the moments of analysis delivery and feedback to check on patterns around timing and problematic stakeholders.

- A linear sequence of feedback in the decision-making process, where feedback from stakeholders builds up and adds to the final reports to decision-makers.

- An open feedback channel between stakeholders and the people running the analytics, so that changes can be made dynamically. Depending on the volume of requests and size of the organization, a ticket system can be placed.

The main concept is to formalize the process, so that everyone can easily understand what is going on, and changes in the team will not affect the strategy.

From the content explored in this book, a good familiarity with metrics, dashboards, and reports are very helpful once a planned strategy is running. While our knowledge of such aspects is an ongoing process of learning, the more we know about reading and adjusting metrics, setting up dashboards, and building reports, the better we can apply and make changes to what we are measuring and how we are reacting to what the data is telling us.

A final point into this stage is to truly understand the decision-making process and facilitate necessary changes as much as possible. The faster we can get through cycles of analysis and actually apply improvements, the better our strategy will be. This sometimes involves questioning decision-makers about time availability and possibilities that other team members may take certain decisions without higher consent.

One simple example of this is a social media director trusting the head of content (or the content team) to adjust the images, the length of the video, the timing of publication, and even the investment budget independently. There will always be the need for a strategic pause and evaluation of the full cycle, when the primary decision-makers have their voices heard. While cycles are ongoing, however, decentralizing the decision-making process on a microlevel can greatly optimize the strategy.

Strategy and Tactics

Tactics are related to the very practical aspects of making the strategy work. A strategic goal is set and then a series of tactics can be proposed and applied to reach such goal.

Some strategists see all the processes under strategy as simply "strategy," while others like to divide strategy further into strategic, tactical, and operational levels. The subdivision of strategy into more levels is recommended, depending on the scale of the strategy and information about the activities. When higher specialization is required to perform certain processes, or people need to be focused on just one part of the process, it can be a good idea to subdivide and create a chain of command.

Different levels of knowledge come into play when dealing with strategy and tactics. The strategic-level decisions require a very good understanding of the tactical aspect and deeper knowledge about major company goals and business science. The tactical level does not require the knowledge of the strategic level and can be focused instead on what it takes to actually perform the tasks under each tactic. Knowledge of the strategic level, however, always benefits the tactical level, so there is no harm in learning more of that level if we are tactical and teaching if we are strategic.

Strategy can then be more or less detailed when it comes to tactics, hence our studies of the planning stage around all the knowledge in this book and beyond. The less detailed a strategy is, the more room there is for the tactical level to take decisions and create its own plans. If the strategic level trusts the tactical to do so, a less detailed plan can be made at a higher level. Otherwise, a very detailed plan can be made, even with the help and insight of the tactical level.

We will look at examples of tactics later in the book. At this point, it is good to keep in mind that such subdivisions are also an option when building our strategy.

Evaluation of a Strategic Analytics Cycle

How much are analytics affecting the business?

The evaluation stage is when we truly connect all the work in analytics to its impact on all relevant areas of the business.

It is a time for questioning.

- Which metrics, dashboards, or reports have generated action and positive changes to the business strategy?

- Any specific cases to highlight where analytics brought in a key insight?

- Which areas of the business were most affected? Which areas can have more focus for the next cycle?

- Which goals were reached?

- Are all the stakeholders happy with the processes?

- Are there new technologies on the market that can be implemented for a next cycle?

- Were there aspects that did not work and need to be changed for the next cycle?

. . . and so forth.

The evaluation stage is then also a time of discovery. We will find out positive aspects about our work, but also negative aspects, and must be brave to make all necessary changes even if they mean we need to take a step back in our overall strategy to grow again in the future.

The material collected during evaluation is the basis for the planning of a next cycle. It is interesting that we can then clearly register the process so that we can always look back from the future and understand our decisions toward improvement. The idea of an internal wiki, or similar system, can be a good idea for a home for such material. The lack of registration creates the risk of repeating the same mistakes.

In cases of very fast-paced workflows with very dynamic content, the evaluation of one cycle can happen during the application of a second cycle. Major adjustments can then be made into a third cycle. The second cycle can have only minor adjustments to critical points, which can be easy to measure before the major changes into the third cycle. This can give the team enough time to properly evaluate every important point.

For example, if we are working on monthly cycles, we start a major evaluation after the first month, work on it during the second month, in parallel to our ongoing strategy, and apply all changes into the third month. The third month becomes the first month of a truly new cycle.

The dynamics of evaluation can be flexible. If we don't have major adjustments to be made, we can just keep going into new cycles until we feel that we need the extra time to evaluate and change. Processes are created to help us and not to waste our time if they are not needed.

In time, with experience and a structured approach, we have high chances to find an ideal analytics strategy—a perfect workflow that collects all relevant data, generates relevant insights, and follows the improvement into new cycles. Once there, the analytics workload is much smaller, and there is a lot of room for innovation and experimentation. At that stage, we can then start pulling more data points, creating experimental apps, and artificial intelligence projects, automating adjustments to the timing and frequency of our content based on a connection between analytics and our publishing platform, and so forth.

To reach that point, it is vital that we understand how much we can handle at each step. Too much too soon easily becomes a problem and hinders our progress. It is better to start with simple strategies and simple analytics processes, even if they don't fully cover all of the points that we are studying in this book. Once we feel comfortable with one strategy, it is easier to push forward and add more elements to the mix.

In some cases, especially when we feel overwhelmed, we can separate processes and send part of our analytics needs to third parties. We can keep the short-term actionable metrics to ourselves and request the more complex correlations from external teams. However, if the analytics process is being handled by separate teams, such as in the context of agency and client, or agencies working with other agencies, or even between different branches of a larger company, it is important to create a unified storage of all the data and analyses for future reference.

From the evaluation stage, many discoveries push us into applying new tactics into our strategy. The example of branching out to third parties is one such case. Tactics involve practical approaches to processes and workflows. They can involve adjustments in metrics, adding or removing competitors, working closely with the content team to promote growth, creating and measuring experiments, and so forth.

Detecting a Hidden Strategy

A new strategy does not have to be built from scratch. In many cases, we can reveal what is already in place to then make certain adjustments. With time being a key resource to our projects, an initial analysis of what is already in place can be a great way to save a lot of time.

This process requires investigation into all areas that will be part of the new strategy. An initial study can focus on pulling simple numbers to find out what is already performing well and what is not. From there, areas of further research can be detected.

In cases where a company is successful without social media, when implementing a new social analytics strategy, the team can investigate how the company works on its current channels. How does it measure the performance on nonsocial channels? How does it improve its processes with the use of any kind of analytics?

This study can reveal fascinating strategies that can then be applied into social media analytics as well. It can often reveal more about the relationship between stakeholders and their relationship with measurement and improvement cycles.

Building a Good Social Analytics Strategy

The ideal analytics strategy manages to be so in tune with the activities of the company, that it becomes a natural part of the process, and not a hassle for the people involved.

This is why we have been exploring so many different elements that go beyond analytics itself and are apparently disconnected, but in truth are very much entangled.

A good starting point, therefore, is to understand the people, their activities, and the assets that directly relate to the company's social media channels.

With an initial view on that, we can then define goals for analytics and the roles of stakeholders, moving into further information on what we need to search for in the perfect technology setup.

From there, with a basic understanding of the people, assets, and the ideal technology in hand, we can move deeper into the details of technology setup, metrics, dashboards, timing on reporting cycles, formats, feedback, and so forth.

The goal is to reach a strategy that does not require major adjustments, but instead leaves room for experimentation and innovation. Once we have a basic workflow well covered, and we are reaching enough insights to continuously improve results from social into the business, we can move to more advanced applications, such as machine learning, artificial intelligence, and the predictive aspect of analytics.

Another key point regarding the ideal strategy is that there is no clear rule of what to do. Rules can be very dangerous when each company has a very different context to work with. This is another reason why we explore so many different elements in this book. The idea is to fill ourselves with relevant knowledge, to the point where we can easily perceive what is best for our specific case and context.

Key Takeaways

- Analytics strategy affects social media strategy, which affects the business strategy; it is all connected.

- There is an entangled relationship between analytics and the process or activity being measured. Understanding this relationship is important to understand the concept of strategy related to analytics.

- If we implement analytics but don't go beyond to make sure that it is generating a positive impact in the business, we are leaving the outcome of our analytics strategy to chance or luck.

- Registration of all that we do in analytics creates a knowledge base to grow upon; it is used to avoid repeating mistakes.

- Strategy can be divided into three main stages: planning, application, and evaluation.

- Strategic planning is open to brainstorming and creativity; we can bring in all ideas and evaluate them during such stage.

- Strategy can be applied at a campaign level or a global company level with short- and long-term applications.

- Strategy will likely involve making compromises. We need to decide how to invest resources, time being one of them.

- Knowledge beyond social media is vital to a social analytics strategy. When analytics takes into consideration what is beyond the tools, it can truly deliver insights that are relevant for the company as a whole.

- ROI in social media starts with understanding the investment (the I) to then understand the return (the R). Knowledge beyond social media plays an important role in this process.

- Jumping straight into application without planning creates the risk of becoming stuck under high delivery pressures and less than optimal results. When this happens, we can start a parallel planning process to adjust the strategy in the future.

- The better the team and the team preparation, the higher the chances of success.

- Clear goals are the basis of a good strategy.

- Improvement must be continuous; there is always a good way of reaching such improvement cycle. No excuses; make it happen.

- Contingency plans can include excessively positive effects as well as negative; we can be prepared to scale into further success and also deal with a sudden crisis.

- During the application stage, it is important that we can act quickly and be prepared to handle the need for changes.

- The evaluation stage is a time for questioning and discovery. How are analytics affecting the business?

- The more detailed the strategic plan, the less tactical planning we need. This balance shifts, depending on the qualities of each team and the context of the business.

- The ideal analytics strategy is one that manages to be so in tune with the activities of the company that it becomes a natural part of the process and not a hassle for the people involved.

Tactics

Practical Elements to Include in Social Analytics Strategies

Tactics come into play when it is time to put strategy into practice. Depending on how detailed the strategy is, the tactical level has more or less room to explore and create.

Strategies usually give a lot of room to tactics, because it is on the tactical level that the team can better adjust and experiment to reach a strategic objective.

A strategy can point out, for example, that it is vital to have a view of performance on a per-product basis, assuming the brand has many different products. Tactics then come in and resolve the best way to deliver that. Filtering metrics with keywords and hashtags or tagging posts in the publishing tool can work well. There are also choices on the best ways to display results. Also, certain products may be so popular that they deserve their own social channels, and this suggestion may be then given from the tactical to the strategic level.

Even with a very detailed strategy in place, it is still likely that many specifics around metrics, dashboards, data, insights, and suggestions for improvement will remain an open topic. Tactics can then play a major role in the success of a certain strategy.

© April Ursula Fox 2022
A. U. Fox, *Social Media Analytics Strategy*,
https://doi.org/10.1007/978-1-4842-8306-6_16

While the study of possible tactics in social media analytics is an ongoing process, and we come across new tactics all the time, we can explore a list of tactics to include in our strategies and inspire our research into more on the tactical level.

Tactics for Analytics Strategies

Examples of tactics bring specific practical points and certain concepts that help us develop our tactical view and build new tactics to serve different project needs in our analyst life.

Please note that examples can be transposed from one social network to another, so please consider it when reading terms such as *posts, fans, timeline,* and so forth. The main idea is the concept.

The following is a list of the tactical areas that we will explore:

- **Correlation**: metrics that can be linked to each other
- **Filtering**: keywords, expressions, and hashtags
- **Ranking**: from best to worst and vice versa
- **Aggregation**: metrics that can work better together
- **Conversions and rates**: formulas to speed analysis
- **Goals and success rates**: defining and adjusting the meaning of success
- **Competitive benchmarking**: industry competitors, dispute for audience time, partnerships, and inspiration
- **Discovery**: analytics without clear goals

Correlation

Can metrics be correlated? Will we find that one metric always affects another in a similar way? Can our assumptions be broken or confirmed to reveal insights?

Under this set of tactics, we explore metrics that can eventually correlate in some way, and even if we find out that they don't, we still have a trigger on an insight in the end. So the noncorrelation can also have meaning.

On the practical side, we can display these metrics next to each other on a dashboard or report, for example. Another practical idea is to look beyond snapshots and understand the behavior of this potential correlation through time. We can eventually find that there has been correlation during a certain period and that it fluctuates. This can push us into further research around certain time periods to understand other aspects affecting the results.

Let's go over a few examples of correlation research.

Posts, User Posts, and User Questions

This examines audience behavioral patterns.

Do we always get user posts on our timeline when we post? Do we get more if we post more? Do the user posts include questions? Do we get more questions from having more user posts?

User questions can reveal positive interest, or people wanting to know more, or confusion about any aspect of the content or the object of the content. It can also reveal dissatisfaction.

The interesting aspect here is that we are not yet looking at the questions. We are first detecting if there is a pattern that can lead us into a major insight. The questions are important, naturally, and they will be dealt with, but here we are looking for elements that can support or change our strategy.

This concept can be expanded into the comments section, however, that may be a more complex task. Determining whether questions in comments are made to the brand or to other comments is not a very straightforward approach. Also, a discussion could come up in the comments section, generating a lot more questions and comments around it. So it may not fill the initial objective in this case.

Questions and Mentions with a Per-User View

This examines the value in the number of mentions and questions.

Do we always get questions and mentions from the same people? In the event that we do, are they lovers or haters of our content or brand? With mentions, are they spammers? Are they simply promoting the content into their channels to get interactions? Should we block them? Promote them within our content? Partner with them as influencers?

This initial search can trigger our research into certain primary users affecting our overall number of mentions and questions.

Total Followers and Follower Change

This examines the audience growth and consistency.

Do we get more followers as we grow our channel? The bigger it is, the more new followers it gets? Or is there an opposite trend? Was there a period when the trend happened, but then it stopped?

It is important that we move away from percentages with this study. It is important that we clearly understand the dimension of the numbers.

This is particularly useful in competitive benchmarking. It prevents assuming that smaller or larger pages always get more or fewer new fans. We will look for the truth on a case-by-case basis.

Total Interactions, Average Interactions, and Post Frequency

This examines the effectiveness of post frequency.

An increase in total interactions shows an increase in the average per post? How has this evolved over time? Is the average higher because of fewer posts? Is the total lower even with more posts?

This is a very simple and initial search that can lead to detailed research in specific posts, their interactions, and the effectiveness of the frequency strategy. Maybe the audience is bored with so many posts. Maybe they want more. Maybe the algorithm of the network is limiting exposure with more posts. This initial trigger leads to such research.

Post Types, Interactions, and Types of Interactions by Post Type

This examines the effectiveness of post types.

Do we get more interactions with a certain post type? Do we get more of a certain type of interaction with a certain post type?

Percentages do not help in this study. We need an overview of the number of interactions. A higher comparative percentage can translate to a lower actual number, and we need to understand the true volume we are working with.

We can then work with each post type and understand the distribution of interaction types within them. This can lead us into further research and experimentation to see if an increase in this post type also promotes an increase in a certain interaction type.

Filtering

When we need to go into the details about the content but don't have the time, filtering tactics can come into play. The main idea is that we can filter out what is most important to us and try to reach what we need without having to go into a manual research of the content.

This is similar to the core process in traditional social listening tools. The difference is that listening searches for the presence of terms independent of a specific source, while in this example we define our universe of search, have access to the entirety of its content, and then filter out from there what we need. This means that traditional listening can eventually miss certain results from sources that can be important to us, while filtering is all about covering such sources. On the other hand, listening can bring very interesting results from unexpected sources. Both processes have their use and importance for different use cases.

Filtering also uses terms and expressions, and the actual search can be very similar to the traditional listening search. Because we are separating content from the same source, it is important to find unique terms for our filters. This could be the name of a certain product, a unique hashtag, or specific keywords that are added to the content for filtering.

Next, let's look at a few examples of filtering.

Performance per Topic

A common need for social media channels is to separate the performance by a certain topic-related criteria. The channel may publish content about products, company events, open positions, free training—you name it. All of these topics published by the same channel can make it complicated to understand what exactly is driving performance and how. To better deal with that, an initial filtering can be made, and all other metrics after that can see the performance on a per-topic basis.

Competitive Research

Competition also happens on a per-topic level. Maybe we only compete with a certain product line of a big manufacturer, so we can filter just that content to use as a comparison. Perhaps we are curious about whether they are using certain buzzwords in their content and if that is helping them drive engagement. Maybe we want to detect the use of nonbranded hashtags and tag along to a certain trend or seasonal event. There are many cases in which a filtered search of competitor content can be great.

Influencer and Partnership Analysis

It is common to have external profiles sharing our content, mentioning our channels, or simply sharing content that touches our brand in any way. To evaluate the effectiveness of such activity, we can filter from such channels only the relevant content related to us. This can be greatly helpful if we are paying for influencers to promote us. We don't have to depend on a report from them and can have a good view of the results on our own.

Another interesting case is when we are researching for potential partners. We can evaluate their performance per topic to detect if a certain potential partner is better suited to speak about our brand. This can happen when choosing certain media channels to invest in. Whether the media channel is small and local or huge and global, it helps to quickly understand if they fit well into our overall branding strategy.

Ranking

Rankings single out events very quickly while giving us a view of a sequence following the criteria we used. The significance of this tactical approach is to approach the use of ranking from every possible angle.

Top-Down and Bottom-Up

It is common to only use rankings from the top-down. It is important to understand the other side of things. Usually, when we decide to change something, it is because it is not working very well. So why do we tend to skip an analysis of the worst and register only what works best?

While we can always scroll down the entire ranking and reach the bottom, with interactive tables inside analytics platforms, this approach can be more direct, and we can select a certain number of posts to look at from each angle, for example, the top ten and the bottom ten.

This includes top and bottom days and longer periods. Whatever we decide to use ranking for can be subject to a top and bottom approach.

Ranking Multiple Attributes of an Object

Beyond an overall ranking of certain fundamental objects, such as content pieces, days, and defined periods, we can add a ranked view to multiple attributes of such objects.

The objective is to have a more detailed view of the object before having to go into manual research.

As an example, we can rank content by total interactions, but then also rank it by each type of interactions. This gives a comparative result of more attributes of a certain content piece. Our top overall content can be ranked tenth in amount of shares, for example, and twenty-third in the number of comments. This can help us deal with very broken numbers that usually compose the many attributes related to objects of study. Instead of seeing *Likes: 479, Shares: 132, Comments: 19,* we would see *Likes: 1st, Shares: 10th, Comments 23rd.* The ranked view can be next to the actual numbers, so that we are also familiar with the volume of interactions in our ranking.

Aggregation

Many metrics are so closely aligned that they can actually become part of the same metric. They complement each other in certain ways that we will end up constantly using such metrics together. When we see ourselves doing that, we can likely aggregate these metrics into one.

We are not yet creating a rate in this tactic. We are simply putting together two metrics into a view where we can see the relationship between them, but we can also see each one individually.

The choice of chart type plays a key role when aggregating metrics. We can always add many metrics into a table, but is a table our best option? To save time and quickly understand the main points behind what we see, it is likely that other chart types will be better than a table.

When looking at trends and spikes over a long period, the very traditional line chart can do the trick. When looking at competitive snapshots, we can have a bubble chart.

Scale is also an element to consider when bringing metrics together. In many charts, we will end up having more than one scale as a reference or one scale for each metric, which is something we must pay careful attention to and become comfortable working with.

A few examples of possible aggregation:

- **Response rate vs. number of questions**: Can brands properly handle the number of questions?

- **Total interactions vs. posts or fans**: Do more posts or fans equal more interactions?

- **Impressions or reach vs. interactions**: Does a higher number of impressions or reach always result in more interactions?

- **Post type distribution vs. interactions by post type**: Do more posts of one type equal more interactions to that post type?

Conversions and Rates

Rates are great when they are very clear and give immediate meaning to an analysis. In some cases, however, rates can complicate things more than they will help.

The reason is that, in such cases, the rate will display the result of a calculation between metrics that are not so closely related or that fluctuate in a way that the result hides a crucial part of the story behind their relationship.

This is the case with the competitive engagement rate, in which we are not sure why it changes, as it can be a result of gain or loss in either audience or interactions, which are its two metrics. An open view of such a relationship can likely be more insightful.

Conversions, on the other hand, are rates that work very well and offer insights even before we investigate further. So even before we know the number of clicks we had, for example, if we see a higher CTR, or *click-through rate*, we already know that such performance was better overall.

The logic behind conversions is helpful when building a rate. In simple terms, we are following a logic along the lines of, *If this happened, then how much of that happened?* or, *If I had this many impressions, how many people clicked on my link?* Both metrics are closely related, even to the point where one thing needs to happen for another thing to happen. People need to see the post to click the link.

Another type of comparison can be made between two different results: one result that is not so good against another that is ideal. An example of this is a version of the *view-through rate*, also known as *audience retention* or *view retention*. Videos can deliver metrics on the people who watched a video for 3 seconds and those who watched 30 seconds. With 30 seconds being ideal, it is possible to build a rate between the number of people who watched to 30 seconds against the number who watched for 3 seconds. The closer this rate is to 100% as a result, the better. The higher the rate, the more people watching for 30 seconds than for only 3 seconds.

Goals and Success Rates

When building metrics to measure goals, the first challenge is to understand the goals that can be reached. This tactic, as you can imagine, requires adjustments and experimentation until a reliable model is found. A success rate is then created from the results of all of our goals, giving us an initial measurement of the overall goal-oriented performance.

Two approaches into this tactic can work, for different levels of insights and different kinds of goals.

A first approach can be very simple, where we establish a goal based only on what we desire and believe is possible to reach. Some study into past performance and other pages similar to ours can help, as well as an overall view of the planning strategy for future content and company activities.

From there, we set goals to every metric that we are working with and establish a continuous improvement cycle where we can adjust until we reach a good model. A good model is a set of goals that we will likely reach. And if we don't, it is because of some failure along the way and not because the goal was set incorrectly.

A second approach can be more complex, following what we have seen under conversions tactics and the concept of connecting elements that are highly related. So if we wish to reach a certain goal, what are we doing to get there? How does the goal relate to our activity? Are we getting ideal types of engagement, such as in the view-through rate?

For this, we first establish a series of relevant rates and, from there, create our goals. The difference is that, in this approach, we can be more dynamic and build on top of a reference. If one of our goals is, for example, to reach 0.5 on the view-through rate, the total number of video views does not matter; the rate is independent of the number of total views and videos posted.

Once we find a working model, we can then relate the success rate to our activities, for example, if we have higher success with more posts or with fewer posts, and if audience growth, timing, and the number of posts influence results.

Competitive Benchmarking

Tactics in competitive benchmarking start by choosing the right competitors or any relevant external channel. Tracking and comparing against relevant channels is crucial to finding insights from this process.

There is no definitive rule on what is a relevant channel. It is under the discretion of the team to determine and define what is relevant to the analysis. In marketing, competition goes beyond the sphere of specific products and services offered by the companies. It is about engagement and how much time a certain audience spends with a company. We are competing for audience time.

With an open mind about competition, we can then be creative about benchmarking and explore a list of possibilities:

- **Industry "real-life" competitors**: Companies that compete in all levels, including market share.

- **Volume**: Similar volume in audience and content frequency strategy. Some strategies also benefit from benchmarking higher volume channels as reference.

- **Audience**: Similar audience is even better when we are sure that there is an overlap.

- **Visual style**: Similar or simply amazing visuals can feed inspiration and even new tricks for content creation.

- **Creative content**: Reference for content creation, in general, can relate to good text, images, video, use of new media, live broadcast, or all of it at once.

- **Influencers**: True influencers of the industry and/ or audience. This can range from executives to media professionals and artists. Detecting relevance of such channels needs thorough evaluation; many apparent influencers may not actually influence the relevant audience.

Social listening can be useful when searching for relevant channels to benchmark. Because it looks for mentions of terms independent of the source, it potentially reveals relevant sources.

Listening alone, however, does not handle the entire benchmarking process. Metrics such as share of voice, checking for volume of mentions of competitors, are only a very small part of the benchmarking process. We need to go beyond listening and make use of tools that can review a lot of information about a large number of channels at once. We want to know all the strategy details of the channel being benchmarked.

The initial stage of competitive benchmarking can also benefit from a landscape study or from brainstorming when we are feeling highly creative about potential competition. This is a period when we add as many channels as we can to the analysis—basically, everything that we believe can be relevant. So we put these channels to the test.

Discovery: Analytics Without Clear Goals

Although goals are the cornerstone of analytics, it can also be interesting to follow a discovery approach and be open to unexpected tools, triggers, or insights. This is easier said than done, however. A discovery process involves technical aspects and the human side, the mindset, and the curiosity of the analyst. It is also not a process that we can turn on and off; it is always on.

To discover something new while not having a specific goal means to observe and simply be aware of anything relevant that we come across.

When discovering new potential benchmarking channels, for example, a trip to the supermarket or any store can trigger the interest for a new brand that we didn't think about initially.

In the search for new potential graphs and metrics, an investigation of fields different from marketing can be great, such as the financial market, or even the manufacturing sector. A review of traditional business intelligence concepts and statistics may also bring new ideas.

Within analytics tools, we can approach discovery in different ways. An initial approach is to create "the obvious path" and see if anything will break from the obvious. We can create a dashboard where we place metrics that always correlate in the same way next to each other, but do have a small chance of breaking that pattern.

Another approach can be to investigate metrics that we rarely use, maybe because we are not the ones who set up the tool before we started to work on the project, or because we tend to always stick to the same metrics.

A third approach can be to think about the data sources and go into "mad scientist" mode. What can we put together that has not been put together yet and can deliver new insights? It will be an interesting experiment. Even if we are not very technical, we can still explore data sources. Many tools have a list of available data sources—or data points—that are not hard to understand, such as the following for Facebook:

- time (TEXT)
- fans (NUMERIC)
- fansChange (NUMERIC)

When looking at such a list, certain data sources, or data points, can be perfectly related to stand-alone metrics (from a graphic point of view). This happens, for example, with the number of total fans. However, many of the data points or metrics (from the data point of view) need to be put into a certain context or even combined with other points or metrics to express a more useful reading, such as viewing the fans change along a period of time. This is where our "mad scientist" approach comes in: with the creative combination of the data points we come across.

If we get stuck or need to clarify information, we can then reach out to the analytics tool we work with, or to friends that are savvy with such details, and ultimately to the social networks themselves.

Discovery can be fun. We don't need to become stressed about the process. It is an optional approach that we can explore or not; it is really up to us.

We also don't need to make it complicated, and even with discovery mode being always on, we can take an easy route when relating to it. When we work from 9 to 5 with analytics, for example, we usually run away from it when we are not on the job; the discovery process can then be very light. We can simply add small notes into our mobile notepad, or physical pocketbook of ideas when we come across something interesting, and then dedicate proper time to it during our working hours.

Key Takeaways

- Tactics come into play when it is time to put strategy into practice. Depending on how detailed the strategy is, the tactical level will have more or less room to explore and create.

- We can explore metrics that can eventually correlate in some way, and even if we find out that they don't, we still have a trigger on an insight in the end.

- When we need to go into the details about the content but don't have the time, filtering tactics can come into play.

- Rankings single out events very quickly while giving us a view of a sequence following the criteria we used. We can approach the use of ranking from every possible angle.

- Many metrics are so closely aligned that they can actually become part of the same metric.

- Rates can be great when they are very clear and give immediate meaning to an analysis.

- When building metrics to measure goals, the first challenge is to understand the goals that can be reached.

- Tactics in competitive benchmarking start by choosing the right competitors or any relevant external channel.

- While goals are the cornerstone of analytics, it is good to also follow a discovery approach and be open to find unexpected tools, triggers, or insights.

Michael Wu

Chief Scientist at Lithium Technologies

Michael Wu is an influential and inspirational data scientist. The projection of his work reaches and moves the global community of analysts, data professionals, and data enthusiasts. He is also an influence for many global C-level decision-makers that understand and embrace the data-driven world we live in.

He is a leader and a vital member of the visionary team behind the innovative technology of Lithium Technologies, a company pushing the boundaries of digital customer experience. His work at Lithium touches directly many points that are extremely relevant for us in this book—social media marketing, analytics, data management, customer relationship management, and the creation of true communities around brands.

Beyond his work at Lithium, Michael influences the global discussion by speaking in many events and publishing articles and books on many topics related to data science, data analytics, artificial intelligence, machine learning, and on the "human side," which he mentions as the top-down approach, considering the connection of social sciences and human behavior to the development and use of technology.

I first came across his work through one of his books, *The Science of Social* (Lithium Technologies, 2013), years ago, during a peculiar moment in my life. I had just been given a Kindle e-reader and was excited that I could easily

© April Ursula Fox 2022
A. U. Fox, *Social Media Analytics Strategy*,
https://doi.org/10.1007/978-1-4842-8306-6_17

continue reading everything as I commuted through the subways of Prague to work and home, so I was on the hunt for new reads. During that time, as it happens to many of us riding in public transportation, my mind while catching those trains and watching all those people would flutter over ideas, observations, and assumptions of what could motivate each person to do what they did.

I would try to relate what I saw to what I was learning in my work with marketing and social media, asking myself, *What shaped their habits?* Their attitude? Were they influenced by the advertising around them? Why were they using a certain brand of headphones? Why wear the sports team jersey? Were they comfortable with themselves or trying to become a new version of themselves? Were they experimenting in life? Would they take risks? And the key questions to us in this book, would social media influence any of this? How? How could I measure it? How could I collect such data? How could someone improve that human connection through social channels? How could the voice of people be heard by brands? Where was the connection between people as a community more than an audience? How to use data to reveal all of that?

Then came along *The Science of Social* with a holistic take into the universe of social media. I was immediately hooked. That content was speaking to all my questions and giving me possibilities that I had not considered before. It spoke of data, analytics, but also of community, true engagement, gamification tactics, and more. I read book one and two in three days with my new e-reader and bumping into everyone in the subway. Then I began to hunt for more content by Dr. Michael Wu.

I reached out to him back then just to be in touch, basically as a fan and admirer of his work, which I am even more today. When the time came to write this book, I immediately reached out to Michael again, to capture some of his views and thoughts and broaden the range of our studies here. In this interview, I then tried my best to capture a little bit of everything that he studies which can be related to social and to this book. It is a conversational material which will likely open our minds to thinking "outside the box" when it comes to social media analytics strategy. Michael also inspired me in adding prescriptive analytics into this book, explaining to us—as you will see in this interview—that the technology for doing so is already here.

You can find Michael Wu and *The Science of Social* directly through the following links:

- www.linkedin.com/in/michaelwuphd/
- http://pages.lithium.com/science-of-social
- http://pages.lithium.com/science-of-social-2

Question 1

One area of your work that I feel is very interesting can greatly add to our need for broader knowledge when working with social media analytics and making sense of the data. This is the concept of building a true community. This understanding can help analysts better interpret their results and better suggest solutions for improvement.

Exploring your view on the concept of community related to social networks, how can we differentiate a true community, understand the differences to a network, and eventually explore more details into elements that compose the concept of a community?

To summarize the difference between community and network, we can start by truly separating social media into these two main categories—community or social network—and know that sometimes they can eventually be a hybrid. We can see this as two ends of the spectrum, where in the middle are the hybrids, and some are more community-like, others are more social network-like.

The main difference that distinguishes one from the other can be seen when we look at what actually holds them together. What holds the group together? Both social networks and communities are groups of people. What holds a social network is essentially interpersonal relationships. And what holds a community together is basically a common interest.

Many social media technologies are seen as networks, when they're actually a community, with a common interest. The common interest for YouTube is basically videos. The common interest for Instagram is photos. Blogs are basically the written content. The more specific the common interest is, the more niche the community becomes. There are communities around, for example, HDR photography. That's a very specific kind of community.

The social network, on the other hand, is held together by interpersonal relationship. For example, Facebook is a social network. It is held together by interpersonal friendship. There's also LinkedIn, also a social network, held together by interpersonal relationship in the professional realm. There are a lot fewer of these social networks, and the kinds of relationships that people care about there are then friendship, kinship, the professional relationship, and so forth. Everything else in between will be a hybrid.

Twitter, for example, is a hybrid. You could follow someone because you know someone, so there is interpersonal relationship, and you could also simply follow someone because you find what they say interesting, the common interest that holds these groups of people together.

Author's note: The conversation on this topic continues throughout the interview, but if you have further interest, the article at `http://lith.tc/2u1M8ZO` *can give you a lot more information.*

Question 2

Going further into that line of thought, how do you see these concepts fitting into a marketing strategy?

We can approach it from a more scientific perspective first and then look at the application in marketing.

In our life, in everybody's physical life, we actually have a single social network that consists of pretty much all the people that have any relationship with us. That is our social network. It includes our friends, our colleagues, our relatives, as well as anybody who has any relationship with us. That's our physical kind of social network in the real world.

Technology, or a technological platform like Facebook, will typically highlight a part of our social network through a social graph that captures some relationships. For example, Facebook captures our "friendship graph"; the relationship that it captures is obviously friendship. Whereas LinkedIn tries to capture a different kind of relationship in our social network, that can be called the "coworkers graph" or "colleagues graph."

We all have our unique social network consisting of many different social graphs, but at the same time, we are part of many different communities. Some people, who are connected to us on social network, will also be connected to us through common interest. I am a photographer, for example, so I like photography and have some photography friends. Other people may have friends from grade school, university, or companies where they worked, and still keep in touch with these friends and colleagues. This is also my case; I am still in touch with my friends from when I was pursuing my PhD in neuroscience.

That's how it works in our real life. Anthropologically, that is how community complements social network. There are actually functions for each one of them. The functional difference between community and social network is that community is where you build relationships and social network is where you keep those relationships even when you moved on from those communities.

If you take a look at your own social network, and you look at all your Facebook friends, for example, you actually share some common community with them in the past—whether they were in the same kindergarten as you or same college or same company. It is actually within those physical communities that you have built relationships.

I think that community and social network could actually complement each other a lot more when it comes to marketing. Many marketers will overlook the importance of communities and only try to find the big numbers, always driven by the idea that anything big is good. Consequently, they tend to focus only on the big social networks and miss out on the more niched communities. Social networks tend to be bigger because they're more generic. Everyone has relationships. Communities tend to be niche, because people have all kinds of different interests that can be very specific, which tends to result in smaller groups for each. As a result, the marketer who is only looking for the big numbers will gravitate toward platforms like Facebook or LinkedIn and forget that where you actually build a relationship with your customers is within a community.

That's actually where Lithium comes in to help. We can provide a platform that will help marketers and companies engage with their customers so that they can build a strong relationship with their customers. Once they build these relationships, they will see the positive results.

A strong relationship with a customer is typically manifested in loyalty. If you've built a strong relationship with your customer, then your customer is going to be a lot more loyal to you because relationships are pretty long term. You don't just get rid of your friends. Once you develop this friendship, once you develop a weak tie into a strong tie, and they become a stable part of your social network, those relationships tend to last quite a long time. Before they become a strong tie, of course, things could still be fluid, but once that relationship is built, then it becomes stable. And if that strong relationship is with customers, then these customers will tend to stay with the brand much longer. That's what I mean by loyalty.

The manifestation of loyalty is then essentially repeated business. They will do business with you for a much longer period of time and hence have much greater customer lifetime value.

Question 3

A main keyword for us in this book is strategy. With this in mind, and part of the reason why I'm so curious about topics apparently unrelated to analytics, is because people arrive at analytics with some kind of goal in mind, which in many cases may not be yet well defined. They will be asking, and sometimes looking for a direct answer from analytics, on questions such as, "How can analytics help me have my customers buy more?" Analytics will help, but many times the ultimate answer will also relate to a broader strategic approach, such as the better use of community. With this in mind, how do you see the use of analytics related to goals and broader strategic options?

I think it is important to have a goal in mind. What are you trying to accomplish? That is actually one thing that we advise. Even if you're trying to start a community, what are you trying to accomplish with that community? Are you going to use a community to reduce your support costs through peer support, or are you trying to use it to drive more awareness of your product and your brand? Are you trying to get the community to talk about your product so that you can improve upon it and build better products? What is the use case? What are you trying to do with the community? After you have that, then you can formulate a strategy around, "Okay, I'm going to use this community to do a certain thing." I think it is important to have the end goal in mind from the start.

In terms of analytics, looking at descriptive analytics, it typically tells you how you perform related to your goal. This can start from zero, when you don't have anyone in the community yet, no content, nothing. Then the goal comes in: What are you trying to get? Are you trying to get to a million members by the end of year one or year two? Are you trying to get to a community with lots of content, say, a million member posts by the end of year one? What are you trying to do?

Then you can go into further goals. What are those members and posts supposed to drive? Are they supposed to drive more discussion about your product? Or recommendations about your product? Or reviews about your product? Or other business outcomes? What do you want the community to do for you? The descriptive analytics will tell you how you progress along this trajectory.

It can happen, for example, that your goal is to have a million posts by the end of the year, and by month eight you're not even halfway there, so you know you probably will miss the target. You know you need to do something about it. Maybe the answer is then to use gamification to motivate people to drive more activity, or run a contest, or launch a superusers program. There will be many different tactics that you can employ once you know where you want to go and your progress toward this goal.

Question 4

Within this descriptive field, how do you see, for example, things like competitive benchmarking, thinking about the benchmarking of communities and social networks? When can it be interesting to bring such elements into analytics and strategy?

That is very interesting. We also have a benchmarking service in Lithium. The beauty of being a SaaS platform is that we basically host all the communities on our platform. What that means is that not only do we have access to one community's data, but we also have access to all of them. We can actually benchmark, to some degree, on whatever similarity or criteria that's relevant to you.

For example, if you are a retail brand manager and you say, "I want to benchmark against all the retail communities that are as old as mine," you can. We will filter out all the other irrelevant communities that are not retail focused and that are too young or too old. Say you are a community that is three years old, we can then look at communities that have between two and four years. We could take a look at their data and then look at how they progress from day one, the launch, all the way to their current stage.

There are privacy restrictions, however, so typically we would do this benchmarking service if there's actually more than five communities in the benchmarking group. The averages over communities within the benchmark group will then hide details of who is in the group and what exactly they are doing. If there are not enough communities in the benchmark group, either we will have to relax the similarity criteria or we will not offer benchmarking.

Going beyond communities, competitive benchmarking on social media will follow the same concept as doing any competitive study. Why do you want to know anything about your competitor? It will help you focus on what you do best and not compete head-to-head on what your competitor does best. Maybe instead you can focus on improving something that they're doing poorly. Having the customer's voice in this process is actually very important. This is basically the realm of, I would say, social media monitoring services.

Social media monitoring can listen to a social media conversation and tell you how many people are talking about a competing brand compared to yours. It can also tell you the sentiment around their conversation about the brands. How many mentions have positive sentiment? How many mentions have a negative sentiment? All that will tell you something about where should you focus, and therefore help you formulate a strategy to win in this hypercompetitive market.

Question 5

How does the idea of community and social network come into play when a brand is trying to use channels such as Facebook and Twitter?

I think it is important for marketers to also engage on these social networks precisely because they're big. These channels become amplification platforms for the content created by the community. If you only have content that stays within the brand community, and you don't have any medium of propagation, then the community doesn't actually get anywhere. You could certainly build a community that's pretty big, but then typically communities don't get too big because people don't just have only one interest, and those interests go beyond your brand.

The key is then really to use community and social network together, to have them complement each other. You use the community to build relationships to create relevant and trusted contents about your brand, and you use the social network as a propagation medium to help you spread these contents and reach a wider audience.

For example, if someone wrote an excellent review about your product within the community, you should try to propagate that out onto social networks and let them create what is sometimes called the "viral loop." Bringing analytics into that, thinking on the example with social media monitoring, you can then monitor the propagation of this content and see if it will increase the positive sentiment about the brand. That will help you formulate your strategy and decide what to do next. If you see the positive effect growing dramatically and it's actually improving sales, you know that this specific propagation strategy is something that you should continue to do. If there is growth in activity but no correlation to sales, then maybe it's ultimately not that useful. Maybe you should focus on doing something else.

Question 6

Going a little further into communities, and taking reference from social media channels where there is a member of the brand as a moderator, or participating in the discussion to answer questions, and so forth, how does the flow of interactions happen within communities?

Within the communities that we host for the brands, typically all the members are actually customers of the brand. This is another important difference between off-domain social channels (like Facebook or Twitter) vs. on-domain communities. Social channels like Facebook and Twitter are often perceived as the voice of the brand, whereas the communities we host are perceived as voices of the peer (i.e., other customers). One of the consequences of this difference in customer perception is that customers are much more critical and negative on social channels than they are in communities. We have many customers that have both community and off-domain social channels, which we encourage. They often see many complaints on the off-domain social channels and are surprised to find their members so cooperative and helpful within the community.

Even though there's nothing stopping the employee of the brand to participate in the community, they are a very small fraction of the community's population. These customers within the community are the ones who will essentially influence others, and they're just like you or any other customer. They're not experts in the product nor do they get paid by the brand. If they're helpful to other people, then that actually creates value and people appreciate it. They slowly grow their influence in the community and eventually become recognized by the company or the brand as an expert. The company can then reward them positively for what they have done. Maybe not necessarily monetarily, but they could certainly reward them by other nonmonetary means to encourage them to continue their positive behaviors.

For example, "we invite you to beta test our new product," or "maybe you could come help us design the next version of this feature?" Or "would you like to come over and meet our senior leader team or have dinner with our CEO?" Or "I'll give you a ticket to come to our conference" or offers like that. All these are ways that the company could reward these influencers, which sometimes we call the "superfans" and the "superusers" within the community.

Question 7

Going into a different topic and looking to the future, how do you see the arrival of technologies such as machine learning and artificial intelligence? What challenges and limitations are we facing? Why isn't everyone using these technologies yet? Is the technology truly available, or are we not quite there yet?

The current limitation is that most companies don't collect enough data to train the AI model. That is the issue. Companies that have enough data are already able to produce predictions that are very good. They could even prescribe actions that are somewhat optimal or better than a human could. So why isn't everyone using these predictive and prescriptive analytics yet? Because most people don't have all the data that they need to build this type of AI model. It's not that the technology is not there. The technology is actually already here.

Examples that go from algorithmic trading, automatic loan origination, or even self-driving cars, which I wrote in many of my articles, show that the technology is already here. The reason why they are here now, however, is because there are efforts, huge efforts, invested in collecting lots and lots of data.

Google is spending lots of money to have cars driving around collecting data about the road conditions, traffic patterns, and different kinds of weather conditions. They will then have lots of data, right? That's why there are self-driving cars and the artificial intelligence that tells the car how to drive from point A to B. The AI is able to drive the car very well, just as well as a human.

In investment, algorithmic trading already exists, although not fully automated. But capital-trading companies have years and years of data. It is not huge data, though. You could load the past 20 years of the entire stock market into your laptop. It's not that big; it's all just numbers. Today, there are actually a lot of other data that we could collect and add to the stock market data, such as the market conditions, news, public sentiments, political events, even weather and disasters like earthquakes, and so forth. Having enough data, the investment firms can then build something like a robo-advisor that can automatically trade for us. I actually signed up for one of these robo-advisor types of services myself. There are several such companies out there doing that, like Wealthfront and Betterment. So the technology is here. I think a lot of companies simply don't have the data that is needed to fully utilize these technologies yet.

In the case of marketing, we can then question ourselves, "Can I actually make the AI smart enough to help me send, for example, the right emails to potential buyers so that I don't have to do marketing?" You could, but you have to train your AI so that it knows what to do. You have to show your AI what to do with data, for example, "Okay, this is what should happen when a customer exhibits this behavior, and these are all the different behaviors of a potential buyer. So first, you send them this, then you do that," and so forth.

You need to have all this data so that your AI can learn from it first, before you could actually have an AI that is smart enough. Without enough training, the AI will be very "dumb." Your AI can only be as good as the data that you have. If you don't have the data, then your AI is just a "stupid" or "dumb" computer.

Question 8

That is very interesting. It makes me curious to ask you about the need for data integration in this process. How do you see the integration factor coming into play within this challenge of collecting enough good data to be able to train the AI? Is data integration a challenge?

Yes, I think that is a real issue. Many companies have lots of data, but the data is dispersed. That is not very useful because the AI has to be able to see everything in order to learn from it. If you only feed the AI financial data, for example, and build a model, the model will be able to forecast the financial aspect very well, but may not be able to respond to the other conditions, such as marketing.

It is important to have what we call a "fairly complete coverage" of how your business operates. That's why one of the themes that is very heavily discussed nowadays is the idea of *digital transformation*. Why do you want to digitally transform your company? When you digitally transform your company, eventually everything, every part of your business operation, becomes digitized.

When that happens, it means you can have data on every part of the business operation, whether it's marketing, sales, support, or just a day-to-day operation; everything can be digitized and become data. Those data can be integrated. You could then actually build a very massive model about how your business operates by feeding it all these integrated data.

By providing all the business operation data, you essentially teach the AI how to operate your business, so that eventually it will be smart enough. Then it could help executives make decisions instead of the executives having to go through all the data themselves, which is actually what we are doing at this point. We look at all the data from different parts of the business and then we make a decision. Once you feed all that data to the AI, and you train it with your strategy, for example, "under this situation, I make this decision, and under that situation, then I make that decision," the AI will learn to mimic how you make decisions. It eventually makes decisions like you would have, because you used your data to train it.

Question 9

Stepping into the role of the marketer, to create an even better bridge with the concept of this book, and taking our conversation so far as a basis, how do you see the marketer navigating through this data-driven world? Would a marketer need to code, for example? How far would a marketer need to go to fully participate in the digital world?

I don't think it's necessary for marketers to do coding. That's not what they're necessarily best at doing. They need to know enough about coding to work with a data scientist who can code. They need to be able to, for example, tell the data scientist that, "Okay, I think these are important variables that we should consider, this is the context."

They definitely need to know how to collect data. That's an important skill for future marketers. They also need to be able to explain to the data scientist how to collect it. Are there any systematic bias? How did they sample their audience? Those are concepts around data sampling that marketers need to understand well.

If a non-savvy marketer goes out and collects some data, say, from smartphones, and tells the data scientist, "Okay, I built this app and I collected the data." The data scientist then asks, "So is this biased or not biased?" The marketer answers, "Oh, I collected from everyone. It's not biased." That would be an incorrect assessment of the bases within the data. The market for the brand will likely consist of a subset of the entire population. When it comes to smart devices, not everyone has them, so you are actually sampling the data, collecting the data from only a biased group among this entire population.

These are the things that marketers need to learn and understand better at the conceptual level. They need to understand statistics and data sampling and biases so that they can actually talk to the data scientist. The data scientist would then write the code and maybe try to adjust for the bias when they know what is causing the bias.

In a certain region, for example, where not everyone has a smartphone, it could be known that only about 70% of the people have smartphones, and the poorest 30% don't. Results can then be adjusted based on the fraction of the population that actually has a smartphone.

For marketers who come from a creative type of background, the data collection aspect is very important. Without good data, everything is off. You need to collect good data and understand how your instruments do that.

If there is any bias, you need to understand what the bias might be and what created such bias. Sometimes you may intend to collect data from everyone, but maybe there is some bias that crept in there just from the design of your app. Maybe the design of the app, or whatever data collection device you have, is not completely free of bias. You designed it in a certain way. Inadvertently, you created some bias by designing it a certain way and not choosing to design it in 100 other different ways, and so forth. Not only you need to understand what those biases are, you must understand what is creating those biases also.

Question 10

Going into the last question and taking such broader aspects around the understanding of data and the business into account, how important can it be for a social media marketer to step out of the social media "bubble" and into further aspects of the business and of the technology landscape?

Stepping out of social is actually the first step toward proving the ROI of social. If you only stay in social, all the data and all the analytics and metrics that you're going to get are what we call *social operation metrics*. You're never going to get financial data or business KPI data. You're never going to get that from your social media platforms.

You have to step outside of it to look at other parts of your business and see how social operation is related, or how it is correlated, to the other parts of the business and their metrics. That's how you can actually prove ROI and prove that your work is actually making a difference in the business.

The Future

Prescriptive Analytics

The Final Stage for Analytics Applications

Prescriptive analytics, as the name suggests, recommend decisions that can be taken using analytics. It is considered the third and final stage of analytics applications because it incorporates the most diverse types of data and data collection processes and pushes on the most advanced capabilities of analytics systems to reach the point of effective recommendation of the best possible decisions.

The process behind prescriptive analytics can be complex and involves the use of many different disciplines under mathematical and computational sciences. On top of its complexity, prescriptive analytics work with the results from descriptive and predictive analytics, which are the two stages considered to happen prior to it from an evolution point of view.

To better understand prescriptive analytics and how it is likely applied and influences social media analytics, let's briefly overview the three stages and then explore a few potential applications.

© April Ursula Fox 2022
A. U. Fox, *Social Media Analytics Strategy*,
https://doi.org/10.1007/978-1-4842-8306-6_18

Three Stages of Analytics

With the evolution of technology, it becomes possible to use the information available in the world in a way that makes future predictions highly accurate. Based on this technology, many practical applications of analytics are moving into delivering fully actionable information, enabling users to make the best possible decisions instantly.

To reach this fully actionable level, analytics technology will go through three stages, which we can look at to better understand the entire process. The following analytics stages are described in Figure 18-1:

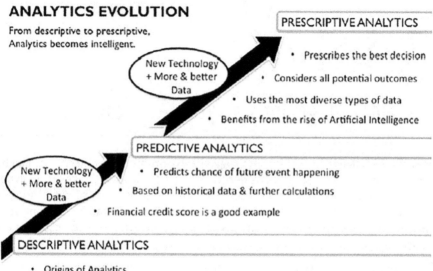

Figure 18-1. Analytics evolution

- Descriptive
- Predictive
- Prescriptive

Descriptive Analytics

Analytics started as descriptive analytics. As the name suggests, it is there to describe what happened. As you can figure out, it deals with historical data, with facts that already happened, as opposed to dealing with predictions and the future.

Descriptive analytics represents the majority of analytics solutions. It is likely that even with the evolution of technology, we will still see many solutions available on the descriptive level. Many organizations are not fully digital and many that are highly digital are not fully integrated. The challenges of gathering and integrating the necessary data to move beyond descriptive analytics will likely keep many organizations from doing so.

Social media analytics is also mainly descriptive. The challenges of social media go even beyond the intention of companies to be more digitalized or not. There is a dependency on the availability of data from the social networks themselves. There are challenges with not only connecting and integrating the data from different networks but also connecting that data to the proprietary data of the organization.

Applications of descriptive analytics are still very useful despite the evolution in the field. They can also be relatively inexpensive and offer a great return on investment. Therefore, they can be a great starting point for any person or organization to begin their use of analytics. Once the descriptive process is well understood, it is easier to understand and apply the second and third stages of predictive and prescriptive analytics.

Descriptive analytics require, as we have been seeing throughout the book, that the analyst creates a link between data and insight. It requires some level of work before reaching the decision-making point. This can happen because of the complexity and connections around many facts occurring at the same time and the different context of each fact and each different connection. Analysts then need to step in and fill the gap of missing knowledge and interpretation with further information from research that may go beyond the analytics system. The human element, therefore, plays a major role in the use of descriptive analytics.

Decision-making is the main point to understand when it comes to analytics. It is really all about making the best possible decisions in the end. The next stages beyond descriptive analysis aim to accelerate the process of reaching a decision-making point and eliminate the need for much of the current work being done by humans. To be able to do that, the next stages work with future predictions in the same way our decisions as humans are highly based on what we predict will happen after we take them.

Predictive Analytics

The goal with predictive analytics is to reach probabilities of possible future outcomes for any object or situation being analyzed. In simple terms, it is based on the probabilities of each variable repeating itself in the future, thus giving a forecast of events based on all variables together.

One simple example is the financial credit score, where institutions verify the financial history of a person and determine if they are likely to pay their debt in the future or not. Law enforcement also makes use of this level of analytics when dealing with its cases.

On social media and in digital marketing, we see this level of analytics highly present in advertising, for example. When we look at a certain product, or interact with certain content, and start seeing ads for that product everywhere, or more of that type of content in our feed, there is some form of predictive analytics in the background thinking that we will likely buy that product or enjoy that content.

When it comes to the analytics platforms themselves, the presence of predictive analytics is currently very limited. Reasons range around costs and complications of dealing with social media data at the predictive level. Many predictive processes can be already applied to social analytics, but currently, they do not provide high enough accuracy and consistency to become an integral part of an analytics tool. We can look out for machine learning and artificial intelligence to change that as analytics platforms evolve.

Certain elements of predictive analytics, however, are already widely present in social analytics platforms. These are elements that make use of the same technology used by predictive and prescriptive analytics, but are only a small part of the entire process.

One example is *sentiment analysis*. The process behind sentiment makes use of *natural language processing*, which in simple terms is a field that develops the connection between humans and machines through the use of real-world language.

Another example is the detection of paid posts using machine learning. The system analyzes each post and detects signals showing that it is potentially paid; much like it would analyze other patterns to determine a probable forecast.

In social media, there is a chance that we will see elements of predictive analytics being used, as we see today, but when the time comes for a full analytics solution to be in place beyond descriptive, we may see a jump straight into the prescriptive level.

The reasoning behind this possibility comes from social media being a multimedia field, which is better handled by the prescriptive level. Also, many advancements are being first implemented in practical marketing activities to then eventually become part of an analytics solution. Chat bots and image recognition are examples of such technologies. They are first applied on very practical aspects of marketing activities, such as advertising, media buying, and marketing campaigns; maybe at some point, they will integrate accessible analytics technologies, but already in a prescriptive level.

Prescriptive Analytics

This is the point where analytics, in simple terms, considers all potential outcomes of a given case, all potential decisions, and all potential effects of such decisions, and suggests the best possible decisions.

An example of this technology that is already in place is GPS. It shows us information on all possible routes and suggests the best route for a trip. This example was mentioned by Dr. Michael Wu during one of his lectures, and it is indeed one of the best examples of how prescriptive analysis is done and how it can work very well.

If you picture GPS working on your mobile device, you can easily grasp the level of interactivity that prescriptive analytics involve. In the example, GPS technology does not only calculate the best route based on external data but also includes data that is very specific, giving routes based on places you normally go and routes you normally take. The analytics from a GPS can also make use of your personal data to blend certain preferences of yours into its results. It helps you make the best decision based on your personal criteria, not just generic criteria.

This dynamic aspect is fundamental to prescriptive analytics. In the ideal prescriptive scenario, the technology can be updated constantly and change the prescription if necessary. The more we think about it, the more we understand how this makes sense. The future is never set in stone; it changes as events in the present affect potential outcomes.

Without going too far into the technical details of prescriptive analytics, we already understand how this process needs enough data and good data to be able to work. When it comes to social media, depending on what exactly is our objective, these two elements will be quite complicated to gather.

Despite challenges, it is likely that we will see such technology coming into play as the field of social media evolves. It is possible that the big initial push will come from paid solutions, on new offerings for advertisers. The investment behind advertising will justify the development of prescriptive technologies toward a broadly accessible model.

Parallel to potential releases of broadly accessible prescriptive analytics for social media and digital marketing, companies are already experimenting with and developing their own solutions and looking to integrate their data with social media for market research, planning, CRM, hiring, sales, and so forth. They will likely run descriptive analytics solutions as a basis, but such predictive and prescriptive models are giving certain companies a valuable competitive advantage already.

Competitive Advantage As a Goal

Competitive advantage is within the core of the need for evolution in analytics. It is all about spending less time and other resources to gain insights and then again spend less time and resources to take the right decisions and perform the best possible business activities. Working well with descriptive analytics already promotes serious competitive advantages. Predictive and prescriptive then take it to a higher level.

Currently, while much of the technology involving predictive and prescriptive analytics is not broadly available or easily accessible, one element we can focus on is competitive advantage. During our studies of analytics, we can try our best to track the impact of analytics in every area of the business that it touches. We can make questions toward discovering points in which this impact occurred and understand which types of resources were involved and how much did we gain or save on them. Time is a major resource, but also sales leads, candidates in recruitment, product feedback, free promotion, and any elements that can be measured and directly relate to the performance of the business overall. By doing this with whatever tools we have at any given time, we start to build focus into what really matters to our business and can then invest toward that when the time comes to spend more resources on new technologies and processes.

Key Takeaways

- There are three stages in analytics: descriptive, predictive, and prescriptive.

- Descriptive is the origin of analytics and represents the majority of analytics solutions available.

- Predictive generates potential outcomes for any object or situation being analyzed.

- Prescriptive taps into all potential outcomes, decisions, and effects of decisions to assist in taking the best possible decision.

- Prescriptive analytics is the final stage because it incorporates the most diverse types of data and data collection processes and pushes on the most advanced capabilities of analytics systems to reach the point of effective recommendation of the best possible decisions.

- Social media is challenging for predictive and prescriptive due to cost and complications in gathering and working with social media data. It can also become more complex when integrating to company data.

- Some technologies today, such as sentiment analysis and paid post detection, make use of small parts of a larger set of predictive analytics technologies.

- Competitive advantage is a concept that can be measured toward the effectiveness of analytics in the business. While we evolve our analytics technologies, we can keep track of the impact of each innovation on the overall business to focus on them when moving forward.

The Future of Social Media Analytics

What Can We Expect and How Can We Prepare for It?

In conclusion to our studies in this book, let's put together a few key points from the innovative concepts we have touched upon, and that were mentioned during interviews, to look into the future and project some possibilities.

What is coming up for social media analytics? How can we prepare and invest our time and resources toward making the best out of it? How can we push ourselves into the future and be part of the movement in innovation and disruption?

© April Ursula Fox 2022
A. U. Fox, *Social Media Analytics Strategy*,
https://doi.org/10.1007/978-1-4842-8306-6_19

Naturally, this part of our conversation is very open-ended; it intends, in fact, to be so. We can start by listing a few interesting topics and then briefly look at them a little further:

- The need for more data and the digital transformation
- Integration and "social everywhere, social everything"
- Rise of intelligent machines and how to befriend them
- Behavioral changes and what is measured
- Wise investments: the right step at the right time

The Need for More Data and the Digital Transformation

Data is the fuel of technology. Moving into the future, it is very likely that more data will be needed to run the extremely useful and disruptive technologies that are up and coming, such as artificial intelligence. This means that companies will inevitably need to go through some level of digital transformation to make that happen. Even brick-and-mortar companies will need to find ways to digitize everything about their businesses. We already see a lot of that happening, but there is still a lot that can and needs to be explored in the digitization field.

So in the future of analytics, we can expect that new forms of data collection will be coming up. It will likely happen with hardware and software innovation and can eventually be pushed into an accessible reality by the demand of large companies.

As a tip for analysts today, I would recommend finding ways of storing your data yourself. As much as we trust social media network companies, or data analytics providers, there is nothing safer than having our own data under our own care and then being able to apply our data to any kind of analytical technology we want. Be as independent as possible.

Integration and "Social Everywhere, Social Everything"

With the need to collect all possible useful data comes the need for the integration of all kinds of different data and different systems dealing with different parts of a business in entirely different businesses. This points to new technologies coming up that will help integrate everything very easily.

Taking this line of thought into the evolution of social media as a type of technology, it is likely that we will start seeing less ownership over the social media landscape from branded solutions. So instead of using Facebook, certain technology can eventually be "powered by Facebook," or even just connect and integrate with Facebook to fulfill a certain task or role. This adds to our view on the need for new integration technology.

The "unbranded" landscape of social media, while somewhat hard to imagine at first, becomes easier to grasp and understand when we start including things like the Internet of Things into the mix. Our fridge doesn't care if it buys more ice cream from Amazon or Target directly, or if it sends us a message through WhatsApp, or any kind of app, to tell us that we are running out of ice cream. What matters is the ultimate task. Under such unbranded needs, the ubiquity of social media technologies will also remove the need for a social media brand. As hinted by Tam Su, our guest in the book, it will likely be referred simply as "social," or even "online."

As analysts, we can look into this future as a hint on the use of social media technology today. How much does it matter if we are using a certain social network or all of them? Does it matter if our company has a prominent presence in every single social network? Or does it really matter if we are engaging with our community and growing our business with the benefit of activity and data from social channels? The idea here is then to think "outside the box" when it comes to social strategy and, consequently, social analytics strategy.

The Rise of Intelligent Machines and How to Befriend Them

Intelligent machines require them to be trained. Eventually, machines will reach a point where they can train themselves on a specific use case, but before that can happen, all the basic training needs to be there. With training comes the selection of good data and the use of enough data so that machines can reach the highest levels of accuracy in what they do.

As analysts (especially as marketers and nontechnical business managers going into the analytics field), this future means that we can start to invest some of our time into understanding more about data collection and concepts about good and bad data, biases, and so forth. As mentioned by Dr. Michael Wu in Chapter 17, machines will become as good as the data they have, so to "befriend" them, and have them really become intelligent and truly help us, we need to feed them good data.

When it comes to practical social media analytics applications, the rise of intelligent machines will take us to the prescriptive level, and we will have very accurate predictions of all possible effects of engagement while a bot creates the entire content for us. The bot will also, naturally, make all the choices related to the publication of such content, choose the best channels, best timing, tag relevant people, and use whatever social media resource it has available to it. As mentioned by Frederik Peiniger in Chapter 6, it is likely that such intelligent machines will transform communications and change things from the broadcasting model to the individualized experience, where each person and all that makes them unique is taken into account under the creation of content just for them.

Prescriptive analytics will then take social media truly into the mix with all that matters to businesses. So it could, for example, warn the marketing strategist that a certain piece of content will be so popular that the production will not be able to handle the demand. The marketing strategist then speaks to production to sort it out, or eventually machines will figure that out for themselves as well.

Behavioral Changes and What Is Measured

Measurement on social media will naturally evolve into metrics that are truly relevant to the core of a business. While behavior of new generations will continue to change, and there will always be a "next best thing" to drive buzz around brands, social media will become less isolated within the "social media bubble" and more integrated with the business. The measurement of social will be connected to an integrated system for the entire business.

In practical terms, as marketing managers and social media analysts, we will inevitably have to reach a point where we know exactly who interacted with our content in which way and then keep track of our relationship with each individual. To reach that, it is likely that new models of monetization will come up from social media technologies—models that include a lot more data and the facilitation from these social media technologies on reaching precisely the data we need.

The "stone age" advertising model will also likely change at some point. Whether by the further rise of new technologies, such as the communities being developed by Lithium Technologies, or by the rise of the one-to-one content experience offered by intelligent machines, such ads have to change because they don't truly add a long-term value to businesses.

In conclusion, measurement will be enhanced to the individual level, and we will know if, for example:

John, who always buys ice cream from us, suddenly stopped buying. We know that John started mentioning another brand, and that his mentions include specifically the new flavors he is already consuming by that brand. We are absolutely sure we lost a customer, and not just assuming it. At the same time, we know that John is still following our social channel, and every now and then, he likes a certain piece of content. The day we launch one of his favorite flavors, which we created to compete with that brand that is stealing all of our customers, we are sure to let John know. We will then know if John bought it, and so forth…

So the focus will be on the relationship.

Wise Investments: The Right Step at the Right Time

As a very last point in this book, it is important to understand that there is always a best time for everything. When making our choices about investing in new analytics systems, or pushing the boundaries on what we are currently doing, it is wise to consider all possible consequences of our decisions, especially including the resources allocated to activities we become committed to.

In the movie *Excalibur (1981)*, Merlin, the wizard, told King Arthur, who had a small cake in hand and was asking him about the future, that

Looking at the cake is like looking at the future—until you've tasted it, what do you really know? And then, of course, it's too late!

This means that it can be hard to pull back from certain decisions after we have taken them, hence the value of detailed planning, and of taking small steps to build confidence into taking bigger, more complex ones. It is not because being data driven is essential that we must instantly reach the data-driven level. One step at a time, with enough time for validation of methods and evaluation of results, will be crucial for a solid progression into any goal that we set ourselves against.

A solid foundation is also crucial. If we can store our own data and create processes that don't depend exclusively upon the expertise of certain team members, we will be better off than if we invest on certain technology, for example, then lose a vital member of our team, and waste our investment until we find or train another person.

All of this is part of social analytics strategy. While you can take from this book any amount of insights and learning that you like, from specific increments on adjusting your social media metrics to a broader company-wide analytics setup, it is important that you understand how analytics and measurement connect to an array of elements in your business and relate to apparently unrelated areas.

On a personal level, it is about shaping the best possible version of your "analyst self." It is about opening your mind to everything that is happening in your object of study and your field of work. Question the world, find the truth, don't stop, and don't let anyone tell you it's not possible. Then bring your insights into the community, share what you have found, and participate in pushing the field of social media and analytics forward. It is by exchanging experiences and knowledge that we can all grow together.

I

Index

A

Accounting, 243

Actionable insights, 10, 15, 24, 36, 51, 104, 180, 240

Advertising analytics tools, 66, 74

Aggregating data, 38, 48

Aggregation, 37, 241, 275

AI financial data, 290

Algorithmic trading, 289

Alignment, 214, 227, 254

Ambiguity, 52, 53

Analysis, form of comparison, 126, 127

Analysis of competing hypothesis (ACH), 53

Analyst mindset, 142

Analysts, 305

Analyst selves, 148, 308

Analyst's mindset, 139

Analytics, 4, 57, 84, 125, 128, 130, 173, 249
  actionable, 24
  good analytics tool, 36, 37
  metrics, 23
  metrics/numbers, 110
  process of comparison, 33, 34
  in social media, 35
  strategic planning, 31
  use of technologies, 121

Analytics/channel analytics, 59, 60

Analytics evolution, 296

Analytics in social media
  advertising analytics, 64–66
  analytics/channel analytics, 59, 60
  CMS analytics, 66
  CRM analytics, 67, 68
  listening (see Listening)
  types, 58

Analytics stages, 296, 300

Analytics systems, 295, 301, 307

Analytics technology, 36, 254, 296

Analytics tools, 73, 126, 166, 173, 204, 233

API integration, 242

Application Programming Interface (API), 19, 20

Areas beyond social analytics
  culture and history, 254, 255
  global marketing assets and strategy, 255
  key company employees, 255
  market, 255
  nonmarketing departments activities, 255
  product feedback, 255

Around cross-network analysis, 121

Around image analysis, 121

Artificial intelligence (AI), 6, 16, 17, 34, 72, 91, 92, 120, 122, 189, 252, 256, 264, 289, 298, 304

Artificial intelligence automating, 6

Audience, 161, 170

Audience and interactions relationship, 169

Audience insights, 188

Audience retention/view retention, 276

Audience size, 178

Augmented reality (AR), 223

Automatic loan origination, 289

Automation, 224

Average interactions *vs.* Average hashtags per post, 168

B

Bar chart, 163, 164

Behavior, 99, 104, 105

Being actionable, 24, 28, 37

Benchmarking channels, 279

Best tools, 72

Big data, 43, 46, 54

Branding, on social media, 96

Brands, 97, 140
   to "be social" on social media, 108
   Instagram, 105
   one-on-one conversations, 108
   organic content, 100
   truth, 104
   Twitter, 106

Brick-and-mortar companies, 304

Building and collecting metrics, 159

Business impact, 240

Business intelligence (BI), 85

Business operation data, 291

Business strategy, 142

C

Chat bots, 67

Competitive benchmarking, 87

Calculated metrics, 189

Calculations, 189

Capital-trading companies, 289

Causality, 187, 203

Chart types, 163, 164

Chat bots, 108

C-level decision-makers, 281

Climax points, 229

CMS analytics, 66

CMS tools, 66, 75

Commercial-only channels, 175

Commitment, 150

Communication channels, 241

Communications, 54, 92

Communities, 46

Community activity, 130

Community of customers, 239

Community/social network, 283

Community's population, 288

Company-wide analytics setup, 308

Comparison, 127, 130

Competitive advantage, 300, 301

Competitive analysis, 39, 178

Competitive approach, 151

Competitive benchmark analysis, 109, 166, 169, 176, 272, 277, 278

Competitive engagement rate, 171, 173, 276

Competitive/external analysis, 178

Competitive intelligence, 3, 49–51, 53

Competitive intelligence capability, 53

Competitive interaction rate, 172

Competitive negotiations, 151

Complex development stage, 241

Complexity, 52, 53

Complex/subjective questions, 185

Comprehensive analytics tool, 166

Conflict, 229

Content, 161

Content management systems (CMS), 66

Contingency plans, 261, 267

Continuous and monitored analysis, 149

Conversation, 304

Conversion-based strategy, 15

Conversions, 276

Correlation
   comments, 271
   dashboard/report, 270
   followers and follower change, 272

mentions and questions, 271
post types, 272
total interactions, 272
user posts, 271
user questions, 271
Cost per impression (CPI), 66
Cost per thousand (CPM), 66
Crimson, 113, 116, 120, 121
Crisis management, 131, 135, 260
Critical thinking, 232
CRM system, 245
CRM tools, 75
Custom dashboards, 35, 202, 203
Customer relationship management
    (CRM), 67
Customer support workflow, 67
Customization, 167
Custom metrics, 167, 168, 179, 192
Custom reports, 219

D

Dashboards, 36, 189
busy nightclub, 208
chart, 206
content table, 196
custom dashboards, 202, 203
default dashboards, 202
definition, 195
essence of a good dashboard, 214
final layout, 201
key metrics table, 196
"maximum amount of information", 195
metric positioning and correlation, 206
process, 194
process of reshaping, 213
seven-metric performance overview, 201
simple dashboard, 208
templates and structure, 204
Data, 4, 116, 117, 243, 244, 304
Data aggregation, 37, 241
Data aggregation companies, 45
Data analytics providers, 304
Data availability, 84

Data-based decisions, 181
Data-based processes, 5
Data-based proof, 168
Data calculations, 37
Data challenge, 85, 86
Data collection, 304
Data collection aspect, 292
Data display, 41–43
Data-driven decision, 244
Data integration, 47, 237, 238, 241
Data integration dashboards, 212
Data integration tools, 71, 78, 79
Data products, 245
Data providers, 245
Data quality, 84
Data sources, 58, 59, 161, 279
Decision-making process, 16, 54, 297
Dedicated tools, 71, 72
advantages, 75
advertising analytics tools, 74
analytics tools, 73
CMS and social CRM tools, 75
disadvantages, 75, 76
with hybrid features, 77
listening tools, 74
Default dashboards, 202
Default metrics, 159, 165, 166, 192
Descriptive analytics
analysts, 297
analytics solutions, 297
applications, 297
data and insight, 297
decision-making point, 297
historical data, 297
social media analytics, 297
Digital, 52
Digital and social advertising, 65
Digital assets, 107
Digital communication, 178
Digital customer experience, 281
Digital data, 167

Digital gap, 4

Digital marketing, 83, 167, 204

Digital transformation, 290

Digitization field, 304

Discovery processes, 259, 279

Diversified technology landscape, 244

Divide and Conquer metrics, 160

Dynamic cycles, 134

Dynamics, 131

E

Ecommerce, 7, 241

Ecosystem, 90

Effectiveness, 166

Email, 7

Engagement rate, 38–41, 115, 169

Engagement rate metrics, 169, 170

Enterprises, 242

Estimated metrics, 187, 188
    applications, 189–191
    calculated by third-party technology,
        188, 189
    categories, 188
    causality, 187
    facts, 188
    performance metrics, 187
    social networks, 188

Evaluation stage, 268

Evolution of data, 6

Experimentation, 187

External knowledge, 254

F

Facebook, 19, 67, 96–99, 103, 106, 116–118,
    122, 195, 199, 305

Familiarity, 157

Fast-paced topic, 157

Fast-paced workflows, 264

Feedback, 221, 232

Filtering
    competitive research, 273

    core process, 273
    influencer/partnership analysis, 274
    performance per topic, 273
    terms and expressions, 273

Filtering metrics, 269

Flexibility, 167

Foodie, 138

Freakonomics series, 118

Friendship graph, 284

Full KPIs, 223, 225

G

General guidance, 168

Goal-oriented approach, 226, 227

Goal-oriented performance, 277

Good model, 277

Google, 122

Graphic/visual approach, 179

Graphs, 231

Graph types, 162

Guidelines, 187

H

Hard system, 243

Hashtag detection, 26, 27

Hashtags, 101–103, 169

HDR photography, 283

High-level performance analysis, 159

Highlights, 224

Hiring process, 148

Hockey stick approach, 51

Human-driven process, 34

Human social media actions, 12

Hybrid tools, 71, 72, 76
    ads, 76
    advantages, 77
    analytics, 76
    differences and variations, 76
    disadvantages, 77, 78
    listening, 76
    publishing, 76

I, J

IBM, 120, 121
Ideal dashboard, 203
Impressions, 176, 188
Improvement cycle, 267
Indexes, 37, 38
Indicators, 152
Innovation, 150
Insights, 126, 127
    analysis process, 128
    aspect, 127
    comprehensive report, 133
    truth, 127
Instagram, 96–98, 101, 103, 105, 106
Instagram performance, 167
Integration capabilities, 245
Integration technologies and services, 238
Integration tools, 72
Intelligence, 54
Intelligent machines, 305
Intelligent platforms, 10
Interaction rate/engagement rate, 159
Interactions, 14, 161, 170, 184
Interactions distribution metric, 25, 27
Interactions vs. paid posts graphs, 176
Interactivity, 99, 103
Internet, 7, 8
Interpretation, 174
Investments, 87, 90

K

Keboola, 237
Key performance indicators (KPIs), 35, 135,
    136, 225
Knowledge sharing, 259

L

Lego blocks analogy, 242
Linearity, 186
LinkedIn, 98, 105, 106, 283

Listening
    challenges, tools, 62
    demographics, 63
    interests and sentiment, 63, 64
    keyword-based search, 61
    keyword "Toyota", 62
    official brand channels, 61
    process, 61
    search in Google, 61
    as social media monitoring, 61
    tools, 74
Longer periods, 136

M

Machine learning, 34, 45, 91, 176, 245
Mad scientist mode, 279
Marketing, 277, 290
Marketing communications, 51
Marketing managers, 306
Marketing optimization, 11
Massive model, 290
Measurements, 254, 306
Media streaming, 7
Medium, 221
Message, 220
Metrics, 23, 135
    analytics system, 155
    collection, 186
    customization, 159, 173
    and dashboard graphic design, 211, 212
    and dashboard layout, 210, 211
    data availability, 158
    data interpretation, 158
    deck, 159
    estimation, 181
    events/facts, 157, 191
    interaction rate, 156, 157
    rational and precision-oriented
        thinking, 158
    selection, 179, 180
    separation, 171
    simple and straightforward, 155
    simple/complex, 191
    strategic goals, 192
    tables, 191

Michael Wu, 281

Milan Veverka, 237

Mobile applications, 7

Multimedia field, 299

N

Naked truth, 178

Negotiation techniques, 147, 151

New data sources, 167

New tools, 80

Nike, 120

Nonbranded hashtags, 273

Noncompetitive analysis, 39

Noncompetitive engagement rate, 171

Noncorrelation, 270

Nonmonetary, 289

Non-savvy marketer, 291

Noun, 57

O

Objective goals, 30

Off-category metrics, 162

Off-domain social channels, 288

Online devices, 7

Online sources, 7

Open dashboard tools, 79

Optimization of processes, 15

Organization, 150

Own Posts Table metric, 26

P, Q

Paid promotion, 65, 125

Paid social media strategies, 15

Paid-to-conversions channel, 175

Paid *vs.* organic posts and interactions, 178

Paid *vs.* organic strategy, 175

Paid *vs.* organic table, 175, 176

Parallel planning process, 267

Periodic measurements, 152

Per-product basis, 269

"Personal AI", 46, 47

Personality analysis, 121

Personal preference, 162

Per-user view, 271

Pinterest, 96, 100, 104

Post-by-post approach, 168

Posts/interactions comparison metric, 24, 25, 181

Potential metrics
    content ranking tables, 182
    interactions by content type, 182
    interactions distribution by post type, 184, 185
    interactions types, 183, 184

Predictive analytics
    analytics platforms, 298
    digital marketing, 298
    elements, 298
    financial credit score, 298
    machine learning, 298
    practical marketing activities, 299
    probabilities of possible future outcomes, 298
    sentiment analysis, 298

Predictive and prescriptive analytics, 289

Prescription, 174

Prescriptive analytics, 282
    businesses, 306
    data and data collection, 301
    dynamic aspect, 299
    GPS technology, 299
    mathematical and computational sciences, 295
    potential releases, 300
    in social media, 299
    technical details, 299

Pricing, 257

Primary decision-makers, 262

Private data, 16, 17

Private-level data, 160

Private-level metrics, 160

Professional analytics tools, 60

Project indicators, 149

Project management, 147–149, 151, 152

Project requirements, 180

Public data, 16, 21, 169

Public-level data, 160

Public/private-level data, 159

Public transportation, 282

Publishing tool, 166

R

Ranking
  bottom-up, 274
  multiple attributes, 274, 275
  top-down, 274

Rare resources, 252

Reach, 176, 188

Reading terms, 270

Receiver, 221

Reebok, 120

Reference, 178

Relationship, 151

Reporting
  analytics goal, 219
  analytics tools, 219
  animation and effects, 231
  approaches, 222, 223
  cycles, 260
  drivers to success, 234
  element qualities, 220, 221
  elements, 220
  formats, 223
  images, graphs and numbers, 231, 232
  stakeholders and feedback, 232, 233
  unstructured approach, 222

Reporting with teams
  clear tasks, 234
  deadlines, 234
  education, 233, 234
  feedback sessions, 234
  individual tasks, 233
  project, 233

Reports, 189

Resource management, 147

Resources, 130, 303

Restaurant chain, 240, 242

Return on investment (ROI), 64, 254

Rich data, 240

Road conditions, 289

Robo-advisor, 290

Rule of thumb, 71, 72, 78

S

Self-driving cars, 289

Sender, 220

Sentiment analysis, 62–64, 67, 298, 301

Services, 81

Shares, 200

Short cycle, 131

Short-term actionable metrics, 265

Simple-to-answer objectives, 35

Skill requirements, 242

Social market intelligence (SMINT), 50–52

Snapchat, 96, 100

Social analytics, 49, 84

Social business strategy, 51

Social channels, 155, 288

Social CRM tools, 75

Social data, 114

Social in social, 175

Social interaction, 97

Social listening, 278

Social media, 7, 87, 109, 113, 114, 119, 128, 282
  analytics (see Analytics in social media)
  audience information, 141
  and big data, 43
  and challenges, 44, 45
  common goals, 110
  communication channel, 239
  conversations, 103
  conversions, examples, 65
  evolution, 305
  Facebook/Twitter, 238
  marketing impact, 238
  monitoring, 239

Social media (*cont.*)
    network companies, 304
    paid promotion, 65
    paid *vs.* organic, 64
    promotion, 14, 170
    text analytics, 241
    as a two-way channel, 107–109
    unbranded landscape, 305

Social media analysis, 3, 208

Social media analysts, 306

Social media analytics
    application, 261, 262
    applications, 306
    contingency plans, 260, 261
    data availability, 252, 253
    data sources, 252, 253
    descriptive, 297
    development, 266
    evaluation, 263–265
    goals and objectives, 259, 260
    hidden strategy detection, 265
    impacts, 249
    knowledge, 253, 254, 256
    reporting cycles and timelines, 260
    strategic planning, 250, 252
    strategy and tactics, 262, 263
    team preparation, 257–259
    tools and technology preparation,
        256, 257

Social media analytics market, 159

Social media analytics platform, 5

Social media analytics tools, 99

Social media bubble, 306

Social media channel, 128, 130

Social media command center, 212, 213

Social media data, 43, 44, 46, 47
    community growth, 46
    competitive intelligence, 3
    definition, 11
    estimated metrics *vs.* factual data
        sources, 13–16
    marketing and targeting, 46
    reference, 46

Social media data sources
    competitor mentions, 9, 10
    demographic, 9

Internet, 8
    offline originated data, 7
    online originated data, 7
    people mentioning, 9
    region, 8

Social media index, 38

Social media network, 7, 18, 95
    concept and UX, 96–98

Social media networks, 18–20, 59, 167

Social media post, 7, 32

Social media ROI, 254

Social media technologies, 306

Social media technology, 305

Social media tool companies, 81

Social media tools, 10

Social network, 84–86, 89, 95, 181, 284
    community, 284, 285
    Facebook/LinkedIn, 285
    interpersonal relationships, 283
    marketers, 287
    propagation medium, 288
    propagation strategy, 288
    social graphs, 284
    technological platform, 284

Social operation metrics, 292

Soft data stack, 243

Soft system, 243

Solid foundation, 307

Sophisticated machine learning
        algorithm, 240

Special access channels, 18

Speed, 252

Sponsored interactions, 178

Sponsored posts *vs.* total
        interactions, 177

Stakeholders, 232

Statistics and data sampling, 291

Storytelling, 229, 230

Stranger than Fiction (movie), 157

Strategic analytics, 128

Strategic goal, 262

Strategic-level decisions, 263

Strategy, 263

Studio TSU, 113, 114

Subjective goals, 29

Subjectivity, 222

Success rate approach, 174, 276

Superfans, 289

Superusers, 289

T

Tactics, 191, 265
   analytics strategies, 270
   role in success, 269
   strategies, 269

Tactics, social media analytics strategies
   aggregation, 275, 276
   analytics without clear goals, 278–280
   competitive benchmarking, 277, 278
   conversions and rates, 276
   correlation, 270–272
   filtering, 273–275
   goals and success rates, 276, 277

Tagging, 103

Team members, 258

Technology, 50, 52, 54

Text, 232

The Project Management Institute (PMI), 261

The Science of Social (book), 281, 282

The "stone age" advertising model, 306

360 approach, 228

Time, 173, 300, 303

Time-consuming tasks, 132, 187

Tiresome, 187

Topic-related criteria, 273

Traditional business intelligence, 3, 279

Traditional social listening tools, 273

Transform communications, 306

Twitter, 10, 67, 68, 96, 98, 99, 101, 103, 106, 115, 116, 283

Twitter Firehose, 19

U

Use of data, 4, 6

User experience (UX), 96–98, 104

User questions, 271

V

Validation, 307

Vanity metrics, 239

Viral loop, 288

Virtual reality (VR), 223

Visual graph, 158

Voice, 148

W, X, Y, Z

Wealthfront and Betterment, 290

Web, 118

Web 1.0, 121

Web 2.0, 121

Web crawling, 20

Web crawling/scraping, 17, 18, 20

Websites, 7

Wikipedia, 258

GPSR Compliance
The European Union's (EU) General Product Safety Regulation (GPSR) is a set
of rules that requires consumer products to be safe and our obligations to
ensure this.

If you have any concerns about our products, you can contact us on

ProductSafety@springernature.com

In case Publisher is established outside the EU, the EU authorized
representative is:

Springer Nature Customer Service Center GmbH
Europaplatz 3
69115 Heidelberg, Germany